This book is dedicated to my wife Tricia
and our twin daughters Megan and Elizabeth.

Building a Family
with the Assistance of Donor Insemination

Ken Daniels

First Published in 2004 by Dunmore Press Ltd

Reprinted (third printing) in 2012 by Dunmore Publishing Ltd
P.O. Box 25080
Wellington 6146
New Zealand
http://www.dunmore.co.nz

Republished in 2020 by Donor Conception Network

Books may be ordered from:

Donor Conception Network
www.dcnetwork.org

Text: Minion, 10.5/13.5
Cover Design: Central Media, Wellington

ISBN 978-1-912886-07-4

This edition produced in partnership between Ken Daniels and DC Network. All profits from the sale of this edition of the book are being donated by Ken Daniels to further the work of the Donor Conceived Network

Contents

Acknowledgements

A very special thanks to those parents who have been prepared to share their lives and experiences, first with me and now with you, the reader. Without their contribution, there would be no book. Thanks also to all those with whom I have had contact over the years. Your insights, thoughts, and feelings have taught me so much and have added greatly to the depth of this book.

Three research assistants have been involved in the preparation of this book. The late Kathy Hanson provided a sound beginning before her untimely death. Melanie Boursnell was then involved for a short period before Annie Oliver joined me. Annie's contribution has been outstanding, and I acknowledge her wisdom, efficiency, and skill. Her contribution to the final production of this book has been tremendous.

A grant from the Bertarelli Foundation in Switzerland paid in part for the research assistance needed, and a special thanks is extended to the Trustees for this contribution.

Foreword

Welcome to a book that for many of you will be a life-changing experience. I hope that Ken Daniels will inspire you as he did me at our first meeting over ten years ago at a Toronto infertility conference. We both spoke about the emotionally charged topic of Donor Conception. We approach this issue from starkly different directions. Professor Daniels has a broad background of encounters with doctors, infertility patients, parents of donor-conceived children, sperm donors and people conceived through anonymous sperm. He has devoted over twenty-seven years of his professional career striving to understand the complex issues from multiple perspectives. His views are richly based on a depth of understanding rarely seen in this field. As a result of his studies, his influence has been phenomenal, leading to a worldwide revolution in thinking about donor conception. I came to the conference with a different perspective rarely heard in those days: the experience of living the life of a person conceived through anonymous sperm donation, surviving 37 years of secrecy before my mother's disclosure. Professor Daniels and I agreed on many points and disagreed sharply on others. He came as a calm, reassuring professional who counseled hope for change in the profession that has made a tenet of absolute secrecy. I came as a man angered by the injustice this paternalistic medical profession has inflicted on countless vulnerable children.

As I grew to know Ken better over several communications since then, my respect for this man has likewise grown. He has taught me the value of empathy and persuasion over aggressive attack. When I received the drafts of this book, my admiration increased. Although I still have a few points to argue with him, I know we are both after the same thing: honesty and openness in family relations.

Ken speaks about the various emotions that will arise from reading this book. I have one emotion that he didn't mention. This book fills me with regret. Where were such enlightened people like Ken Daniels in 1944 when my parents chose to use donor sperm? They faced these issues without knowledge of the profound effects their actions would have on me and on their marriage. They had no counseling, no proper informed consent, and no wise guide to dissuade them against sharing the truth with me. Their doctor advised them to keep my conception secret, assuring them I would never suspect. He reinforced the prevailing stigma of infertility, instilling shame in my father. The social attitudes of adoption at that time were also based on shame and the prevalence of secrecy and deception. No one knew how these children came to terms with their struggle for identity, as they became adults. Even today, long after adoption has evolved into a more positive social system, donor conception remains primarily secretive.

This honest book is long overdue. Books on infertility often talk about the positive aspects of donor conception and gloss over the inevitable areas of controversy. They strive to make infertile people "comfortable" with their decisions, even if they decide to deceive their children. Other books are highly critical of the ethics of reproductive technology and show little empathy for the pain of infertility.

Infertility is one of life's deepest sources of pain. There is no comfortable resolution to this suffering, this loss of hope for children who come from the magical mixture of genealogical heritage between you and your partner. If you adopt a child, there are many losses; for the adopting couple, the birthparents and even the child. If you choose a childfree life despite your desire for a child, the everyday encounters with other people's children will cause grief. If you decide to use medical interventions and choose donor insemination, egg donation, or embryo transfer, you will also suffer from the loss of a full genealogical connection with that child. The experiences of these children will eventually come out in another book that needs to be read by every DI parent. I hope to be a part of that project soon.

For over a century, most DI parents have chosen to keep DI a secret from their children. Although some people would say I am judgemental to presume this, I know that secrecy is a serious mistake with toxic effects. Children trust the people who care for them the most. They expect parents to tell the truth. Parents have a duty to instill the love of truth in their children's character, in order to prepare them for the realities everyone has to face, no matter how unpleasant or harsh. Yet some parents will deceive their children out of fear of causing pain, for themselves as well as for their children, by choosing the path of comfort. Pain is inevitable in life. It contributes to the richness of human experience and makes us strong. We all have to learn the art of facing pain with courage and integrity. As the Trappist Monk and Philosopher Thomas Merton wrote: "The more you try to avoid suffering, the more you suffer, because smaller and more insignificant things begin to torture you in proportion to your fears of being hurt. The one who does the most to avoid suffering is, in the end, the one who suffers the most."

Bill Cordroy
Salt Lake City
USA

1 Building confident and healthy families – the goal of this book

Welcome to this book. The fact that you have it in your hands means that you have an interest in families built with the assistance of donor insemination (DI), i.e. families that have used sperm 'donated' by a man who is not usually known to them. Your interest may be as:

- a potential user of DI, considering it as an option for building your family
- a parent of a child or children already born as a result of DI
- a person created as a result of your parent/s choosing to use DI
- a man who has provided, or intends to provide, semen to a clinic to enable others to have a child
- a relative or friend of any of these people

No-one involved with DI will be immune from the views and attitudes of others about DI in the community, particularly family, friends and professionals. Such views and attitudes can have a powerful impact on how DI is approached and it is for this reason I hope that, beyond the families who are directly involved, others may also want to learn more from the personal experiences recorded here.

This includes the health professionals involved in the treatment – doctors, nurses, counsellors and social workers – as well as lawyers, scientists and members of the clergy. The book is also likely to be relevant to those concerned with the development of social policies for families who use

DI. In addition, academics who study the family – particularly the various ways in which families are formed – may find the book enlightening in terms of the insights it gives to family building and family dynamics when DI has been utilised.

All of the people mentioned above play a unique part in the achievement of the central goal of this book, namely to build confident and healthy families. However, while it would be a bonus, no book – including this one – can possibly respond to *all* of their varied interests. Therefore, as the foundations of families are primarily laid by parents or would-be parents, the focus of the book is on providing the support and guidance for couples and individuals as they contemplate, experience and live with family building using DI.

People who use DI to build a family are in the minority. Most people don't need to seek the assistance of health professionals in creating their families, and of those who do, only a small proportion will use DI. Consequently, there is not a lot of public knowledge about DI, and many people do not even realise that it is an option for building families. As with most minority groups, other people tend to have some concerns that DI users are not conforming to the norm and are therefore 'abnormal' or 'strange'. This may be particularly so for lesbian couples and single women who choose to become parents through the use of DI. A more appropriate and positive way of viewing this, however, is to recognise that there are many different ways in which families are built and DI is just one of these. Families built with the assistance of DI are not better or worse than other families. They are merely different. This difference, however, added to the lack of understanding by others, leads some users of DI to avoid acknowledging that this is the way they have built their family.

Other parents have chosen to be more open about their family creation and it is their experiences that have provided me with the most important source of information for this book. I want to salute their courage in being prepared to share their stories with me and therefore, with you as a reader. In their own words, they recount their journeys, experiences, thoughts, anxieties and joys. They have not all had the same experiences, nor do they necessarily think that how they managed their experiences is the way others should manage theirs. On the other hand, readers may well be able to identify with some of the parents' comments and find in them strength, inspiration and support, as well as some practical ideas to use.

These parents are not meant to be representative and this is not an account of a study based on scientific research. Rather, it is a story of pioneers, who have invariably moved into unchartered territory, experiencing the associated risks, uncertainties, conflicts and tensions. They all wanted to identify themselves and are happy to be contacted if you would like to discuss their experiences further. Rather than publish their individual email addresses in this book, however, it was decided that it would be more appropriate for you to send any messages to my email address and I will forward them on. They will then correspond with you directly. My email address is ken.daniels@canterbury.ac.nz.

Each of the named parents has also provided a 'pen picture' of themselves and their family situation, and these appear at the end of the book. The parents come from a number of different countries.

Throughout the book I have attributed quotes from the parents I have spoken to either individually or as a couple, but unfortunately I am not able to identify quotes from the parents who took part in the three focus group discussions that I organised – in London, Sydney and Melbourne. This is not because the parents didn't want to be identified, but rather because it was impossible when transcribing the discussions to know who had said what.

While the experiences of the parents appearing in the book have been very different, they all share one vital ingredient, that is, they have shared with their children how their families were created. By choosing to do so, these parents have swum against the long-existing tide – many were advised not to share information and others were cautioned against it – but although they have faced many challenges surrounding their decision to be open, they remain positive that it was the right thing to do. These parents are convinced that to build a healthy and happy family, it is important to be open and honest about their use of DI. To not share this information would convey the view that it is something to be ashamed of.

Throughout the book I have also included quotes from various written sources that are publicly available, including a series of extremely helpful letters to would-be parents. These letters, which contain very rich and helpful insights for those considering DI, are prepared by and are available from Donor Conception Network in the United Kingdom.

A further source of information for this book is that which results from my own work over the past 27 years. Like the parents who have shared their experiences with me, I have also been on a journey in relation to my understanding of DI. When I was appointed to a full time academic position at the University of Canterbury in New Zealand, it followed several years as a counsellor and a social work practitioner. As I wished to retain some involvement in counselling, Marion Ward, the then social worker at Christchurch Women's Hospital, invited me to join her in the 'assessment of couples who were seeking AID'. (DI was previously known as Artificial Insemination by Donor). I had to ask the question, 'AID – what is that?' As a result of Marion's request, a whole new world opened up to me, one that has been full of excitement, stimulation, challenges and on occasions, frustrations. My journey had begun.

Working with would-be parents who were considering what it would mean to use DI was a fast learning curve. The more I became involved in this area of work, the more I realised that Marion and I knew very little about it. We drew on the experience of adoption but that had its limitations. I also became aware of the many issues that could emerge in the future, especially for the children and their families. I'm sure that my experience as a father of adopted twin daughters gave me added insights into this area.

My journey into research – part of every academic's life and work – meant that I began to collect information from couples and doctors. I also sought views from the community on DI and the emergence of *in vitro* fertilisation (IVF). The sharing of this information included writing academic papers for journals that were read by doctors, social workers, counsellors, psychologists and lawyers, as well as writing articles for the emerging consumer groups for infertile couples. Up until that time, very little information was available on what was happening with DI – it was, after all, practised under a cloud of secrecy.

That early information I gathered, together with the research that I and others have carried out since, has contributed to a greater understanding of the issues experienced by families built with DI, and by the men who provide their semen. Much of my writing is designed to contribute to the education of health professionals and those concerned with the development of social policies. In several countries my research has supported submissions made to the government regarding policies that enhance family well-being and uphold the rights and responsibilities of all parties involved.

However, my first commitment has always been to the members of families that have been built as a result of DI. I retain a very strong commitment to their needs and am very grateful that my research continues to give me the opportunity to stay involved with many of them. I am also very grateful for the invitations to speak at consumer group meetings in a number of countries around the world. This ongoing contact is immensely helpful in deepening my understanding of what it means for parents and their sons and daughters to be part of a family that has been built with the use of DI.

While I have not specifically gathered material from those born as a result of DI, many have shared their thoughts and feelings with me over the years, including Bill Cordray, who at age 58 is the oldest person I have met who was conceived as a result of DI. I asked Bill, to write the foreword to the book as his journey has been an inspiration to me and many others. He reminds us of many things surrounding the use of DI – the influence of professionals, the power of social attitudes, the impact of family life on the growing child, the need for greater protection and recognition for children, and the fact that children become adults.

As I move to the concluding phase of the journey in my professional work and career, this book in a sense brings me back to my beginnings in DI, which were very much with people who are considering and preparing themselves for the use of DI. I want to be able to offer the insights and experiences of those who have already walked some way along this path, which in turn, I hope will make family building with the use of DI a richer and more satisfying experience for others. Ultimately it is parents who can best provide for the protection, health and well-being of their children, as they 'set the scene' by making and acting on the major decisions concerning their family. If the book contributes, as I hope it will, to their being able to parent to their highest potential, then the many offspring who follow in Bill Cordray's footsteps will have richer lives and more open and trusting relationships with their parents.

One of the themes throughout the book is the use of appropriate terminology, as the words we use when conveying important messages can be extremely significant. For example, finding one appropriate word for describing people conceived as a result of DI presents a challenge, and as you will notice throughout the book, different people use different terms. The word 'child' has been used for many years, and still is by some people, but clearly this is not an appropriate term for Bill or other adults. The word 'offspring' is being increasingly used, but some people object to this, believing it is more appropriate for animals than humans.

I was recently at a meeting, where it was argued that 'DI conceived person' was the most appropriate term. I would reverse the words to 'person conceived as a result of DI', thus emphasising the person first and the means of conception second. My preferred phrase is long and presents difficulties in terms of the number of times it would be used in this book but as I did of course need to choose a word or phrase, I have settled on 'offspring', except when I am specifically referring to a child. I apologise to anyone who finds my choice inappropriate. I certainly do not use, or think of, the term in anything other than a human and personal sense.

The title, *Building a Family with the Assistance of Donor Insemination* was chosen very carefully. All families have to be built. There is the physical building, but equally as important, there is what may be described as the ongoing psychological and social building. As you read the stories of the parents who contributed to this book, you will see that most of the issues they are concerned with regarding their families are psychological and social, and as this is also where my expertise lies, it is the area I have focused on throughout the book. The physical aspect of DI (the medical treatment) is not covered, as that information can be obtained from other sources and there are such references at the end of the book.

The notion of building a family means that consideration has to be given to a plan, thinking about the resources that are available, making decisions, laying foundations and using experts, both professional and lay. The 'treatment' of DI is only one stage in that building plan, and in tracing the journey of parents who have used DI, the book places as much emphasis on the experiences leading up to and including treatment, as it does on the ongoing experiences throughout the following years. None of these parents would say that they have *built* their family, but rather that they are *continuing to build* their family. Their desire to share their experiences with you is based on their hope that you may gain something from their reflections and insights, an opportunity that was not available to them as they began their own journey into DI.

In effect, other people's experiences can be viewed as part of the preparation process for DI, a notion that was first talked about by Patty Mahlstedt and Dorothy Greenfeld in the U.S.A some twenty years ago. This notion of preparation has become increasingly important to me in recent times and one that my German colleague, Petra Thorn, and I, have been developing. We feel that too much emphasis in DI is placed on the treatment phase because that is the phase in which the health professionals are involved.

This is brought home to me very clearly every time I go into a clinic and see a pinboard with pictures of babies. In many ways, these pictures are the signs of success for the clinic staff: somebody came seeking DI, the treatment was provided and the outcome is seen in this photo of a beautiful baby. I have, however, never seen pictures of teenagers or families on these pinboards and yet, of course, each of these babies is part of a nurturing and sharing family.

It may well be that photos of families are not there because of the privacy or secrecy that has been associated with DI; it may be that parents have felt that the clinic was more interested in seeing pictures of the baby than of them; it could also be that pictures of teenagers weren't there because by the time they have reached that age, parents may have thought the clinics had forgotten or would not be interested. Whatever the reason, like the treatment phase, the baby phase is only one stage in the building of the family, and in this book I prefer to take a holistic view – from the time of discovering the need for assistance in building your family, through the period of treatment, conception and birth, and continuing into the many years of family life that follow.

You will see that I adopt a strong and clear position on the benefits of openness and honesty surrounding DI family building. The personal stories, together with the academic and professional work I have been involved in, show that love is stronger than fear, and that love is also the basis for building healthy, honest and open communication within families. Fear only leads to stigma, shame and secrecy, which have an adverse effect on the well-being and healthy functioning of children and families.

Many professionals, especially in some parts of the world, claim that being open with children and others is too strong a position to adopt. Some of my colleagues have even argued that until we have clear research evidence that secrecy in DI has a negative effect, we should not be encouraging parents to be open and honest with their families. In response, this book asks the question, 'Why would you not be honest and open with your children?' If you wish to teach your children the values of honesty, openness, trust, truth and love, then how can you not mirror these in your own relationship with them?

Apart from this more philosophical and moral response, some research evidence is now available. Emma Lycett, Susan Golombok, Ruth Curson (from London, England) and I have recently published an academic paper based on a research study of 46 families with a child aged between four and eight, where some of the families had disclosed to their children the use of DI and some had not. We were able to conclude:

> The differences that were identified between the two groups of families indicated fewer difficulties among the disclosers than the non-disclosers. Mothers who were inclined toward disclosure reported less frequent, and less severe, arguments with their children. They also considered their children to show a lower level of conduct problems, and to be less of a strain. In addition, disclosing couples viewed themselves as more competent as parents than did their non-disclosing counterparts.
>
> These findings are of particular interest as they replicate those of an earlier study with a different sample. In the 12–year-old follow-up of the European Study of Assisted Reproduction Families, children who had been told about donor insemination had less frequent and less severe disputes with their mothers, and perceived their mothers as less strict, than those who had not been told. Although the number of children who had been told was small, both children and mothers independently reported such conflicts, thus reducing the likelihood that the finding was produced by chance. The replication of this result in the present study

> further suggests that this is a genuine finding rather than a chance effect. Moreover, the variables that differed significantly between groups were not independent of each other but instead formed a coherent pattern in that child conduct problems, mother-child conflict, perception of the child as a strain and reduced parenting competence are related constructs. With respect to fathers, there were no differences in the present investigation between disclosing and non-disclosing fathers regarding their relationship with their child or their reports of child adjustment. The same was true of fathers in the earlier investigation.[1]

I am very fortunate to live in New Zealand, where we have a social and professional climate that for some fifteen years has strongly supported the view that family well-being is enhanced when there is openness and honesty about the use of DI. As a result of these attitudes, studies have shown that around three quarters of the New Zealand families who have used DI have told, or are planning to tell, their children about the way in which their family was built.

Over the past two decades, there have been several factors that have contributed to New Zealand currently being one of the countries at the forefront of the movement towards more openness and honesty. The shift began in the early 1980s, when counsellors started questioning the negative aspects of secrecy surrounding DI and in particular, how that secrecy impacted on the children born as a result. Adoption literature supported their views, as did the growing recognition and acceptance of Maori (the indigenous people of New Zealand) perspectives on children and family relationships.

For Maori, there is acknowledgement that there are two kinds of family, the nuclear family and *whanau*. *Whanau* is a group of relatives connected by an ancestor (*Tupuna*) and comprising of several generations, several nuclear families and several households. When children are born into their *whanau*, all people involved have a responsibility to ensure that the interests of the child are paramount. The concept of *whanau* is closely related to *whakapapa*, which is similar to genealogy, in that Maori can trace their origins back to the beginnings of life. It is crucial for people to know their lineage, as *whakapapa* links determine certain entitlements, such as land, and also defines the relationships between people. Any seed that is shared between people to create life is therefore regarded by Maori as *tapu* or sacred, which of course, has important implications for both assisted human reproduction and adoption.

Another factor impacting on the New Zealand DI climate was the formation in 1988 of the New Zealand Infertility Society (now Fertility New Zealand), which recognised the valuable contribution consumers could make to encouraging openness. Perhaps most significantly, however, New Zealand doctors also began to change their thinking, embracing the psychosocial perspectives of this type of family creation and incorporating them into their policies and practices. In his report of a 1990 New Zealand Infertility Society workshop held specifically on DI, Dr John Peek said that many fertility clinics were looking for donors prepared to be identifiable and, contrary to previous belief, most donors were prepared to do this.[2]

In our continuing journey, New Zealand will introduce legislation in 2004, enabling future offspring to gain access to information about the identity of the man whose semen contributed to their conception. This legislation will not cause major changes to DI practice; rather it will confirm what the professionals are already doing. (This is in sharp contrast to some other countries where the law and social policy has sought to establish a change, the consequences of which have been somewhat negative and conflictual.) It needs to be acknowledged that New Zealand did not reach this position without many struggles but the fact that men and women who donate their gametes are not accepted unless they are prepared to be identified to offspring in the future – and this has been the case for approximately fifteen years – indicates the commitment of the professionals involved in this field.

One of the privileges of being involved in international policy and research on DI is that I have been able to travel to many countries and meet many families. It is of note, however, that I failed in my attempts to find a family in Sweden who was willing to contribute to this book. Sweden was the first country to introduce legislation enabling offspring to identify the man whose semen helped create them and it is a country in which I have carried out research, but despite the legislation which supports openness, the consumer organisation and some of my colleagues in Sweden could not locate any parents willing to talk about their experiences with me. This suggests that the purpose of the legislation, namely to encourage a more healthy and open approach, has not been as successful as hoped for.

The lack of success has also been suggested by the results of a Swedish study reported in 2000, which shows that 89% of parents in the study had not told their children that they had been conceived as a result of DI. Of the 105 parents who chose to comment further, 61 were going to inform their children, 28 were not going to inform them and 16 were unsure.[3] It needs to be acknowledged that while many of the families in this study still had very young children, who were to be acquainted with their family stories as they grew older, a number of other parents had opted quite purposefully not to share this information with their children. The main message emerging from this is that legislation itself does not achieve the kind of change that has been witnessed in New Zealand, for example, where legislation is following the changes, rather than forcing them.

This book has been written at a time when there is continuing publicity about semen, egg and embryo donation. There has been a significant growth in support groups around the world, both those that meet in person and those established via the Internet. The Internet now provides a great range of information, online access to offspring and sibling contact groups and the opportunity to exchange ideas through chat rooms. Support groups invariably involve parents, offspring and the providers of gametes, and have had a dramatic impact, not just at a personal level but also at the policy level. Looking at the material that has emerged from a number of these groups, especially those in Australia, New Zealand, England and Canada, it is remarkable to see how well they have provided the three key functions of a support group:

- making information available
- providing support to individuals
- trying to improve social policy and legislation for the benefit of their members

It is also a time of historical significance for DI, in that many countries are considering changes to their laws regarding access to information about donors. Debates concerning prospective changes have been acrimonious and heated. The topic of information sharing in families is one that arouses strong feelings, especially amongst some professionals who believe they speak on behalf of many of their patients and donors, in arguing that anonymity, privacy and secrecy should be maintained. This book is clearly a challenge to these professionals and also to the politicians who seek guidance and take advice from them.

As a current example, Canada's consideration of information sharing is fascinating. Many consumers, who are directly involved in and concerned by the lack of information about donors, have battled against the professionals, who argue that they will not be able to offer services if there is a change to the current system of anonymity for the men and women who provide their gametes. These are the same arguments that were made in Sweden, when the government prepared to introduce legislation there. However, my colleague Othon Lalos and I have shown that the number of men who are prepared to provide semen has in fact increased since the introduction of the Swedish legislation in 1985, although they have different characteristics than the men who provided semen in the past.[4] (This is discussed more fully in Chapter Nine.)

This book is also being written at a time when a decision is awaited about a significant court case in the United Kingdom where two individuals, Joanna Rose and an unnamed child, are challenging the Human Fertilisation and Embryology Authority and the Department of Health over access to information. The outcome of this court case is likely to impact significantly on future policy in the United Kingdom and perhaps in other countries as well. At the beginning of 2004, the United Kingdom government announced that from 2005, children born as a result of gamete donation would be able to access information about their donors, including their identity.

These brief overviews of New Zealand, Sweden, Canada and the United Kingdom show that each country has its own DI 'culture', which plays a part in influencing the views people are exposed to when considering it as a means of family building.

Whatever the different views may be, there are certain stages that people are likely to experience on their journey to building a confident and healthy family and I have organised the book to follow these stages. While some readers may wish to dip into certain sections, which hopefully will be beneficial, my own view is that what the contributing parents say at any particular stage of their journey is best seen in the context of what has gone before. Maori have a saying that they walk into the future backwards, which means that the present and the future are shaped by the past. In other words, we should always be aware of, and acknowledge, those people and events that have shaped us into the people we now are.

I want to conclude this chapter by expressing my thanks, first of all to my employer, the University of Canterbury, for providing me with a job that has been extremely stimulating and challenging. The part of my work that has involved DI has been particularly rewarding. In addition, I would not have been able to interview the families you meet in this book if it had not been for a twelve-month study leave the University granted me.

My special thanks go to the families represented in this book and to the many other people whose lives and stories I have had the privilege of sharing over the years. You have been very powerful educators. I am also grateful to the consumer groups for keeping me in touch with many people I have not met personally but whose stories I know through magazines and the Internet.

I would also like to thank the many colleagues who have facilitated my meetings with parents, as well as for the many discussions we have had over the years. You too have contributed to my education and this book is therefore a reflection, not just of my work, but of the ideas and views of many people, both consumers and professionals.

Finally, I thank you, the reader, for starting the journey of reading this book. I, along with the families who have contributed to it, hope your understanding of DI will be enriched by the knowledge that is shared and I hope the book provides an inspiration to help you manage your own feelings, thoughts and behaviour that surround the building of a family with the assistance of DI.

2 Arriving at the need for assistance in building your family

Tom and I married in 1980. We were both young, 24, and had always dreamed of filling our house in the country with three children. Ali

Ali and Tom's dream of a family is one that is shared by most couples who marry or enter into a long term permanent relationship, almost as if it is 'a natural expectation' that children will result from such relationships. It is also a natural expectation for many women who are not in a relationship that they will one day form a partnership and have children too. This expectation of a family is not only shared by the individuals themselves; it is also something that is highly valued by society. Some researchers have talked about societies being 'pronatalist', in that families with children are particularly valued and catered for, and that they play a vital role in how the society functions. Consequently, the dream and expectation of having children is very strong, and causes many people to experience powerful reactions when they are unable to fulfil this desire.

Finding out that I wasn't going to be able to produce kids naturally was probably the biggest blow to me. Tom

The news was devastating. That was the first time I had seen Tom cry. Ali

I had a feeling of loss. My dreams were shattered. Evelyn

I remember weeping, weeping. Susan

When they said that it was him, it was a massive shock and he said that he was finished now. He was devastated. Marie

The words 'devastation', 'shock' and 'shattered' all indicate the typical strength of reactions. Part of the reason for such strong reactions is that the discovery of infertility is usually unexpected. Even if tests and examinations have indicated a problem, couples are still likely to believe they will soon be able to fulfil their desire of having a child and becoming a family.

It was possible that we might not be able to have children. I guess that we live in denial sometimes and I think that's probably what Laurie was doing and consequently I did too probably. Evelyn

As with most unexpected events, the shock leads to significant questioning and disbelief.

It was shocking and disturbing. It took me awhile to get used to the idea; it's not something you want to hear. Part of my process was trying to think, 'Why is this happening to me?' Greg

I couldn't believe this magic run I was on had come to an end. I felt that everything I had done wrong in the past had caught up with me. Romana

I was really devastated but I kept thinking that since it wasn't me, maybe I could get pregnant. And it was this crazy combination of positive and negative at the same time. Susan

Professionals often talk about the impact of infertility on a person's identity. Previously that person may have imagined being pregnant (or having their partner pregnant), kicking a ball with their son, or taking their daughter to ballet classes. People who discover they will not be able to have children, however, will begin to view and possibly label themselves differently, and be faced with re-evaluating their identity for the future.

It was really sad because I had dreamt of having a family and being

a mother all my life. It was really important to me, being able to have a family with Warren. Leonie

In heterosexual couples, the male partner in particular is likely to suffer from an altered self-identity because he is the one diagnosed as being infertile. Many couples, however, say they find it more helpful to think of infertility as being something that they both experience and that *they*, as a couple, cannot have the children *they* wish for. The dream and desire of having children who are biologically related to the two of them has been shattered.

When we found out that we couldn't have a child together, there was a definite grief for me that I wouldn't have a child that would have any of Walt's characteristics, as there were qualities in him that I would have liked to have seen reproduced in our children. Olivia

While Tom felt that he had nothing to offer a marriage if he couldn't have children, I insisted that it was our *problem, not his. He hadn't done anything to cause this condition; it was simply the way he was.* Ali

We quite often say that it's not just me that's infertile, it's, 'We're infertile'. Warren

The loss of the dream of being able to have children is sometimes likened to the pain of death, and is accompanied by a feeling of grief. While the couple may not be mourning an actual person, they are in effect suffering from the death of their potential child and the hopes and expectations of their potential family.

It was very tough. I was in total shock at first, we both were. It's just as if there was a death in the family. You go through the same processes. You are shocked; it turns to anger; you try to find a resolution. Tom

Loss of fertility can feel like a bereavement and the emotions

surrounding it and the time it takes to put it in perspective are similar. Letter from Walter to would-be DI Dads

Researchers who have studied reactions to death often talk about the range of feelings and responses that bereaved people experience. One of the most influential writers in this respect, Elisabeth Kübler-Ross, has described the reactions in terms of stages that people pass through: denial, anger, bargaining, depression, and finally, acceptance.[1]

Those who suffer a 'death' through infertility often talk about these same stages and the impacts they have, although individuals will, of course, experience these stages differently and may spend longer at one stage than another. It is useful having this information because of the reassurance people gain in knowing that many of the reactions experienced are 'normal' and to be expected.

One issue to be aware of is that well-meaning friends, relatives or professionals, may want you to move on to the next stage before you are ready. In particular, this can occur if people are encouraging you to begin having treatment when you are still managing your thoughts and feelings of an earlier stage, such as coming to terms with the loss of your potential biologically-connected family.

Couples can also feel a huge number of other losses when discovering they are infertile, including the loss of self esteem and the sexual identity that is normally associated with the ability to become parents.

I was worried people would think less of us because we couldn't have babies like everybody else. I thought that there was shame associated with the infertility. Romana

From talking to other women, it was like their husband's ego had taken a big hit and it was too much to reveal to the world that they were infertile. It was like equating his fertility with sexual potency. Susan

Another loss many people find difficult to face is that of the 'genetic line'. There is an expectation that family life continues on beyond the present and for some families, this has a great significance and meaning.

> *Feelings about inheritance are born and bred in us. We inherit our fathers' names because we inherit our fathers' blood. The simplest family tree tracks the blood line. There's going to be something missing and it's going to be my genes that have gone missing. I'm going to be the end of the line.* Letter from Walter to would-be DI Dads

Another common emotion is the strong sense of injustice at being unable to achieve something that comes so easily to others and that is a natural expectation in life.

> *When Tom's sister-in-law told us at a family gathering that she was expecting her fourth baby, I just broke down completely. I thought this is just not fair. 'You're having your fourth baby and we have been struggling for two and a half years to have our first baby and you're Tom's brother.' To me, there was just no justice in that whatsoever. I became really angry inside that this was not going the way that I had planned.* Ali

> *I felt a tad jealous of couples that could have babies naturally, without even thinking about it. I thought, 'If you knew what we were going through right now. If you had to go through what we have gone through, you'd have a different perspective on life.' There we were, not able to have kids naturally, and we're looking at other couples that could. They'd say, 'Oh, we're going to try for another child' and have one immediately. It wasn't a healthy thing internally because it brings you down.* Tom

> *What have we done to deserve this, I thought. It's so unfair – all our friends just seem to be having children without any trouble. They didn't have to go off to special clinics, being told to be sure to have sex at particular times, wear loose pants, demean themselves by having to produce sperm samples. They seem to have ordinary sex lives and pregnancies just happen for them.* Letter from Walter to would-be DI Dads

As well as a man having to deal with the impact infertility has on his own thoughts and feelings, he may also suffer feelings of guilt about the effect his infertility has on his partner.

> *To me, if children came along that would be fine but if they didn't, it wasn't a big deal at the time. But when I found out I was infertile, I was more concerned that my own infertility had stopped Leonie from having children.* Warren

Sometimes a man who finds he cannot father children believes he had almost entered the marriage or relationship under false pretences. This may lead him to feel that he needs to offer his partner the opportunity to reassess, reconsider and even leave their relationship.

> *They say that females choose their mates from men they want to father their children. Now it's obvious I can't even do that, would she really want to stay with me? She wants kids, wants them desperately.* Letter from Walter to would-be DI Dads

> *When I found out I was infertile, one of my first reactions was to say to Leonie, 'You don't have to stay with me; you're free to go and find someone else who can give you children.' I felt I shouldn't deny her the opportunity. If I didn't, I'd probably feel guilty having tied Leonie to me and her not being able to have children and I would have to live with that for the rest of my life.* Warren

Reassuring comments by Leonie and Ali show, however, that they married their partners because of love, rather than to have children.

> *I remember Tom saying, 'I can't give you what you want'. And I just thought,* 'You're *what I want*'. Ali

> *Warren was basically saying, 'You can leave me and have a divorce'. That was ridiculous. I didn't know where that thought pattern came from. I hadn't even thought I would want to leave my husband just because we can't have kids. I said, 'Don't be stupid. I didn't marry you for your ability to have children; I married you because I love you.'* Leonie

Male infertility is only one of the reasons people need assistance in building their family. Single women and lesbian couples do not of course experience infertility in the same way that we have been talking about, but their inability to have a child without assistance – often described as 'social infertility' – is just as significant. The desire for these women to be a parent is no different from people in a heterosexual relationship and although there may not be a physical base to their infertility, they have personal and social reasons for wanting to use DI.

Another group of people, who are not infertile in the traditional sense of the word but may have the need to use DI, are those who suffer from a physical or genetic condition that could be passed on to any children conceived with their gametes.

> *I am fertile but there's a fairly big risk that any children I father naturally will have fairly severe defects and that's why we chose DI. I think that I'm used to it now that I won't father kids naturally but it was a blow. Maybe a lot of people would jump at the chance to have a kid naturally, whether it be so-called normal or not, so I've struggled with that too.* Male, Melbourne Focus Group

The story of another family faced with a genetic condition appeared in an article in a German newspaper in July 2000:

> I always wanted children but it was clear to me that our society cannot deal adequately with handicapped people. I suffer from a spastic spinal paralysis, an inherited disability which gets worse over the years. The risk was great that our child would also be handicapped and then I decided, 'I don't want that, neither for my offspring nor for me, myself'. With every wrong step of a child, I would have thought, 'Well there you are, that was your fault, you are responsible for it'.[2]

Some individuals and couples know beforehand that they will not be able to conceive without assistance, perhaps because of a medical condition or a prior vasectomy. One such person is Tony Ferns, who related his story at a meeting of DI Network (now known as DC Network).

> I was successfully treated for lymphatic cancer when I was younger. The chemotherapy, whilst sorting out the more immediate problem, enabled

my sperm count to be calculated on the fingers of one hand. So we always knew that DI would be route one for our own family.[3]

Although this means there is not the shock of an unexpected discovery, there are still issues that need to be faced and resolved.

My body doesn't make enough testosterone and I was told when I was 14 or 15 that I wouldn't be able to have kids naturally. At first that was fantastic but when I met June, she had this thing about kids and I found it very hard to tell her. I was really scared and worried that I'd lose her. But from the time she found out what was going on, she said that we should go to a doctor and see what we could do. Male, Melbourne Focus Group

When I met Grant, I knew he'd had a vasectomy when he was 24 and because I felt I was running under a lucky star, I just assumed the reversal would work and I would start to have my family. So we didn't even rush into it. We waited a couple of years after we married and then he had the operation and we were told it didn't work. That was very shocking to me. Romana

I had a vasectomy as I'd been married before with two children. Then when I met Pam, your views change, there is something missing, you want a child. So we went through the reversal of the vasectomy. Male, Sydney Focus Group. *Yet all the attention was on me. That went on for sometime, not realising that his sperm count was going down, down, down every year. That wasn't picked up.* Female, Sydney Focus Group

The discovery of infertility and/or facing the need for assistance in building your family is, of course, where the DI journey begins. How the journey develops depends to a large extent on the manner in which issues are faced at this stage, in particular, the level and quality of communication.

Firstly, there is the communication and contact that couples and individuals have with professionals. Professionals need to recognise the devastating effects on a couple when they discover their infertility and to allow them time to be together to manage this news. The couple need to share the news of their loss and to communicate their thoughts and feelings with each other, before thinking about what they will do as a result of this news. (The need to be able to digest the discovery of infertility before being able to move on is discussed more fully in the next chapter.)

Professionals also need to be aware of the stress involved for people having to seek assistance in conceiving. It is likely they will be asked a great many personal questions on matters that would normally be contained within the privacy of their relationship, and this 'invasion' into their private life can be seen as a further 'punishment' for their infertility.

> *After the initial shock, there was the highly self-conscious nature of infertility that involves other people in the methodology.* Male, London Focus Group

Most doctors are understanding and empathetic when carrying out tests and delivering the diagnosis of infertility.

> *It was so degrading. Our doctor was terrific though, he was really supportive. You could see he was broken up about having to tell us.* Ali

> *The gratitude and satisfaction that we got from the support staff here and all the doctors and nurses being able to help us through this – you can't put it into words. They are like saviours to us.* Tom

Unfortunately, though, there are also doctors with a 'bedside manner' that is not so tactful, particularly when it comes to understanding the pain, distress and embarrassment a person may be feeling. The matter-of-fact way that this significant news is conveyed by a doctor can be very distressing.

> *It was a bit of a shock and it hurt me that suddenly this result came back rather brutally.* Male, London Focus Group

> *My advice to doctors, nurses and counsellors is that they should be concerned about the mental health of the infertile person and the partner of that infertile person at the time of giving the diagnosis.*

The way they break bad news, how do they support that person? The way they treat men who are infertile, it's criminal really. To leave my husband walking the streets of Sydney after giving him that diagnosis over the phone – it's insensitive. Where was the support for my husband upon learning about his infertility? Leonie

We turn now to communication that takes place between partners and invariably, we think of verbal communication. However, non-verbal communication – such as smiling at each other when happy, weeping together or holding each other when upset, or transmitting messages of love and understanding through the eyes – is also very significant within a relationship, particularly when it is as a result of receiving such important news as infertility. Whatever form communication takes, it is vital for partners to share their thoughts and feelings with each other, which in turn, will benefit them both individually and as a couple. Not only will they better understand what their partner is experiencing but many couples find they can draw support from each other and become closer as a result.

If it wasn't something that we were working on together, if it hadn't been for Ali there to support me through it, it would have been a lot more devastating than it was. It was a team effort. Tom

I think it brought us closer together, not pushing us apart. Warren

It was very traumatic for me. And I remember bringing you toast in bed in the middle of the day because you were lying in bed crying. Grant. *Yes. Avocado toast, which is your favourite toast but I ate it because it was so comforting.* Romana

Other people find that the strong emotions accompanying the discovery of infertility, added to the stress of undergoing tests and treatment, have a negative impact on their relationship.

The infertility did more [to the break up of our marriage]. The DI was only because of the infertility. Marie

> *The infertility had an impact. It was just a real strain and stress to be going through infertility testing. It became a focal point. I felt pretty upset about the whole infertility thing.* Susan

> *If we hadn't had children, if this programme hadn't been available, I'm not sure we would still be married to each other because that was first and foremost in our minds and in our big vision.* Ali

Some people find that their partner is in such a state of shock and in need of support that he or she is not in a position to provide it in return. If both partners are already distressed, they may also feel that they don't want to burden each other further. When both partners are preoccupied with their own thoughts and feelings, however, it becomes difficult to reach out and understand what message the other person is conveying. The desire to protect each other and avoid causing additional pain can make it extremely difficult for partners to communicate honestly with the person closest to them. My experience of working with couples consistently shows that communication about infertility can be as stressful and demanding as dealing with the infertility itself.

Being able to communicate honestly with your partner and with others is one of the most positive and beneficial ways of managing the impact of infertility. What is very clear though, from the preparation seminars Petra Thorn and myself run in Germany for couples seeking DI, is that they feel a great deal of uncertainty about communication and also of each other's expectations. To facilitate better communication and understanding between partners, we find it important that they recognise the effects of infertility in three main areas – their feelings, thoughts and behaviour – and how these can differ between genders.

When men and women split into two separate discussion groups at the seminars, we find that their issues are often similar but are dealt with in quite different ways. Women tend to respond predominantly with their feelings. They usually need to discuss and explore the issues fully, expressing their emotions and seeking the support and love of their partners. They often describe their male partners as being practical and seemingly lacking in any emotion and feeling for them.

Men generally respond much more with their thoughts and behaviour.

This is often reflected by men saying that they don't know how to respond and be supportive to their female partner, particularly if she becomes very emotional at the time of her period, when reminded of the lost opportunity for a child. Men often report that they also find it unhelpful and distressing to have endless discussions, constantly going over the same issues. They would prefer a much more pragmatic approach by just making the decisions and moving on.

These of course are gender stereotypes and as with all stereotypes, there are many, many exceptions. My own observation is that both men and women experience emotions quite strongly and are very thoughtful about the way in which they approach issues or resolve matters, but they may have different ways of expressing themselves. While this is challenging in terms of communication within a relationship, it is immensely helpful to understand that your partner may be merely communicating in the mode he or she is most comfortable with and it doesn't mean there is a lack of understanding of your position.

Communication of course extends beyond the couple, to their family members and friends. Perhaps one of the first decisions a couple needs to make when discovering infertility is who they will share this important information with and on what basis. It is not helpful for people to find that their partner has already talked with others, without first discussing the possibility of that happening.

> *There can be issues about, 'Well my wife has told a number of her friends but I haven't told anybody'. The man says, 'Well I don't really want or need emotional support but my wife seems to have a group of woman-friends she tells everything that's going on', and that rather alarms the man.* Walter

> *First of all, I didn't realise I wasn't supposed to tell people. So I went and told people. And then when Romana asked me not to, I couldn't remember who I told and who I hadn't told and it was confusing for me.* Grant

Some women feel that by talking to others, they are in some way letting their husband down. They often struggle with the conflict of trying to balance their need to gain support from others, with their desire to protect their partner from what is sometimes seen as a social stigma.

> *I think women who have infertile partners have an automatic button in their brain. We must protect them. I don't feel I do that now, but in those days I probably used to.* Leonie

> *I wanted to protect Grant. He was a wonderful human being who I love dearly and people like him, he's competent at his work and I didn't want people to think that he was less than he was because he couldn't have babies. I had to protect him and I know that within the whole thing, women do tend to protect their partners.* Romana

By talking about something that is important to us, the need to share our feelings can be satisfied, but at the same time it can raise questions as to the response we will receive. If we are fearful that others may respond in a negative way or that they may view us differently and make us feel less than normal, then we may avoid talking with them and as a result, alienate or isolate ourselves even more. Because some people associate infertility with a perceived stigma or shame, those who use assisted human reproduction methods sometimes choose to keep the nature of their child's conception a secret. (Secrecy surrounding DI is discussed in detail in Chapter Four.)

It is important to recognise that people we talk to about infertility will each have their own views and own reactions, based on a whole variety of personal experiences. Some may not know how to react and may respond in very inappropriate ways. They may feel very sad for you, or they could find it so difficult to cope with your sadness that they avoid the issue by pretending they haven't heard what you have said. Other people may want to find solutions and advise what you should be doing. The chances are that you will have some idea of their likely reactions by the way they have responded to other people's powerful and meaningful experiences.

Some of the more negative ways in which friends can respond is by asking, 'Why do you want to have children anyway?' It is difficult to know how to answer that question, particularly as couples who can have children without assistance don't usually get asked that question. Also, there can be the unhelpful jokes and comments such as, 'You're only shooting blanks' and this may not just be from friends but may even be from professionals, as some people have reported.

> *How could you talk about this anyway? Anyone you might think of talking to about it might just burst out laughing. An infertile man. Sterile. A jaffa – no pips. You've heard plenty of jokes about all this, now they will be laughing at you.* Letter from Walter to would-be DI Dads

> *I quote one doctor who said to me, 'Did you spit in [the sample container] or something?'* Male, London Focus Group

There is also a lack of understanding of the differences between sexuality and reproduction by some people, who mistakenly believe that infertility impedes a satisfactory sexual relationship. Whether it is because of this belief, because they think it's expected of them, or because they just don't feel any sympathy about infertility, friends may jokingly offer to be the sexual partner in place of the male whose sperm count is low or non-existent. It can indeed be a very unhelpful and painful experience coping with the comments of others who do not seem to understand.

Infertility can certainly be a considerable challenge to relatives and friends, and one that is well illustrated by a research assistant who worked with me for a couple of years. She told me one day how her mother had said that her daughter and son-in-law's lack of children presented her with quite a difficulty – her friends would all talk about their grandchildren and she had no grandchildren to talk about. Other subtle or not-so-subtle hints given by potential grandparents include knitting baby clothes, putting money aside for future grandchildren or lamenting the fact that they are getting older and would like to be around to enjoy grandchildren growing up.

Parents are likely to feel they have a considerable investment in potential grandchildren and for this reason, their need to be a grandparent may get in the way of their ability to see your need to be a parent. On the other hand, it may well be that these needs coincide and that there is a great deal of understanding and empathy for the situation the couple is experiencing. Some individuals or couples have even talked about how other family members have offered to act as surrogates or to assist in some other ways, e.g. the provision of eggs or sperm, so that they can achieve their goal.

> *We were concerned with, 'How are we going to tell our family that we cannot have children?' We had to have our family hold us and hug us and say, 'We're sorry this has happened to you. We know this is terrible news.'* Ali

It is also possible that people find their parents blame themselves and question whether they had in some way contributed to the infertility. Therefore, it is worth remembering that while parents may be potential sources of support, they may also need support and understanding themselves.

> *I remember the devastation of my Mum when she found out. It was obvious that she thought she had done something wrong or raised me improperly or there was something that she hadn't done to protect me, to cause this. We had to keep reassuring her as a couple that it wasn't her fault. Nothing that she had done, it's just a physical defect.* Tom

It is helpful to understand that friends and relatives are often as unprepared and as uneducated as you were when first discovering infertility. Even though their intentions may be good, they may not know how to respond appropriately or the best way to offer and provide support. And of course, when you are feeling bereft and under stress yourself, it's unlikely that you will want to be spending time educating them on how they can be helpful to you!

One infertile woman who was a member of a support group in New Zealand said 'insensitive comments can cause quiet agony for the childless'. She prepared the following list to help other people recognise which responses can be helpful and which can be unhelpful.

Unhelpful Responses

1. Joking about the infertility problem.
2. Offering advice such as 'Just relax and you'll get pregnant' or 'Let nature take its course'.

3. Telling us to 'hurry up' and have a family and constant reminders that 'time is running out' – we are well aware of the biological clock ticking on.
4. Having people who want to 'fix it' and tell us that all will be 'ok'. In effect that is ignoring the problem as it doesn't feel 'ok'.
5. Saying: 'I'll pray for you' – that can be seen as a cop out unless it is followed by practical and caring help.
6. Cheerful Cherub 'Everything will be alright' – comments like that show lots of optimism but little realism and DO NOT HELP!
7. Telling us about 'Aunt Martha' who didn't get pregnant until she was 41 and then she had four more!
8. Being ignored/left alone.
9. Matching the problem e.g. 'It took me 15 years to get pregnant, then I had 3 miscarriages and look at me now – I have 6 of them!'
10. Going into great detail about your obvious pregnant state.

Helpful Responses

1. Tread lightly when discussing our infertility. Broach the subject only if we have already told you about our problem and if we appear to want to talk about it.
2. Mostly we want someone to listen, understand and show that they care.
3. Ask 'Is there anything I can do to help?'
4. Sometimes we need to excuse ourselves from difficult situations (baby showers, christenings, family gatherings) – please understand and allow us some breathing space.
5. Allow us to be sad around you. It will protect us from withdrawing.
6. Treat us as you would any good friend – we still need friendship.[4]

In addition to gaining the support of friends and family members, two other sources provide specific and valuable support. Firstly, there are the support groups or self-help organisations that have sprung up around the world and offer an absolutely vital source of understanding. They provide the opportunity to talk with, and listen to, others who have travelled (or are still travelling) on a similar journey and who have experienced many of the issues people face as a result of infertility. These consumer groups also extend their service to providing information and advocacy. (The main groups in the Western World are listed at the end of this book and are divided into general infertility organisations and those that are specifically for families formed with the assistance of egg or semen donation.)

> *Support groups are just tremendous. I think people need to know that they're not alone. Everybody has the same issues.* Ali

> *Who better to talk to than somebody that knows exactly what you're going through?* Evelyn

By talking with those who have a personal understanding of what infertility means, anxieties are acknowledged and dealt with. Fears of what the other partner may be thinking or feeling are also more openly expressed and quite often found to be fantasies, rather than reality. Communication between partners can then become more meaningful and helpful.

> *Until we found the support group, we'd never talked about our experience and we didn't know any other couples that had been through DI.* Evelyn

> *It would help for there to be a support group for men, where they could say what they need to say without feeling, 'I don't want my wife to hear this because I know how much she wants this but in my heart this is really how I feel'.* Ali

A further source of support is counsellors, who have invariably had specialised training and are skilled in recognising and understanding the issues people need to work through when dealing with the distress of infertility. While counsellors also provide couples with information and assist them to clarify their options, their main functions are to encourage and enhance communication between partners, and to help them find ways of managing their pain, grief and decision-making. Couples are then better prepared for undertaking treatment and building a family in an alternative manner.

> *We were really working through the issues and I think the counsellors were delighted they had met someone who wanted to talk about it. They gave us heaps of time and it was terrific.* Male, Sydney Focus Group

Counsellors are not a homogeneous group, in that some of them have been trained in psychology, some in social work, some in counselling, some have been nurses who have moved into counselling and others are doctors who have developed a specialist interest in counselling. Clearly each of these different professions may view counselling in different ways and will therefore function from a particular orientation or standpoint. It is important to know the background and orientation of those from whom counselling is sought. It is also important to know that professionally qualified counsellors will be encouraging you to come to your own decisions rather than advising you what to think or do.

One concern I have about counselling services, is that they are invariably located within infertility clinics, which means they are offered in association with the services provided by those clinics. In my view, it is at the time of diagnosis – often conveyed by a general practitioner – that counselling could be particularly beneficial for couples, rather than having to wait until they had decided to use assisted human reproduction, being referred to a clinic and only then finding that counselling is available.

The provision of counselling is a relatively new development in assisted human reproduction and although many clinics around the world do not have counsellors available or see them as relevant, others have become very understanding and supportive of their contribution towards the building of healthy families.

Some people raise a concern over the gender of the counsellor, feeling more comfortable with a counsellor of a particular gender. If this is the case, they may need to ask for a referral to another service, as most clinics do not have the luxury of having both male and female counsellors available. In my experience, most counsellors in this area are female, which may be highly appropriate in terms of recognising and understanding the emotional aspects of infertility, but having said that, all counsellors are expected to be able to respond to whatever issues are presented, in whatever mode they are presented (i.e., cognitive, emotional or behavioural), and by both males and females.

It is not uncommon for people to approach counselling with some apprehension. Their anxieties include beliefs such as:

- If I go to see a counsellor, it's because I have deep psychological problems.

- I'm going mad.
- If the doctor has referred me to counselling then she or he thinks I am going mad.
- If I become upset and distressed this will impact on whether I can have access to treatment because I will be seen as unstable.
- It is not appropriate to talk to a counsellor as I should be able to sort these things out on my own.

> *We went to a counsellor once. We thought that we were going there to be decided on whether or not we could be parents and we felt that it was a make-or-break night. We acted as though we were going to be able to handle this because we didn't want them to see that we were crumbling and hurting.* Female, Melbourne Focus Group

I think a helpful way of viewing counselling is that it is a resource available to people who are affected by infertility and who are facing choices regarding their options. It enables them to talk with somebody who is objective, but who is also caring, understanding and able to provide support and assistance with communication. Whether people choose to avail themselves of that resource is, in many cases, an entirely personal decision but there are also a number of clinics who require anyone undergoing DI to see a counsellor, regarding this as part of the total healthcare programme provided by the clinic. Seeing a counsellor gives people the opportunity to ensure they are as fully prepared as possible, for whatever option they choose. However, as the following extract shows, the benefits of counselling may not be realised until later.

> *The counselling session is the first thing which, with the benefit of hindsight, I might have done quite differently. My own fears of being judged led me to see it as a hurdle rather than an opportunity and once I'd 'got through' I wouldn't have dreamed of going back for more. Now, I think it would have been good to take up the opportunity to talk through some things to which I wasn't giving much thought … I was surprised to find it a fascinating, thought provoking and enjoyable session but I was oblivious to some significant issues.*

Letter from Emily to single women

For most couples, facing the challenge of infertility will be the biggest test they encounter in their lives together and some will not be able to survive or overcome it. The two things that are likely to help them deal with the negatives are their ability to communicate with each other and their recognition of the love that brought them together in the first place.

> *This was something that was happening to us as a couple and we had to face it together as a couple. Perhaps it brought us together in an intimacy that we hadn't had before.* Olivia

3 Deciding to use donor insemination to build your family

In the previous chapter I discussed the importance of acknowledging the feelings of loss and grief that are associated with being told you are infertile and how support from those who are significant in our lives can be of great help in managing these feelings. The feeling of loss, however, is likely to be lifelong; it is not something that can be packaged away in a closet and forgotten, nor is it something that one ever 'gets over'.

> *I think that I'm used to it now, that I won't father kids naturally but it was a blow. Maybe it's still affecting me – I'm not sure.* Male, Melbourne Focus Group

> *You never forget you're infertile but having a child is a distraction.* Warren

> *Some of the feelings of grief and sadness don't go away fast but we learn to live with mixed feelings – the feelings of loss for the children we could never have, mixed with the feelings of excitement and joy for the children we do have.* Letter from Walter to would-be DI Dads

There is a sense, as one person said to me, of a 'sinking-in process' that occurs, as the message of infertility and its impact gradually takes hold and becomes something of a reality. Some people have said that it's a question of coming to terms with infertility, but I doubt whether people ever come to terms with infertility. You may adjust to it, but the loss is so significant that there is always likely to be a gap, and a pain associated with that gap.

It is during the adjustment process that couples will begin to question their options. After a period of time – and it varies from person to person and from couple to couple – the mind starts to question that if Plan A (natural conception) is not achievable, is there a Plan B? For some people – quite often men – this questioning will come very quickly. It's almost as if the thinking (or cognitive) aspects of a man's mind takes over, and desires to seek information about the alternatives. Some would describe this as the 'typical, practical male response'.

> *I snapped into a decision very quickly and simply. I knew there were only three options and I said, 'We're not going to stay childless, we're not going to adopt, so it was obvious. I approached it in a logical way.* Male, London Focus Group

> *The driving force was that we both wanted children so desperately and wanted to have them naturally and if that was not possible, to move on and find a way out of this that would satisfy both of us. If you wallow in self-pity and anger, it's not healthy. I found the more I worried about it, the more it just drove me down. So you have a choice, keep going down or find a solution.* Tom

Finding a solution is often determined by when and how the appropriate information is passed on to the couple or the individual. It is hoped that the professionals passing on such information will recognise that emotional issues may emerge at any time and may present themselves in a variety of ways, including everything from sadness to anger.

It is also hoped that professionals will recognise that passing on information too soon means that it is not always heard or received. Some doctors, by the very nature of their work, have a major focus on problem-solving and are particularly at risk of advising about the options before the emotional work of grief and loss has been undertaken. This was very much borne out in some of the early work I was involved with in Christchurch, New Zealand, where a group of social workers and psychologists met out of concern that many infertile couples were being told in one breath that they were infertile, while in the next breath, the doctor was picking up the telephone to make an appointment for them to see the adoption service or an assisted human reproduction clinic. While this outcome-oriented approach may be fine for some people, others will need support, understanding and time to take in the meaning and significance of infertility, and to communicate with each other about it, before being able to consider their options.

> *When they're breaking bad news about the diagnosis of infertility, they must be aware that this is really sad news. They are delivering bad news to a person who has had an image of themselves as being able to have a family. It's not a matter of, 'Sorry about that, here are your options, DI or adoption. Go away and decide'. Why should you be told your options in the same sentence as being told you are infertile? You need to be given a chance to come to terms with that sad information and there should be a follow-up visit and there you are told your options.* Leonie

In recounting their personal story for a 2002 Australian Donor Conception Support Group newsletter, one couple showed how they needed time to explore the issues before making a decision.

> Our first encounter with the fertility clinic's doctor was most off-putting. He seemed to rush us to sign up onto the programme. We felt we were being enlisted in the army and that the next years of our lives were being signed away. We opted to have counselling which soothed our concerns and we chose to pursue professional advice, both from a social worker (associated with the clinic) and an outside source.[1]

Describing in detail the options open to infertile couples or those who are unable to have children without assistance is not what this book is about, as there are many other books available that discuss the physical and medical aspects of the different options. However, the following is a brief, general summary that may be useful.

One of the options is to decide not to have children. It is interesting how the word 'childless' is often used in this context, indicating that you are somehow less because you do not have a child. Some people who have decided not to have children or who cannot have children describe themselves as 'childfree', seeing this as a much more positive term. On the other hand, to use the term 'childfree' could imply that those who do have children are 'child-captive'! As with all words, there are advantages and disadvantages, hence the difficulties of finding words that are appropriate for everyone.

The second choice is to consider adoption or fostering, although adopting children at birth has, in the Western World, become a rarity. Conversely, the number of adoptions of babies and children from another culture and country has been increasing, and this is a subject that is frequently discussed by infertility consumer groups.

The third option is to use one of the many procedures classified under the term 'assisted human reproduction'. Some people will be able to use procedures that involve gametes from the two partners (if there is a male and female), while others may need to use eggs, semen or embryos from a person/s with whom they have no intimate relationship. The ability to use different procedures is determined, of course, by the medical condition or the social circumstances of those involved.

Practical issues can often play a part in would-be parents deciding to choose DI, including the length of the waiting period for adoption.

> *We looked at adoption; we found it was a 5-7 year waiting list. We didn't want to wait that long.* Tom

> *We set off down the path to adopt and were told there was a ten year waiting list and we had to accept that. It took me 13 months before realising it was going to take a long time to be on the top of that adoption list.* Leonie

> *To me DI was just a logical thing to do. If you wanted to have children, a ten year wait is a long time and we would have been pretty old by the time we adopted a child.* Warren

DI is also seen by many as the easiest option in terms of the success rate, the health risks and the level of effort required to undergo the process.

I went to the Royal Children's Hospital for an evening where they had a comparison of methods for people to have children. They had a nurse there who talked about the donor programme and the success rate was pretty striking. Grant

We both agreed that we wanted to have children but I said we wanted to have children without paying any price for it. 'The price' I meant was not money, the price meant health risks, physical risks – especially for my wife. I think having children should be an easy thing and not such a complicated thing where you need a lot of unnatural medical assistance, and DI is quite natural. You don't want to invest so much time and energy into getting the children because we need that energy when we have the children. It's more important. So that was another argument for DI. Sven

Another reason couples choose DI is because of the strong, natural desire for the woman to be pregnant and give birth.

We floundered a while, looking at our options and decided that DI was the best, as I wanted desperately to experience pregnancy. Ali

I was able – if it was successful – to fulfil my prime need to become a momma. Evelyn

It could be said that a man is giving a gift of love to his partner by enabling her to meet that strong desire of having a pregnancy and giving birth.

I was really happy for Susan at the prospect of her getting pregnant because we had spoken a little bit about adoption but really, what she wanted was to be pregnant. She would be related to these kids and it wouldn't be fair of me to just deny her this. Greg

If he can please somebody, he will. And I think that he put me first and he was pleasing me. To this day, sometimes I don't know whether he had doubts – and that's being honest. Evelyn. *I didn't have any doubts at that time. It was for me too. I'm sure of that.* Laurie

If a man has a certain amount of reluctance to use DI and only does so in order to please his partner, there is a high risk of a negative impact on the family, as reported in a newspaper article in Scotland in 2002, when Shirley Brailey (then 52) talked of her experiences of being conceived by DI.

> My mother told me my father went along with the donor insemination because it was she that wanted it. I believe he never felt comfortable about this choice. He had never come to terms with his own fertility and was reminded of that every time he looked at me. He resented me and wasn't a loving father to me.[2]

Being sensitive to your partner's feelings is crucial when considering the use of DI and many women, at the time of discovering infertility, perceive a need to protect their partner.

> *We were really excited that we were going to have a chance at being a family. That's the really important word, 'family', not just a baby. I remember feeling, 'How can I say to Warren that I'm really excited about this? And will he be hurt by these feelings? There must be sadness for him.' There was sadness for me but I remember having to be just a little more sensitive to him. But now, I know I don't have to be protective and maternalistic towards him; he's very secure.* Leonie

Although single women and lesbian couples who want to become parents will not be faced with protecting a male partner in the same way, there will still be a need to consider the many different issues, some of which may not be encountered by heterosexual couples. Andrea and Bridget took time to work through these.

> *We go into things really deeply. It took us two years to decide that yes, we could be parents – not in a physical way but just that we were up to the job. And then, 'How are we going to do it? Some friends had done it themselves with the use of a friend but it wasn't necessarily the experience that we wanted to go through.* Andrea

> *The issues were, should we bring a child into our same-sex*

household, is that fair on the child? What about knowing or not knowing the father and where would that fit in with us? So there were all those complicated dynamics which took us a long time to mull over. Bridget

We really wanted to make an informed decision and one person at a clinic, who was very honest with me, said, 'No, we don't treat lesbian couples. The issue is not your sexuality; the issue is whether you're married or unmarried.' So that furnished me with another question to put to other clinics, 'Do you treat unmarried women?' And all except one said, 'No'. Bridget

Like Andrea and Bridget, many people feel the need to take time when considering the use of DI.

When we were making a decision to take on DI, we went through a very long process of discovering all the options and working through them. Male, Sydney Focus Group

In contrast, other people are so eager to have a child that they don't think through all the implications. Focusing on the short-term goal of having a baby to cuddle in their arms may in fact blind many people to the longer term issues of managing a teenager! While this could be said of potential parents in general, looking only as far as having a baby may prevent people from exploring the full impact of building a family with the assistance of DI.

This information could be part of a discussion for people taking this on – to realise that babies are different from teenagers and different from adults. Female, London Focus Group

I didn't really look at the issues to be quite honest. I didn't look at the implications further down the track when we first started talking about it. It was just a solution to the problems. Warren

I wanted to have babies with Grant. I didn't want to have babies with army clerks or whoever else was available on this sheet of paper. But I was so hungry for a baby, I didn't realise these were the feelings.

> *I ignored them, I denied them. They came out as things became better, when I felt safer to deal with them.* Romana

> *In retrospect, I probably gave it an inadequate amount of thought, to be truthful. What I remember is that it seemed a blindingly obvious decision and one that I was not going to find a great deal of difficulty accommodating myself to. I don't think I thought through many of the complexities that I have obviously now had the chance to reflect on.* Walter

> *We had a known donor. We went [to a counsellor] and the four of us sat there and discussed it and I still didn't want to know about [the implications]. I just wanted a baby.* Female, Sydney Focus Group

> *We would like to see it like adoption, where it's mandatory that you go in there and listen and make decisions based on being taught decision-making skills instead of rushing into something that doesn't necessarily fix a marriage.* Evelyn

Effective counselling is one way of couples having the opportunity to acknowledge the past issues (infertility), exploring the present issues (options) and anticipating the future issues emerging from their decisions. The following comments by Karen and Terry, who spoke at a forum in Melbourne, Australia, in 1995, show the different ways in which a man and a woman can view the issues. Terry sees his infertility more as a practical problem needing a practical solution, while Karen is focused on dealing with the emotional issues when considering DI.

> At counselling, once we knew the legal situation and background to the programme, it was then I had to deal with the emotional and social issues which I felt was the toughest for me to deal with. For example, how would Terry really feel when I got pregnant? Will he accept the baby truly as his? How would I feel when I was pregnant? What if the child is disabled, etc? *Karen*

> Karen has dealt with all the emotional bits so I'll do the typical man rationale .... I was disappointed but I rationalised my problem by

> remembering that life had been good so far and so I couldn't complain and besides I had no control over the problem so why worry about it? Luckily my self-esteem and ego aren't really centred around my virility, but more around my achievements.[3] *Terry*

The process of a couple coming to the decision to use DI is very heavily influenced by professionals. In many ways, this is to be expected because they do have a great deal of knowledge and skill in this area. On the other hand, the following comments indicate that a number of couples – certainly in retrospect – have concerns about the way in which some professionals operate in this particular area.

> *I know many people go to clinics and feel that they become part of a conveyer belt and that the social and emotional issues that are going on personally for them are not relieved. They get the perception that they are not being taken seriously by clinic staff because the staff come across people with various infertility conditions every day of the week. People are not treated as individuals and feel very undermined by that.* Female, London Focus Group

> *They need to quit thinking DI and medical procedures and, 'You get the baby, the infertility is finished, the baby is yours, you can go home and forget about it.' Wrong! They have to make that quantum leap into seeing adoption and DI as synonymous and then they'll be better practitioners of DI.* Romana

> *Being told, 'When you get that baby in your arms, you'll forget all about your infertility'. It is so wrong to send that message.* Leonie

Clearly these comments show that some couples may experience a lack of validation of their feelings and a sense of powerlessness in the face of professionals. Many seem to feel that they lose their ability to be independent and self-determining with regard to the choices surrounding their family building. Most people like to be in control of their own lives (in as much as this is possible!) and their own decision making. Combining this desire with the need for the expertise and knowledge of professionals is ideal. Perhaps the goal is for control to be shared equally by the couple and the professionals, rather than one being dependent on the other.

What people want is a degree of empowerment to make their own decisions and be allowed permission to talk about it and think about it. Couples going through this need to be allowed the confidence to feel that this is something positive for them and [the professionals] shouldn't see this as a problem. Male, London Focus Group

I think it's not a doctor's right to be a social engineer; it's not their right to say who can and who cannot have children. Female, Sydney Focus Group

We had no control over conceiving together so I wanted to go into a private clinic because I felt that there wouldn't be waiting lists and I could control what was happening. I wanted to get that control back and that felt very important. Female, London Focus Group

When people feel as if they don't have much control over a situation, it is never easy to be assertive and ask lots of questions. This was highlighted in a group discussion that was recorded on the video *Why Me*? for the New Zealand Infertility Society (now known as InfertilityNZ).[4] One couple said they went to a consultation with their doctor with a number of questions they wanted to ask, yet came out of the consultation frustrated that they hadn't asked any of them. Being overwhelmed by the emotional impact of the discussion, they had forgotten about their questions. So, before the next consultation, they wrote down their questions, but at the end of that session were frustrated again because they had forgotten to take the list out of the female partner's purse! Encounters between professionals and an individual or couple can be very powerful occasions and it is important for professionals to recognise this and to acknowledge the feelings and issues that couples can be facing. They need to seek these out, rather than expect to be told them.

Doctors don't treat infertility. They never ask you emotionally how you are going. Female, Melbourne Focus Group

I would say, 'Think beyond the medical side of what you are doing, as you are dealing with people and relationships and the production of another human being'. Male, London Focus Group

The professionals, the clinicians, are in the business of getting you pregnant and they are not necessarily in the business of family creation with all its long-term implications. Female, London Focus Group

These comments relate back to the way in which clinics view their task and whether success for them is the conception and subsequent birth of the baby, or whether it's about creating a confident family.

When considering the use of DI, many people find it invaluable to be able to talk with those who have already travelled this path. Although clinics may place notices on the notice boards about support groups, most support group workers themselves, feel that something much more pro-active needs to take place. They say there is no substitute for talking with those who have already been through the process.

There should be information nights where they actually come face-to-face with a donor, a recipient parent and an offspring. Leonie

There are people who feel very isolated in this process. One of the reasons we continue to [provide support for others] is partly because it's incredibly rewarding for us, how little time and effort you have to give, to give somebody an enormous amount of relief and encouragement, just the notion of talking to somebody who's been through this process. For instance, I'm on the phone with somebody and they hear William coming in and saying, 'Dad, I'm just going out, can I borrow a couple of quid?' And I'll say, 'Yes, sure.' They'll say, 'Was that a DI child? He sounded so nice and natural.' And even that is so reassuring to people, to feel there are families who haven't broken up, just a normal family, doing normal things. Walter

I've spoken to people who have been undecided if DI was the right thing or the wrong thing. I used to say, 'Just come and have afternoon tea with us and see how we interact as a family and imagine how it

> *would be for you because it really is right for us. We're just a normal family.' People came and when they walked away, they said, 'It is normal. They don't have horns coming out of their heads!' I didn't really have to say anything; the kids did it for me. It was good for them to see that it actually worked, that you do get children at the end of this.* Female, Melbourne Focus Group

> *By talking to other people, you find out what they have done and how they dealt with it. You realise how many more possibilities there are than you thought.* Female, Sydney Focus Group

> *The thing that really helped us was an arrangement to meet a couple that had children through DI. They could communicate something to us that the professionals who were dealing with us just couldn't. So that helped us make that decision. I found it absolutely invaluable.* Male, Sydney Focus Group

Parents who already have children conceived with the use of DI feel their experiences are also invaluable for helping professionals become better equipped in dealing with prospective parents.

> *I would wish the professionals who talk to people who are considering DI would meet the families who have been through the process and come out the other end 10 or 20 years down the track. There is no substitute to actually having talked to these people and worked with them and listened to them.* Male, London Focus Group

> *They should certainly be including the experienced families in providing more education. They should be letting people make decisions for themselves over whether they want to talk to other families, rather than thinking they know it all because there's a lot out there that they don't know. Who can they learn off best but the ones who have been through it?* Evelyn

> *I would want professionals to take a longer-term view than they currently take. They can only do that by having access and exposure to the people who have done it in the past and to hear their stories.*

Female, London Focus Group

We'd like them to know that they are creating adults – not just babies. They've been told it but we want them to really focus on it. Evelyn

I'd like to think that the support group has been pretty influential in the attitudes amongst the doctors because there has certainly been a lot of two-way communication. Female, Sydney Focus Group

When it comes to decision-making, couples need to work through the issues together – a process that begins by both partners being equally informed.

We had always gone together to the clinics and we want to send a message to the clinic that it's not just important to the mother, it's important to the Dad to get this information as well. It's important to both of us, we're a team. Leonie

As well as having discussions, some people also find it helpful to write down the pros and cons of using DI, to help clarify their feelings.

We did a list about the good and the bad things about having a donor child. We wrote down, 'We'll be a family, we'll get to experience pregnancy, we'll get to love a child'. There was never on the negatives, 'I won't be able to love this child'. Leonie

It is important to recognise that partners may have differing views and it can take time to reach a decision that both partners are happy with.

I didn't want to do it. I was adamant that if David couldn't have a child, then I wouldn't have a child and we would adopt or travel the world. He basically had to talk me into it. He had to work hard to get me to agree. Female, Melbourne Focus Group

Warren didn't try to coerce me into having a baby this way. The greatest gift Warren gave me was tolerance and no pressure and it was my decision. If I didn't want a family this way, then that was the

> *end of it. He would accept whatever I felt comfortable with.* Leonie

There is also the risk of each person becoming so preoccupied with their own feelings that they may not be aware of or take into account their partner's feelings, or even consider their choices from the perspective of their future child.

> *There was very little discussion on our first visit about what the needs of the child might be. I probably didn't even consider Laurie's feelings a great deal, I must confess, because my goal was a baby.* Evelyn

> *I was just so desperate for a baby and I think I really pushed him and my husband went along with it.* Marie

> *One thing that we didn't really talk about at the time was that I wasn't quite sure about my wife's feelings about not having my child. People often want their partner's biological child. At one of the first support meetings, I thought that we must talk about that – the assumption that the women wouldn't mind as long as they had a baby.* Male, London Focus Group

Of course, some men may feel that as a result of their being infertile, they have lost the right to take part in the decision-making process.

> *He thought his rights had been taken away because he couldn't give me children – that it was basically my choice. He felt that he didn't always have the right to say what should happen when it came to having children.* Female, Melbourne Focus Group

This situation is a parallel to the one referred to earlier, showing how the loss of control and power that can occur between professionals and couples may also occur between partners.

> *I think women feel a little bit sorry for the man if he is infertile, especially if she is the mothering type of woman and they feel that*

> *they have to do this for them.* Marie

> *We looked at microinjection and it was a straining part of our relationship. I had two children from DI without taking any drugs and here I was, looking at IVF and I was really worried about the risks of cancer, when I knew that I could have children the other way. He felt rejected yet again because I wasn't prepared to risk those drugs, yet he had, when trying to get his sperm count up initially. So we went through a really struggling time.* Female, Melbourne Focus Group

The above comments illustrate how relationships between partners can become strained in the face of the intense emotional issues. It is helpful to accept that open and honest communication is not just about conveying your own thoughts but also about trying to understand your partner's point of view.

In coming to a decision to use DI, there are likely to be many doubts and challenges along the way. Feelings regarding the loss of the dream of creating a family in the way you had anticipated are likely to continue to surface.

> *It's not about creating a child from a night out of dancing and you come home and you make sweet passionate love. That in itself was a loss. I remember once a donor offspring saying to a person who was adopted, 'At least your parents danced'. I felt sympathetic to that.* Romana

However, some challenges can be turned around and viewed in a more positive light.

> *I would say to a man[considering DI], 'You will have to do things that you thought you'd never have to do and make decisions you never thought you would have to make but the end will justify the means', and I'd show them our family.* Male, Melbourne Focus Group

> *I had a certain amount of reluctance to become a parent anyway*

but that actually disappeared because we were determined to have a child, now that there was a problem! So in a curious way, it produced a positive, engaging attitude. Male, London Focus Group

A medical development that has introduced another option in the past few years for some infertile couples is intracytoplasmic sperm injection (ICSI), available when just one healthy sperm can be retrieved. Many couples are now opting for this, rather than DI, although it needs to be acknowledged that there are some concerns about the impact of using sperm that may carry the gene for infertility onto the next generation. The jury is still out on that issue but it is an option considered by some parents, who already have a child conceived by DI, when planning for another child.

We decided to have a second child in 1995 and at this stage, the medical possibility had improved and the professor would have been able to do something with my own sperm. So we could have said, 'Now we can have our own child, let's try it'. But we said, 'No, both children should have the same donor and method of conception'. They have the same starting position and we are not having to face one of them saying 'I'm better than you'. Sven

Peter (our son) might wonder if we had been dissatisfied with him so we tried to have our 'own' baby. I am happy that I don't have to explain it in this way. Bettina

We were discussing if it would be worth trying ICSI. And I actually wouldn't want to. If we were going to have another child, it should be from the same donor if possible. It wouldn't be a situation I would like, if it would be possible to produce my own child biologically, in addition to Bethany. Male, London Focus Group

If I had a natural child as well as the children we have, I can't imagine it making any difference because I can't imagine loving a child more than I love our two children. Male, Sydney Focus Group

This last comment gives an interesting insight into the importance of genetic linkages – many parents find the need to have a child genetically related to both of them diminishes once the child is born and becomes part of the family. However, if we take a step back to the time couples are considering their options, having some kind of genetic relationship within the family is a major motive for some couples to choose DI.

> *If I'm infertile then it would be much better to have children using a donor because at least the children would then be biologically related to Leonie, have some sort of biological attachment, rather than none.* Warren

> *I still had to deal with the fact that we would be having children that don't have my genes. I still hadn't really gotten over that part of it but to me, having the opportunity of having half of Ali's genes involved in part of our children was enough for me – better than not having any. So that was the deciding point on my side.* Tom

> *One way that I looked at it was that we could adopt and there would be no genetic relationship between our kids and us. The alternative was that we could do DI, when at least my wife would be genetically related.* Greg

Another relevant issue concerning genetics is the 'nature versus nurture' debate. How much of children's make-up is from genes and how much from the environment they grow up in?

> *We just spent a lot of time talking about what being a father is. A father isn't, 'He's got your hair and your height and your build and your smile'. That's not what being a father is all about. And we talked a lot about the mannerisms that they pick up. It's how you laugh, how you talk, how you raise your eyebrow when someone is talking to you. A lot of those things that they pick up are what makes up your child, not just the physical.* Ali

> *The physical make-up of a child is not the bond, it's the character-building and how you raise them, that's more important. People come up and say, 'He's just like you' or, 'She's just like Ali'. They*

> *really exhibit a lot of my character traits and that to me is more satisfying than, 'oh, they look like you'.* Tom

> *We both are very realistic persons and we have the idea of life that 80% is environment and 20% genes.* Bettina

> *I haven't had a real problem with [accepting another man helping us have a child] because I think I'm not so important at this stage. I'm more important when a child is born or when the child grows up but I'm not so [desperate] to transfer my genes to the next generation.* Sven

Most parents of children conceived by DI agree that it is the relationship they build with their children once they are born that is most important. They say it is not necessary to have a genetic link in order to form a close bond with their children and to be a good parent to them.

> *I have this idea that men are not as connected to children until they make themselves connected socially because they're not going to be having the baby and breastfeeding it. Culturally, men are more distant from children, so to become a good father, you have to make yourself a good father socially. If you are a biological father, it doesn't necessarily make you a good father.* Female, London Focus Group

> *Genetic resemblance is just not important. What is important is the relationship, and the quality of that relationship.* Bridget

> *A lot of men do worry that this biological connectiveness means loving relationships that you couldn't have with someone who isn't biologically connected. What happens is that as soon as they have children, that all disappears immediately.* Male, London Focus Group

> *The kids respect Tom. I respect Tom because he is the kind of Dad that he is. And over and over again, it is not about genetics, it is not about physical biological makeup, it is strictly about you being the father and mother that you would like to be.* Ali

The notion of being the parent you would like to be raises the question of what exactly the word 'father' means.

> *I think 'father' means not only the person who gave you life genetically, he's the man who nurtures you, loves you, cares for you.* Female, Melbourne Focus Group

> *I really believe that I was part of the whole conception and child-raising and you're really, in terms of that child's reality, their father. It is much easier if you and they can understand that.* Male, Sydney Focus Group

> *It's quite normal that you think about it not being your sperm, it's the sperm of somebody else. But I think that's not so important. What does it mean? Not much! They are my children; it's just the sperm of this man.* Sven

Echoing the views of these parents, offspring are usually very clear about who is their one and only father, and a lack of genetic connection attachment does not alter that.

> *My father is 100 per cent Walter Merricks – the person who has been there since the day I was born, the man who wants me as his daughter, the man who loves me with all his heart, the man who has always been there for me and always will be.* Susannah Merricks (age 14)

> *He is still in touch with his [estranged] father and he idolises him. He is his Dad and he doesn't want another one.* Marie

> *Ken is absolutely our kids' father in every parent thing. Although they may not understand it properly, they understand that biologically they are not related but Ken is still their Dad.* Female, Sydney Focus Group

There may be some couples who feel anxious that having a child who is genetically related to one parent and not the other will in some ways make for an unequal relationship. The reality is, however, that the relationships between the child and each parent are different only in terms of that genetic connection.

> *One single person on their own, no matter if it's the father or mother, is not really important. The family, the whole family is important.* Sven

> *I don't dwell on the fact that I'm the genetic relation. It's not like I see myself in them in so many ways – except when they are behaving badly sometimes and I see bits of myself that I don't like!* Susan

While it is natural and necessary to question and understand the entire issue of genetic connection, the common thread that comes through most strongly is that love is what holds the family together, not genetics.

> *The babies love you, they need you, so that gives them the bond with you. But an adult may have to grapple with the idea of, 'How am I going to be able to love this little baby that I'm not physically connected to?' It's more of a problem looking at it from the adult angle, I think.* Susan

> *In the end, you are responsible in the same way as if it is your biological child – it makes no difference at all.* Sven

It can be helpful to remember that the two partners of a loving relationship are not linked in any way by genetic connection, yet their love of each other is their biggest bond.

In summary, I believe it is very important to deal with the infertility issues – including the loss, grief, and anger – before moving on to thinking about children and becoming a family. There will still be times when couples or individuals are reminded of their loss through infertility, but it's the way in which that loss is dealt with, that is important. In a sense, it is moving from a reactive position, in which you are responding to the situation that you are confronted with, to a proactive position, in which you look at moving positively into building your family, albeit in a different kind of way than you had expected.

DI remains a relatively unconventional thing to do and like it or not, it means you have got to be prepared to carry on being unconventional. You have to define the family somewhat differently and you have to introduce certain people into the family or define them as part of our family history. You can't [use DI] and carry on just like anybody else. Male, London Focus Group

You are entering a social process, not just a biological or even a parenting process. I think you should be proud of it, as it is almost post-modern parentage. Parenting is changing and evolving. We have the children we have and we chose that way. We can see this as a positive step. Male, London Focus Group

The process of making the decision to use DI is challenging, and it is important that careful consideration is given to all the issues that may arise. DI is not for everyone but there can be a great sense of relief, as well as a huge sense of excitement, for those who feel comfortable that this is the right option to help them fulfil their dream of having children and being a family.

Somehow it seemed really wonderful and I remember thinking to myself what an easy way to solve this problem. The fact that someone had been willing to go there on the stage and share their experience made it like a little door opening. It wasn't this complete unexplored frontier – someone had done it and it was an option that had a certain familiarity about it. I felt really excited at the possibility that maybe we were going to be able to resolve all of this and I was going to be able to get pregnant and breastfeed. So after I went through this mourning period, then I felt like the clouds had broken. There was an end in sight, a potential. Susan

4 Secrecy and donor insemination – an unhealthy partnership

The chapter title, 'Secrecy and donor insemination – an unhealthy partnership' makes a firm statement against one of the oldest elements of DI. Although changes are now occurring, DI has traditionally been shrouded in secrecy and for many people this secrecy has been presented as a natural component of DI. This book challenges that notion, arguing that such a partnership is unhealthy, primarily because it is based on unequal and unsatisfactory relationships. Secrecy, and the inequality it breeds, has the potential to damage everyone involved, but in particular, it damages the well-being and happiness of the families who are built with the assistance of DI.

> *I think we were just appalled when we discovered the cloak of secrecy that surrounds that whole thing and we just recognised that this doesn't work when you are raising children. You can't have this big secret.* Greg

Secrecy means, of course, that certain people know something that others do not. If, for example, I had important information about other people but hadn't shared it with them, it means that I have made the decision that they shouldn't acquire this information. They have not been consulted or involved in the decision making.

Imagine what it would mean to you to discover (or maybe you have already discovered) that people have kept important information about you a secret for many years. Those who have kept that secret information are in a powerful and controlling position, while you may feel powerless at not having been consulted or involved. Worse still, you may feel disillusioned at being deceived by those whom you have trusted, and be left questioning your relationship with them. A natural reaction would be, 'If I can't trust them on this matter, what can I trust them on?' The following comments are typical of people who find out as adults that they have been conceived by DI:

> At first, it was a relief because it helped explain so many incongruities in our lives. As time went on, however, there were a lot of things that bothered me about it. It was like my foundation, which had been so carefully built up under me, had been knocked down. My trust in people was blown away, as well as my sense of identity.[1] Lynne Spencer

> As well as grappling with who I am and where I belong, I have a more difficult obstacle since the secret's been out: trust. I've wondered if there are other secrets being kept from me. I shouldn't have to doubt my mother. But I've found myself questioning whether I was told the truth.[2] Margaret R. Brown

> I had suspected that my dad was not my genetic father since the age of five. I had asked my mother if I were adopted but she said, 'No, you're my child'. When my mother finally told me at age 37 … I was most surprised that my conception was from DI and not from my mother's adultery. So my long-term shame about her vanished but was replaced by resentment that she had not trusted me with the truth. I felt betrayed by her lack of courage. I was deeply saddened by the loss of a possibly closer relationship with my [late] dad and my [late] brother.[3] Bill Cordray

Voicing similar thoughts to Bill Cordray, a child in Australia who knows and understands about being conceived by DI has this to say on what it would mean to have that information withheld:

> If mum and dad had not told me that I was a Donor Inseminated child I would be very angry with them because they had not told me about my history. I would feel they didn't trust me with that information.[4] 11

year old child

With regard to secrecy, I feel there is no need to even discuss its morality (the rightness or the wrongness of such action) because I have never read or heard an argument that supports the stance that it is morally right to lie to children about their family history and their genetic heritage. It is not an argument parents would support either.

> *The key thing was that we wanted a family based on honesty, trust and openness and to not tell Desmond would be to fundamentally compromise.* Grant

What I have heard, however, are many arguments that avoid the moral issue of secrecy and instead focus on what I would call the practical issues. Doctors may say, 'If we don't have secrecy, we won't get enough donors', while parents are likely to say, 'There is a need to protect our children from stigma'. These claims are often perceived as being acceptable because they have the intention of providing for or protecting people. However, the flaw with this type of protection argument is that although they may appear to be saying, 'I have decided that you need to be protected', it is also likely that parents or doctors are in fact also attempting to protect themselves.

In an academic paper Karyn Taylor and I co-authored, we suggested that secrecy was often advocated as protection for the couple, the child, the donor, the medical profession and the ideal of the family.[5] Some parents may initially welcome and support this notion but views about secrecy can, and often do, change over time.

> *You think you are protecting your family, that's the funny thing. You think you are making the whole situation stronger but you weaken the foundations somehow because there's been no truth in the situation.* Female, Sydney Focus Group

> *We were going to tell the children but the doctor advised us not to. We thought back then that we could keep the secret from them. I saw it as protecting us and protecting the donor, and we were quite happy to be protected. But it was very naïve of me to think that;*

I know now that I could never, ever have been a secretive person with my kids. Evelyn

What may be seen as protective at one point in time can clearly be seen very differently later on. For example, it may feel appropriate to protect a child from information that they do not understand, but the child doesn't remain a child forever, and at what point – if any – should information be shared? How will information, or lack of it, impact on the future adult?

The child that results turns into an autonomous human with rights and needs all of its own, separate from the mother and the donor.[6] Shirley Pratten

Keep it secret, it's simpler, advised the doctors. But it is not proving that easy. Someone forgot that gurgling, happy babies grow up into adults with complex needs.[7] Mary Braid

In the past, these complex needs have not been met for many offspring conceived by DI, including Bill Cordray, who sums up the entire web of secrecy and concealment extremely well.

We trusted our parents to tell us the truth, but they had been told to deceive us. We looked for information from doctors who had sworn an oath to do no harm, but they had destroyed our medical records. We hoped for understanding of our emotional experiences from social scientists and psychologists, but they encountered walls of secrecy that prevented them from studying us, or else they studied us as small children and proclaimed that they could see no problems at all. As adult citizens, we asked for justice and equal protection of our rights by governments and the courts, but they placed legal barriers in our way to prevent us from knowing who we are. How long can this go on? When will we earn the rights of ordinary citizens to know our identity, our sense of ancestral heritage? We are left to make sense of ourselves without the roadmap of our genetic blueprint. We are lost in an unfamiliar landscape. We are invisible.[8] Bill Cordray

With secrecy being negatively viewed by so many people, how did it ever come to play such a prominent role in DI? This unhealthy partnership of secrecy and DI is not new, and has in fact been a central feature from as far back as what is commonly cited as the first reported account of DI, by Addison Hard in 1909.[9] Hard was a student of Dr William Pancoast who, while teaching a class at Jefferson Medical College in 1884, discussed a couple's situation in which the male was discovered to be azoospermic and the female was found to be 'perfectly capable of bearing children'. The students in this class suggested that a 'hired man' be called in to solve the problem. As a result, Dr Pancoast took a semen sample from the 'best looking member of the class' and inseminated the woman while she was anaesthetised, without her knowledge or consent.

The doctor later reluctantly told the husband and was relieved to find he approved of the doctor's actions but suggested that his wife not be told. In 1909 Addison Hard went to New York 'to shake the hand of the young man' who had resulted from this procedure. It is speculated that this latter action indicates that Addison Hard was perhaps the student who supplied the sample in 1884 and consequently, the semen provider of the world's first known DI offspring.

In this example, there were several levels at which secrecy operated. Firstly, there was the secrecy of the professionals, in the way they delivered treatment without consent. At a second level, there was secrecy in that the husband accepted the treatment on the basis that his wife was never told. He therefore kept it a secret from her and presumably, also from their son. Thirdly, there appears to be no confirmation – only speculation – of who the semen provider was, thus maintaining secrecy surrounding the son's genetic history.

Clearly, the decisions made in this first reported example were very practical ones: there was a problem which was solved by a very swift, practical solution. A major issue arising from this, however, was that little consideration was given to the long-term consequences and implications.

To understand why there has been a need to move away from secrecy, it is helpful to first consider who actually wants and/or needs secrecy, and why. Certainly in the first half of the twentieth century, social standards contributed heavily to the desire for secrecy. At the time, sexuality and reproduction were not openly discussed or acknowledged.

In 1948, a commission chaired by the Archbishop of Canterbury claimed

DI was a form of adultery.[10] The commission also criticised it for promoting masturbation and demanded it be made a criminal offence.

In France, the French Academy for Moral and Political Sciences formally condemned DI in 1949, a view that was reiterated at a meeting of the Federation of French-speaking Societies of Gynaecology and Obstetrics.[11] As French sociologist, Simone Bateman Novaes has said, 'The historical origins of assisted conception are clearly tainted by doubts about the morality of the acts involved and their legitimacy as medical treatment.'

The Feversham Committee, which examined the legal aspects of DI in Britain, did not believe DI (AID as it was known then) should be declared a crime but still claimed the practice should be discouraged.

> There was no doubt that a child born by AID was illegitimate... A child known to be illegitimate must be registered on birth as such ... One who made a false registration knowingly was guilty of perjury. It had been suggested that persons assisting in AID are guilty of a criminal conspiracy to produce an illegitimate child ... The Committee concluded that AID is undesirable because it is a danger to the institution of marriage and to the resultant children; it dissociated responsibility for rearing children from responsibility for their procreation. And, in view of the weight of medical opinion against its practice, it was questionable whether AID should fall within a doctor's proper responsibilities.[12]

It is understandable therefore, that within this type of social climate, couples who used DI believed it was best not to openly discuss the matter and felt very restricted about who they could safely share this information with.

It is also understandable that doctors who dared to provide DI treatment took considerable risks in terms of the social and professional reactions they were likely to receive. Even though on one hand, they were applauded for their commitment to helping infertile couples, they were also seen as taking the highest risk of those involved in DI. Doctors therefore needed to protect themselves and were not interested in publicly promoting what they were doing.

As the providers of the service, doctors have always played a critical role in the development of the culture surrounding DI, particularly the secrecy. They have traditionally held the view that keeping the nature of the conception secret was in everybody's best interests because it avoided potential problems, including social disapproval.

However, attitudes have changed dramatically and there is now a much greater knowledge and openness of matters associated with sexuality and reproduction. There is also wider public acceptance of the different ways in which families are built – in particular, by using assisted human reproduction – and also a better understanding of the needs and rights of all parties involved.

Such changes have not come easily and many of the people who feel that DI should still be shrouded in secrecy find it difficult to adjust to this evolving culture. There are still a considerable number of doctors, particularly in some parts of the world, who argue that it is not appropriate for parents to share information with their children about the way in which their family was built, or if they do share this information, then it is not appropriate for offspring to be able to access information concerning the identity of the donor.

Dr Arthur Leader, President of the Canadian Fertility and Andrology Society acknowledged recently that 50 per cent of his DI patients at Ottawa Hospital indicated that they intend to tell their children about their origins, compared to only 5 per cent in 1981.[13] He adds that some people are quite firm that they aren't going to tell their children and for this reason, they prefer an anonymous donor. He says that parents have a right to direct the upbringing of their children; that is the choice people make and he cannot impose on them.

> *I think [the doctors] would have supported us if we had opted for secrecy, just as they would support us if we opted not for secrecy. Basically they were not going to take a stand on it; they were just going to support whatever we decided to do.* Greg

> *The idea of living a lie just wouldn't and couldn't occur to me. It really only came up when talking to people at the clinic and realising that it was very unusual to be open. They didn't argue [with us]; they just thought we were very odd and strange.* Olivia

In contrast to parents feeling forced to share information with their children, the opposite has traditionally been true. In the past, there was often pressure from doctors advising parents not to share information – advice that many of them didn't feel comfortable about.

> *The doctor actually said, and he was blatant about it, that we shouldn't ever tell anybody. He said that it would be devastating to tell the child, so we were torn. But the child is something precious and it's the way of handling this precious gift of life that is really wrong. I was ostracised. It was a disgrace, these feelings that I suffered all on my own. No-one should have to do this.* Marie

> *The doctor had said not to tell anybody because it would be better for the child to grow up thinking he was growing up in a family where he belonged.* Female, Melbourne Focus Group

> *It was something to be hidden and something that should not be discussed – even between my husband and I. We didn't discuss things, we pretended it never happened.* Female, Sydney Focus Group

> *When we did DI, it was a secret so no-one knows anything. They aren't to know that the child is not yours.* Male, Sydney Focus Group

This really comes down to the issue of defining the role of the professional. Is it to make information available to people, so they can consider all the issues and implications and then make their decision? Or is it to advise people what to do? In the past, when medical paternalism was very much to the fore, doctors were seen as exerting considerable influence over their patients. As a result, many couples believed they had to follow their doctor's advice, so as not to be denied treatment.

> *It was a very clinical sort of consultation. He just told us our rights – that we couldn't contact the donor and the children couldn't contact the donor or vice versa. We just accepted it. That was our means to get a child.* Evelyn

> *Back in those days, we never questioned our doctor. You were brought up that the doctor knows everything. We weren't as inquisitive as we are nowadays.* Laurie

> *The second time, we asked if it was possible to have the same donor. They said, 'I don't think that's an issue' and dismissed me. We certainly weren't going to argue with him, if that meant we weren't going to get access to the donor.* Evelyn

> *The clinic assumed we were going to keep it a secret. They could not believe that we weren't and we were questioned about what we would be telling the children. They didn't know anything about the way we live our lives; they made incorrect assumptions and made us feel like we should have to play this game to get the sperm.* Female, London Focus Group

Some would say that counsellors are now moving into a similarly risky position, in that they are advising people that secrecy is damaging. The central key in this debate, however, is how information regarding secrecy is presented to parents or would-be parents. As with the medical professionals who provide the DI service, counsellors should present information to the individual or couple, help them work through and understand the issues, and support them as they make their own decisions.

In the past, another concern for doctors was protecting the men they recruited as donors. Part of this protection was to do with the legal ramifications of inheritance – the fear that an offspring might be able to make a claim on the donor's estate if he was known – so to avoid this possibility, the identity of the donor was kept secret. In many countries this issue has now been resolved by the introduction of legislation which makes it quite clear that offspring and donors have no legal rights or responsibilities to each other.

As mentioned earlier, doctors also feared that if secrecy was not maintained and donors were able to be identified, there would be a major decline in the number of men who were prepared to become donors and ultimately, doctors would be unable to assist infertile couples. For this reason, many were very protective of their donors' identities.

> *The one thing that the first doctor made clear to us was that the donors were anonymous and were going to remain anonymous no matter what and they were clear about those circumstances. There was absolutely no way that we could ever change that in the future.* Greg *They said that if at some point in the future we actively pursued it in some aggressive way, the records would disappear. He said that he had guaranteed them their anonymity.* Susan

Some studies that have questioned donors who were recruited under an anonymous system have found that many of these men would not have donated if anonymity wasn't in operation. However, from a number of other studies that colleagues and I have been involved with in Sweden, New Zealand, Australia, the United States and the United Kingdom, there is also increasing evidence that openness does not necessarily lead to a decline in the number of semen donors. (For a general review of the studies on semen donors, see the book *Donor Insemination: International Social Science Perspectives.*[14]) There are men who are comfortable being recruited under an open system and who are willing to be identifiable to future offspring, but these men seem to have different characteristics from those who prefer anonymity. (Chapter Nine covers in more detail the feelings donors have about anonymity and openness, and the factors that contribute to their views.)

Even if the number of semen donors was to decline, this is still not seen as an acceptable reason for discouraging openness, as Louise Priday states in her *Open Letter to the Minister for Public Health* in the United Kingdom.

> It is short sighted and misguided to base policy on the fear that the removal of anonymity would lead to a drop in donor numbers … The question of numbers is, however, a secondary issue. Either something is cruel or it is not; it does not become less cruel because more babies are able to be produced by it.[15]

It has been suggested that another reason doctors have been anxious to continue the system of anonymity is that some of them have been donors themselves, either as a medical student or as a practising doctor. While this reason is based more on anecdotal than factual evidence, it is a view that is often raised.

> *I think that most doctors are not aware of the issues. It's also complicated by the fact that a large number of them are donors, which you don't always know but it does mean that they don't necessarily have an open mind on this issue.* Female, Sydney Focus Group

Even today there are people who still hold the view that DI and other forms of assisted human reproduction are not entirely acceptable, and as a result, some doctors do not want to be identified as being providers of DI services for fear that this may impact on other areas of their work and the number of patients who come to see them. Of course, not all doctors hold this view and in fact, the changing culture surrounding DI in countries such as New Zealand, Sweden and Australia means many doctors have moved into a position of being strong supporters of openness. This is due to their growing recognition of the significant psychosocial aspects of family health and well-being.

Some professionals, especially in certain countries, still argue that secrecy should be maintained. However, it is also interesting to note that in spite of their personal beliefs, there are also those who outwardly support the notion of secrecy because it is expected of them.

> *We were actually counselled to keep it a secret. 'We would counsel you not to tell your families or anybody – keep it between the two of you'. Two and a half years later, the nurses said to me, 'We've changed. We never really believed that but that's what we were told to tell you'.* Ali

Having looked at a variety of reasons why professionals might advocate secrecy, we now turn to the parents, some of whom do not necessarily want or need secrecy at all. Others, while not actually desiring secrecy, avoid being open because they feel vulnerable, apprehensive or insecure. Examples of typical anxieties are summarised below.

(1) There is a fear by some that if they question or challenge a doctor who is advising secrecy, they may be denied access to treatment or to a donor. If this is the case, it represents unprofessional practice and under such circumstances, it is important to gain strength, understanding and practical support from other parents who have children conceived through DI.

(2) For those who have been uncomfortable about acknowledging their infertility, being open about DI could mean that the pain of infertility resurfaces. They may feel that the presence of a child is seen as a cure for infertility and by pretending to be the family they would have been, the matter can be placed in a closet and forgotten.

In the past the denial of infertility has been encouraged by some doctors, who have either mixed the husband's semen with the donor's semen or advised couples to go home and have intercourse after the insemination. The reasoning was that this could help the couple pretend DI was not necessarily responsible for the pregnancy. It kept open the possibility that the husband's sperm, rather than the donor's, may have led to conception, and the baby may in fact be their 'own' biological child. This is not to say that in some cases perhaps intercourse did lead to conception, but the intent was a misguided attempt to try to protect the couple, by helping them avoid acknowledging their infertility.

(3) If they have already felt powerless while undergoing fertility testing and treatment, parents may fear they will suffer those feelings again if they choose to be open.

> *One of the reasons that I think secrecy is adopted is because people are then in control of that information. As soon as you go away from that, you turn to a situation where you aren't in control again.*
> Female, London Focus Group

(4) Some parents fear that relatives may not accept the child as part of the family if they know DI has been utilised. This highlights the need for education for family members, as well as the need for their

understanding and loving support, whatever choice the parents make. Unfortunately some parents report that they have been faced with negative reactions that have been detrimental to their family but others have been pleasantly surprised (and perhaps a little relieved) at the positive support they have received from family members.

The other grandchildren got $50 each when they were born and the one who she knew how he'd been conceived got $20 and that really hurt me. We took a long time to get around that. Female, Melbourne Focus Group

We started to realise that it was in fact the sensible thing to do, to tell people. And then a couple of really good things happened. I was hesitant about how my father would react but in fact he has embraced Desmond as his grandson, just like he has Maxwell. It's been great. Not that we really hesitated about telling him but I was bracing myself for the worst. Grant

(5) There are likely to be people who view DI as an immoral act and therefore could be critical. While some parents may fear this reaction, the families who have contributed to this book and who have talked about their experiences have not had their use of DI perceived in this way. It is also worth remembering that it is beyond our control how other people perceive a particular situation, and what is important is that we are independent and confident in our own beliefs, and not subject to the reactions of other people.

(6) Parents may avoid openness in the belief that they won't have to deal with any potentially difficult issues. While this may appear to be true in the short term when thinking about a new baby, issues are not avoided in the long term, and in fact become more complex and potentially devastating once that baby becomes a teenager or an adult.

(7) A frequently expressed reason for not being open is that parents do not know how or when they should talk to their children or to

other people. Fortunately, more resources are becoming available to overcome this. There are books such as this one which provide information on the experiences of other parents, and there are storybooks for children about DI and different ways of building families. There is also the opportunity to have discussions with other parents through support groups and via the Internet.

(8) Some parents may be concerned that the issues surrounding DI are too complicated for children and they will not be able to understand or grasp the meaning. However, as seen in Chapter Seven, where the topic of sharing information with your children is covered, this is not necessarily so.

(9) Parents will want to ensure their child feels secure and has a sense of belonging within the family. Yet if they mistakenly believe that security only exists for the child when both parents are – or perceived to be – genetically connected, they may avoid acknowledging the use of DI.

Before I really thought too much about it, I would have been quite happy to keep it a secret. I felt that if we were the only two that knew about it, there was no other way the child could find out about it. Why spoil an illusion that can be kept going forever? I think I thought more about it from the child's point of view because I felt that all kids like to feel that their parents are their real parents. They want to be just a normal kid. It was more as a protective measure for the child than to my benefit. Warren

(10) For some parents, there may be a fear that their children will reject them if they know they were conceived as a result of DI. Bill Cordray suggests that it is this kind of fear that leads to some fathers distancing themselves from their children while others become overprotective or over-involved to compensate. Neither situation is desirable.

While it is normal to be curious about information concerning our families and our origins, one of the potential difficulties of donor offsprings' curiosity is that it could be interpreted as rejection of their parents. However, as many offspring have said, it is not a question of rejection; it's a question of adding onto and building up a total picture of their genetic origins, by having as much relevant information as possible.

> I am curious about him – he provided half my genes and I have a natural desire to know about my biological origins. I am fascinated to find out more. Why did he donate? What does he look like? What are his interests, his job? Adult Offspring[16]

> An adult searches because it is natural to want to know your heritage, not because he rejects his parents.[17] Bill Cordray

> It's very hard growing up and not knowing the other side of your genetic background. When you know which bits of you came from your mum and your dad, then you can focus on who you are. Trying to figure that out is hard enough, let alone being a DI child and only knowing half.[18] Susannah Merricks, age 14

> Open adoption is now accepted as humane and practical. It allows a sense of wholeness in the adoptees, without detracting from the adoptive parents' vital and irreplaceable role.[19] Louise Priday

(11) There is also the fear that the father may be thought less of a parent, not a 'real' parent or not good enough to be a parent. In response to this fear, the many offspring who are now old enough to share their thoughts have no question that the real parent in their mind is the one who has loved them, who has been with them through all of the joys and pains of growing up.

> I've never had any doubts about him loving me. To me he is simply my dad. He helps me with my homework, cooks me dinner when I'm not well and is always there for me. I know I can trust him and I love him.[20] Susannah Merricks, age 14

One adult offspring has said she never thinks about the fact that she is not her father's biological daughter and in many ways, she is more similar to him in terms of her interests and sense of humour than she is to her mother.

(12) Some parents may feel that if their child doesn't know, he or she won't tell anyone else and the parents will remain protected from the whole notion of stigma and public misconception surrounding infertility and DI.

If you tell your child you must be aware that they will tell others. But I think it's not right to conclude that, 'I don't want to risk this, so I will keep it a secret from everybody'. I think that's the worst decision. Sven

(13) It is quite likely that other people will be curious about your family because DI is something different. This natural curiosity can cause anxieties for parents, however, if they find it threatening to think of others regarding their family, particularly their child, in a different way. However, this depends entirely on the individual family and whether or not they are celebrating and enjoying the way in which they were built. If there are feelings of shame and anxiety about what they have done, curiosity from other people is going to feed any anxieties and uncertainties the parents may have.

It would be interesting to do some research on what our friends would say – would they say we are odd? Do they say, 'Helena and Keith, they are the interesting people who have got DI children'? Or do they just say, 'he's a teacher and he has an interesting job'? It's the way they characterise you that's interesting. Male, London Focus Group

(14) As well as protecting themselves, parents may feel secrecy protects their child too. However, one mother who was concerned about her son getting teased also recognised that if children want to tease others, they will always find something to tease about – if it wasn't his DI origins, it could be his height, his hair colour or his clothes. She felt the possibility of being teased was not a good enough reason for not being open with her son.

(15) Some parents fear that the donor may claim parental rights to the child or that he will somehow intrude or interfere with their family, but as mentioned earlier, most countries now have legislation to

prevent this. While studies have shown that many donors have a natural curiosity about the children that have been born as a result of their semen donation, they certainly do not see themselves as being a father to those offspring.

(16) There is also the fear for some parents that if their children ever met their donor, they might form more of an attachment to him than their own father. However, Julia Feast of the Children's Society has cited adoption research carried out in 2000 that shows, 'Relationships formed in childhood are strong and don't diminish because of a reunion with the biological parent'.[21]

What is noticeable from this extensive list of points parents raise in their consideration of secrecy is that the word 'fear' keeps emerging over and over again. It is fear of the unknown that causes anxiety, and these natural feelings need to be recognised and appropriately dealt with before entering into a DI treatment programme. One of my concerns is that many people are not given the opportunity to explore their uncertainties, anxieties and fears beforehand, and often it is only after their child is born that issues begin to emerge and need to be dealt with.

In addition to professionals and parents, offspring of course also need to be considered in relation to secrecy. This is easily dealt with however, as there is no evidence that they desire secrecy at all. I have yet to find any offspring who know their family was built as a result of DI, but wish their parents had not shared this information with them. What I do find, and there are many, many examples of this, is that those who do know about their conception, frequently wish they had been told earlier, or that they had been told by parents in a loving way, rather than finding out by accident through another person or at a time of crisis. It is significant that as a result of each of their parents having differing views about the need for openness or secrecy, a number of offspring only learn of their conception when their parents divorce or after one parent has died and the other feels free to share this information.

> Four days after he died, my mother told us 'Your father may not be your real father'. She had wanted to tell us this when we were teenagers, but

my dad made her promise not to tell us. For some reason, after he died, she didn't feel compelled to keep the promise anymore. The timing was terrible though. Rather than grieving the loss of my dad, all I could do was be angry at him for lying to us about our own identities.[22] Lynne Spencer (personal correspondence)

When considering the option of secrecy, parents need to be aware of two distinct outcomes. Firstly, secrecy has an impact on the family's well-being and secondly, offspring unwittingly accept a false genetic history as their own.

Looking first at the impact of secrets, we find that a couple's relationship is compromised and is often unable to survive the huge pressure of maintaining a secret.

It was afterwards that the problems really began. It's hard to keep a secret. It's the hardest thing and it had put an undertone in the marriage. Marie

I think that secrecy was certainly a factor in the marriage break-up. If we'd been able to discuss things openly, I think it would have been a great help. I tried to keep it out as much as possible but the secrecy was always there in the back of my mind. Female, Sydney Focus Group

Secrets are not only developed in response to feelings of insecurity and shame but they also create insecurity and shame. So as parents struggle to maintain secrecy, the need for perpetual lying and deceit, especially to their children, will almost certainly add to their stress.

I think openness is beneficial for the children but it's also beneficial for your relationship because our relationship was based on this lie. We were just perpetuating this lie the whole time we were married. Female, Sydney Focus Group

It would be a heavy burden to carry. When you've got something like that riding on your shoulders, it's an added stress in your marriage to deal with. You'd have to keep on telling lies all through the child's life. It's not that you've told one lie, you just have to keep telling more lies to support your first lie. Warren

> *How could we keep a secret? I knew what secrets did to people. I know that they're really hard, you've got to invest a lot of energy into them and it just didn't make sense. Secrets are horrible things. They go against someone's basic human rights.* Romana

> *I couldn't fathom having a child that I was lying to all the time – it's not like you are just not telling them, you would actively have to lie.* Susan

> *If you lie once, you have to lie again and again and again. It gets worse and you don't want to stop and you don't know when to stop. Then comes the point where lying is impossible and then you will have a conflict with your child.* Bettina

> *You can control it in the beginning but at some stage it is absolutely impossible to control it any more. If you decide to lie your whole life, I think that's a very tough burden.* Sven

While secrecy may appear to be easy to maintain while children are very young, they are, as children, teenagers and adults, able to sense the unease and avoidance that their parents may have around certain topics of conversation. It is not only what is said that can lead offspring to have insecurities and doubts about themselves and their family, but also what *isn't* said.

> *I think children feel if there is a secret – if they start to ask something and you try to avoid the answer. They feel it if you are afraid and you are nervous and want to change the discussion topic.* Bettina

> *If you are ashamed of it and afraid of it and think of it as something you really need to hide, then I think that the child cannot help but pick up on these weird ambivalent feelings. It's hard enough to be a kid, a human being, without that.* Susan

> *The older they get, the more perceptive they get. That's what people have got to realise – that you can't live in a world of pretence. You're only hurting yourself in the end.* Evelyn

> *Lauren Taylor will say her favourite line about parents watching Late Line and there is a discussion on DI and the kids are sleeping and the parents are holding each other's hand and saying, 'No, we don't have to worry about this because little Johnny doesn't know'. But little Johnny is sitting in the bedroom going, 'What's wrong with me? How come I don't look like my Daddy? And no-one ever says to me, 'You look like your grandmother'. And that's the whole point. Do parents know?* Romana

Some offspring, who have found out as adults that their family was built using DI, have said that secrecy suggests that their parents were not confident or secure, and instead felt ashamed. In many cases these insecurities affected offsprings' confidence as a child, making them feel that they didn't belong in their family, or as with Bill Cordray who believed that he resulted from his mother's relationship with another man, their imagination became fuelled by misconceptions. Adult offspring almost always say that before disclosure, they had an undefined sense of a secret being kept from them. They knew something was amiss within their family, even though they didn't know what it was.

> For myself and all the other DI adults, to whom I have spoken, there was always underlying tension, a sense of dislocation and unease in our families prior to the disclosure. Obviously, this was in part the inevitable result of family deceit and secrecy. But it is more than that. It is the knowledge deep within oneself that something is not quite 'right'.[23] Louise Priday

> As a child growing up, I think I was always aware that there were hidden secrets. I just instinctively felt insecure. My father seemed to be irritated by the sight of me sometimes ... My mother was very loving and caring with many cuddles and words of love. However, she was over protective and I got the impression that the outside world was a place full of danger... I was terrified that I was adopted and that my parents would divorce.[24] Amanda Turner

> "I do feel a tremendous amount of regret for [my parents'] sake. They missed out on a fuller relationship with the four of us and spent an inordinate amount of emotional energy to maintain the secret for so long

> … Not being able to know the identity of the donor is far less important to me than the chance for an open relationship with my dad and to see him able to express the deep emotions I know he stifled within him. I still grieve for this loss of emotional connection with him as a child that I finally received from him during the last five years of his [life]."[25] Bill Cordray

It is interesting that for heterosexual couples, a great deal of emphasis is often placed on choosing a donor whose physical characteristics are similar to those of the male partner. In a sense, this helps perpetuate the illusion of the child being genetically related to both parents, therefore avoiding the need for openness and honesty. In other words, if children look similar to their father, it is less likely other people will ask questions that could be embarrassing or difficult, or make insensitive jokes, for example, about the milkman's involvement in the conception. As Andrea points out, however, it is human nature to want to see family resemblances.

> *For the first couple of months after she was born, there was a part of me that was going, 'I really, really hope you look like your Mum' because people put so much emphasis on what you look like, who you are. The thing that everybody wants to do is look for [similarities] in the child. And I do it. And I really should know better. I don't do it with our child but I do it with other people's children. That's incredible because we, as parents of donor-conceived children, should actually know better than that.* Andrea

It does, however, take more than physical similarities to create a secure family environment. The insecurities nurtured by secrecy can prevent closeness and a sense of true bonding between parents and children.

> *It never occurred to us not to tell the children because that would be the ultimate barrier between you and this child. Secrecy is scary, it's absurd. I don't know why people go to so much trouble. They make enormous sacrifices to have these children and then hold them at arm's length for their whole life – it's just crazy.* Susan

Another example of the lack of closeness and bonding is described by Christine Whipp, whose father died when she was six.[7] She was never close to her mother and had always sensed life was somehow a pretence, but it wasn't until she was in her thirties that her mother first referred directly to the secret. Five years later her mother finally agreed to confess all, if Christine would have nothing more to do with her. Afterwards, Christine and her mother, who has since died, never spoke again.

Secrecy surrounding DI has parallels with the secrecy which operated in the field of adoption. For a long time it was believed that children were better served if they were not told they were adopted. In hindsight, it may well be that it was the parents who were better served than the children. Fortunately, adoption policy has now changed dramatically and recognises that it is not only better for the children when there is openness and honesty, but it is also beneficial for the parents. Although there are differences between adoption and DI, there are also similarities which make adoption a field from which we can learn a great deal.

> *I would like to see donor conception be treated exactly like adoption and that means one donor per family. They meet the donor beforehand, the donor has visitation rights with the child, the child knows it's a donor child, the whole community knows and so people can come to terms with their infertility and the child wouldn't have to be protected from its conception. The fact that there aren't names on birth certificates, at least adopted people have that. Donor conception people are totally invisible with their genetic stuff – it's a crime, it really is.* Romana

> *At least adopted children know they can have access to their birth origins. Our children don't and I think this has driven some of the adults who have found out they are DI into extreme camps, simply because the information is not available to them.* Female, London Focus Group

The other major impact of secrecy surrounding DI is the lack of a full, accurate genetic and medical history. If parents have chosen not to be open with their children, those children are denied the knowledge that their genetic history isn't that of their parents, until perhaps the father or a child has an illness that results in unexpected disclosure. The trauma of this disclosure, on top of the event that led to it, is likely to cause a complicated and difficult time for the entire family. For most people this will never arise but there has been a number of cases, such as the story of Robert and Christine Brydon, who Marion Ward and I first saw over twenty years ago in Christchurch, New Zealand.

The Brydons have two sons as a result of DI but had chosen not to tell them about their conception. Robert has since developed an illness for which he receives dialysis treatment and ideally should receive a replacement kidney. When the elder son offered to donate his kidney to his father, the lack of a genetic match made it impossible. As a result, the sons had to be told of the way in which their family had been created, highlighting how the decision the parents made many years ago came back to confront them in a way they had never expected. Robert and Christine are currently seeking to access information on the two donors involved, as they feel it is the right of their adult sons to have this information.

As well as an illness causing unplanned disclosure, it could be that while learning at school about blood grouping and DNA (a subject we are rapidly gaining more knowledge of), offspring discover they cannot possibly be the biological child of their father. This clearly would be a major shock for a young person and one that parents would no doubt be eager to avoid.

> *It's getting more and more difficult to keep these kinds of secrets, connected with biological or medical things. In the future, with all the developments in modern medical treatment and medical science, it will become even more difficult to lie.* Sven

> *Today, kids do basic DNA testing in science and biology at school and even just the colour of eyes and things like that. I'd come home one day and hear them say, 'You can't possibly be my father'. How can you reply to that? You'd have to say, 'Well we've actually been lying to you'.* Warren

Sadly, even if parents have been open with their children about their DI conception, medical information concerning the semen provider and his family is often not readily available. This can lead to unnecessary concern by offspring, some of whom are likely to want information that may have a bearing on their health. For instance, by having a fuller picture of their medical history, offspring would know if there was a history of a certain type of illness. They would then be aware of the need to have appropriate check-ups, or they may choose to avoid certain lifestyle factors or workplace situations that could be detrimental to their health.

Naturally, many offspring have a certain amount of anger and frustration that their medical and genetic history is denied them. This frustration is not with their parents who have been open and honest with them, but with a system that has encouraged secrecy by guaranteeing donors' anonymity. They see it as a system that has given their needs a lower priority than those of the donor, by preventing their legitimate right to access information about their donor, and therefore to information about themselves.

Barry Steven, who produced an award-winning documentary based on his own experience as a DI offspring trying to find his genetic links, talked about how denying somebody their full medical history is malpractice.

> Not to know one's family history is a serious medical disadvantage… In the coming age of genetic medicine, family history is surely going to become more important, not less so. Deliberately to deny a patient (and all his or her descendants) a full medical history should be seen as malpractice.[26] Barry Stevens

Another adult conceived by DI has commented that DI offspring are the only people who are denied the legal right to access genetic information, and that this is due to the convenience of everyone else rather than themselves.

In reviewing why secrecy has traditionally surrounded DI, I have tried in this chapter to explain how the desire for, and decisions about, secrecy were very understandable at the time it began. However, if we continue to accept that shame, stigma and secrecy are associated with infertility and DI, nothing will ever change and the impacts of secrecy will continue. One of the ways to challenge this is by being open about DI. In seeking to educate others to a better understanding and acceptance, community support for families created in this way will grow.

> *I think the problem of infertility is increasing and so more people perhaps will talk more openly on this issue.* Bettina

> *You need to feel like you can talk about it because the more we do, the more you find it normal and the more it helps with all sorts of other ramifications in terms of getting donors etc. If the general community has a better awareness of it, if it's more accepted and more open, then the issues of secrecy around it become easier, the issues for the children will also eventually become easier and people won't get surprised and have misunderstandings because they have heard about it before.* Male, Sydney Focus Group

Times, attitudes and issues surrounding the whole culture of family building with DI are indeed evolving. These changes have been driven by a number of different people: the offspring who know of their origins, parents and consumer groups wanting to avoid the damage associated with secrecy, governments introducing legislation to enable offspring to have access to information, counsellors who are aware of the impacts of secrecy on families, a growing number of doctors who are thinking holistically about all the members of the family and also thinking about the consequences of DI rather than just seeing it as a treatment, scientists who are bringing to light information about the importance of genetic history, and an increasing number of others who publicly challenge the morality of preventing children from being informed about their genetic history.

> *If we want our children to accept this and if we want society to accept the way we have had a family through donation, we have to be prepared to speak out in public. Attitudes won't change unless we speak out.* Leonie

At the United Nations Convention on the Rights of the Child it was said, 'at a political level there is a growing recognition that where a government provides for, or allows a system to operate in which children, and later adults, are deprived of vital information about themselves, that the State is in fact endorsing the notion of secrecy'.[27] Therefore, we must question that if one of the State's responsibilities is to protect the vulnerable, how can secrecy surrounding DI ever be considered acceptable?

Having analysed why secrecy has been adopted in the past and what its impacts have been, there is one crucial point to remember. Privacy and secrecy are two different matters. In looking at DI, secrecy is when offspring are deliberately deprived of vital information about themselves and their family, whereas privacy is defined as keeping information only between the people who need to know, rather than making it publicly available.

> *There's a difference between secrets and privacy. It's not everyone's business but I am not going to hide anything. If it comes up, I'll tell them.* Male, Sydney Focus Group

Throughout this chapter I have challenged the traditional – and unhealthy – partnership of secrecy and DI, by illustrating its adverse effects on the well-being of families. The entire book, in fact, supports the growing recognition that openness and honesty form the basis of healthy family relationships, and we now move on to explore how parents have come to the decision to build their family based on these qualities.

5 Making the decision to have open and honest communication

In the previous chapter, we explored the general issue of why secrecy has been adopted by parents in the past and how it is not in the best interests of family well-being. We now turn to the experiences of parents and the specifics of how they have come to make their own decisions regarding openness. You will see the different perspectives they adopted (e.g. the perspective of the parents, of the child or of the family), and also the factors that played a part in their decision-making.

In the past there was a dearth of information available for parents as they were going through this decision-making process.

> *People should know the full facts about what they are taking on, in terms of their family and bringing up these children. This is what we really lacked. There was no-one with this kind of knowledge and you didn't know what you were buying into and what this would mean in terms of your coping skills with life. Then reality steps in, 'Well, I didn't think it was going to be like this' and you have to find your own solution. Having help to find that solution might be what's passed on, rather than everyone learning it new for the first time.*
> Female, London Focus Group

> *It was about 16 years ago and we call this the blank period of our lives. At the time there was no-one that you could talk to. We didn't*

> *cope with it very well in the beginning.* Female, Melbourne Focus Group

> *People are hungry for information about what other people think and have done.* Male, London Focus Group

The need for discussion and the sharing of ideas is clearly there. Meeting other people, seeking information and gaining support are the main reasons couples attend the preparation seminars Petra Thorn and I run in Germany. Yet, even when parents do gain information about openness and hear how others have communicated with their children and other people, they are still likely to have many uncertainties and anxieties. Some of the questions they may ask themselves are:

- How would I feel about talking with my children about this?
- What do I say?
- When is the best time to talk with them?
- What harm might I cause by talking, or not talking, with my children?
- How will they react?
- Will they still love me? (Often put as, will they reject me?)
- What will it mean to us as a couple? For example, will the children love the mother more than the father?
- Will the children talk to their friends about this?
- Will the children be treated differently by people who know about the DI conception?
- Will we be treated differently by people who know about the DI conception?
- What happens if in the teenage years the children challenge me and say, 'You can't tell me what to do; you're not my 'real' father'?
- What would it mean if the children wanted to meet their donor?
- How would I feel if I met the donor?
- What if the children liked their donor more than me?
- How will this impact on our family relationships?

Some of the questions relate to parents' anxieties about themselves, some relate to anxieties concerning the child, and some relate to the family as a whole. They are all very real feelings and show that moving into building a family by DI represents going into unchartered territory. There are very few signposts to show the way and very few maps to give guidance about what to expect.

What is known, however, is that discovering infertility and arriving at the need to use DI are major life experiences that stir up deep emotions. As with any such experiences, individuals and couples need the support of others, but it is only by being open that they are able to receive this support.

> *People have to tell their family and their friends because if they don't, they don't have support. It's a big lie to them too and that affects that relationship.* Romana

> *I know there are people who are afraid to say anything. They don't want it known. If that's what the couple has decided, I think that needs some extra support. When you can't count on your family for support and you have made a decision to keep this a secret; that is a lifelong commitment. They need to have a sense of family from the people that are involved in helping them with this process because they need to feel there is somewhere they can go, somebody they can talk to.* Ali

An important consideration when making decisions about openness, particularly with family or friends, is thinking about those who already know that you have had difficulty in conceiving. For many women in particular, the inability to conceive leads them to share this information with those who are near and dear to them and who will provide loving support and understanding. Some men will also talk to others but research indicates that men seem to be more reluctant to discuss their difficulty in conceiving than women.

Some couples who have difficulty conceiving may discuss with others the possibility of using DI in advance, whereas others, who feel uncomfortable about using DI or who have concerns about how others will react, have lied about how their pregnancy occurred. Many of these couples have told me that they suspect their friends or relatives have guessed, but because the couple haven't broached the subject, a 'no-talk zone' has developed. They report that this has caused tension and a loss of sharing with people who had previously been special to them. In a sense, this is similar to the situation of children 'knowing' there is a secret but being reluctant to mention it.

On the other hand, by being open with family and friends, couples have not only been able to receive their support, but they have also found it easier to access DI books, literature, websites and support groups, either in person or over the Internet. These different sources have enabled them to learn from the experiences of other parents, and to find out how they have shared information with their own children.

By being open, you are reinforcing to yourself and others that using DI is a positive and acceptable option. Discussions can also give you the opportunity to use their views and comments to examine your own thoughts further and perhaps look at issues you hadn't previously considered.

> *I think people are afraid of opposition and I always say that it helps to confirm your own feelings, even in opposition, not just in people agreeing with you. So that's important.* Romana

> *I always feel that this is the way we have created our family and by talking about it and being open about it, it reinforces the fact that this is okay.* Female, Sydney Focus Group

Having confidence about the nature of your family-building is at the heart of feeling secure, not only in yourself and within your relationship with your partner, but also in your relationships with your child and with other people.

Having the confidence to openly talk about your family-building also means you avoid the difficulty of needing to tell lies.

> *I'd either have to make up lies or I'd have to actually tell what happened.* Female, Sydney Focus Group

> *I couldn't keep looking at my child and lying to him. I just wanted to get it done.* Marie

> *I could never have been deceitful. I'm a very honest and*

straightforward person. That was part of the off-loading of it – that I have been able to be honest to myself, I was being honest with them and I wasn't keeping secrets. Evelyn

In counselling situations, I've frequently heard parents echo what Australian psychologist Suzanne Midford has said, namely that 'secrecy and lies, and the climate in which they live, are worse and create more problems than the truth'.[1]

In a magazine article, adult offspring Nicole Williams talks about how her parents are open now, but while she and her brother were young, her parents lived in constant turmoil trying to maintain secrecy.

> For over 12 years they carried a secret which ate away at their hearts and minds like cancer. Each day they woke up worrying over this secret and each night they went to sleep sickened by this secret. Should we tell the children? How do we tell them? The nucleus of my family was wearing away and breaking down from the constant pressure.[2]

In addition to emotional and relationship problems, the pressure of trying to maintain secrecy can manifest into genuine health problems. People often find that their stress is relieved and their health improves only after openness is decided on.

After the marriage break-up, I was left with the whole secret on my own. I became very ill. I knew I had this guilty secret and thought this could be causing a lot of my problems. I went to talk to somebody about it and she gave me quite a bit of counselling and really helped me. Marie

I was sick and nauseous all the time. They were trying to find out what was wrong with me and I was keeping this secret and didn't even realise myself that that was what was wrong with me. I went to the doctor and burst into tears and said the other doctor told us never to tell anybody and I was stressing because I thought everyone was going to find out. But it changed after the telling. As soon as we started talking openly about it, I felt much better. Once the pressure was released, I felt free and liberated because I wasn't ashamed of my children. Female, Melbourne Focus Group

The notion of being ashamed of how your family was built, or even ashamed of the children who result from your decision-making, is one that will weigh very heavily on some people. Parents may choose to manage this by trying to deny in their minds that it is an issue and therefore, it is not something they need to worry about. However, the mere fact that they feel they need to try and hide this, shows they aren't comfortable or confident about what they have done and aren't entirely able to be proud of the children they have.

In an interesting book, *The Mother Dance: How Children Change Your Life*, author Harriet Lerner talks about the necessity for honesty within a family:

> Kids do best when family members can talk openly together about things that matter. For starters, there is the issue of trust. Our children start out in the world assuming that we will not intentionally lie to them or deliberately conceal information about things that affect them … Children start out expecting straight answers, or at least to be told that some things are private and won't be shared or discussed with them. If our kids can't trust us to tell them the truth about issues that affect them, they have difficulty trusting the universe, including their internal universe of thoughts, feelings, and perceptions.
>
> It's also important to keep in mind that kids have a remarkable capacity to handle difficult facts. They do less well with the falsification, mystification, or silencing of their reality. Kids are also the most dependent family members and, as such, are fiercely loyal to unspoken family rules about communication. If there's an implicit 'don't ask, don't tell' rule surrounding a particular issue, kids catch on. They 'know' at a deep, automatic level what not to ask about and what not to tell.[3]

If parents have feelings of shame associated with their use of DI, children will no doubt pick up these feelings and realise their parents feel discomfort and are unwilling to discuss certain topics. Therefore, shame clearly does not just impact on the parents but has a negative flow-on effect for their children. Conversely, feelings of pride and security between parents can have a positive effect for their children.

I felt very strongly that it was never going to be a secret with anybody because I didn't want my child to think I was at any time ashamed of him. I think he should feel proud of why we decided to use a donor and that we had very good reasons for doing what we did. Female, Melbourne Focus Group

We've got a lot of value on our relationship and as human beings. And we try very hard to make sure that Ellie has the same value of herself, in that she respects herself and is happy with herself. For me, the real worry is that other people will in some way poison her mind about where she comes from, what she is and we are trying to make sure she is empowered enough to know and be comfortable in the way that we are with it. Andrea

We feel it is essential that she understands her beginnings and that she is familiar and confident with it – it's about herself and it's nothing to be ashamed of. Bridget

For most parents, the decision to be open will be made primarily in the interests of, and out of concern for, the children. Part of the reason parents are committed to being open is the desire for a relationship with their child based on honesty and trust, which in turn, builds a strong and healthy family unit.

I would encourage [parents] to think about being honest with their kids – for the connection to be there without barriers. Susan

It felt like a great relief after we had told her [at age five]. For me it just felt like a burden had been lifted off my shoulders that she now knew and there was nothing between us any more. I don't know that it ever felt like a barrier between us but it just felt as if there was something there that needed to be cleared up. Warren

We always wanted to tell the children and have a relationship with them built on trust. Female, Melbourne Focus Group

We were open with the children about it from Day One. Had we

sprung it on them at 14 or 15 and had it been a long-kept secret, we would not have had the comfort level that there is now. So Ali and I made a strong effort to make sure they got the information as they were growing up. Tom

The fact that it is important for children to grow up with the knowledge of their DI conception, rather than being confronted by it later on, is a sentiment echoed by many parents.

There should never be a time that a child didn't know that they are a DI child, what the process is and why the family went through the process. Male, London Focus Group

Both of them say that they have no recollection of a time when they didn't know. Olivia

It should be there from the beginning. 'There is another man who gave something in order that you could grow'. You can explain the particulars later on but [children] should always know, 'I'm a little bit different' or, 'With my family there is something a little bit different'. There should be nothing else before. Bettina

You are never going to change the fact that you have got donor kids. It's better to tell them early and trust in honesty. Do this right from the start and feel comfortable with what you are saying. Female, Sydney Focus Group

Parents report that it is far easier for them to talk with their children from an early age, as they are not confronted with the difficult questions and more complex needs of an older child.

At the age of four, the children can only ask those simple questions. If you do the first step at age 10, 12 or 20, this child can ask very, very tough questions and you are not prepared. But if you do the first step when they are very young, the questions are not so tough. You grow up with answering questions and it's more relaxed for everybody, for the child and for the parents. In the end it's better to tell the children as soon as possible, even if they do not know exactly what's going on. Sven

Grant describes information sharing with his son as a deliberate and planned process. Looking beyond the present, he aims to build a strong foundation for his son's future self-awareness.

I think the main problem is when the kids grow up and when the kids are teenagers or young adults, what is it going to mean for them? And what's it going to mean for the family's relationship, that these kids are donor kids? What we go through now, I don't think is really that significant – what we're doing now is trying to prepare ourselves, trying to prepare Desmond, to place him in the best position for dealing with who he is when he's a teenager and a young adult. Grant

Perhaps the most powerful advantage of talking with children from a young age is that parents avoid the considerable pressure of having to keep a secret from them.

Don't be afraid; go with your instincts and do it as early as possible. I think the longer you leave it, the harder it is, and the years of heartache and torment you put yourself through. Female, Sydney Focus Group

When other people already know about the use of DI, particular care needs to be taken to ensure that information is shared with offspring by the key individuals in their lives – almost certainly their parents.

I wanted to tell the children in our own way and not have them find out through some other means. Warren

I felt the minute we told anybody, then they had information that I would prefer we told our children before anybody else said anything that could confuse them. Even before the children were born, we told people what we were doing, so I already thought there's knowledge out there that could be told to the children by mistake if we don't give

> *it to them more consciously.* Male, London Focus Group

Sven alludes to a greater comfort level, and perhaps also a sense of relief, once information was shared with their children, as relationships amongst all family members, and particularly the children, were on an equal footing.

> *From that day [we told the children], all the members of the family lived their lives based on the same knowledge. Everybody knew what was going on and what had gone on and everybody in the child's world and in the adult's world had the same information.* Sven

Claire Wells, who shared her experiences at a DI Network (now known as DC Network) meeting in London, also felt it was important for all members of a family to be equal in their level of knowledge.

> We didn't want our children growing up in a conspiracy of secrets or a hierarchy of people knowing varying degrees of information at different times ... We know that in being open, we have to make some compromises about people knowing an intimate aspect of our life and information about our children, but we trust we are doing our best.[4]

We will return to the specifics of when and how to talk with your children in Chapter Seven, but to summarise so far, I suspect that most parents want to be open and honest with their children. As we have discussed earlier, however, some of the reasons parents find this difficult include a perceived bogey of shame, a lack of confidence in what to say, or anxiety about how the information will be received. I hope this book, and particularly the accounts of the parents who have broken through those barriers and developed confidence and a sense of security within their families, will be a source of support and inspiration to others who are considering the notion of open and honest communication.

In addition to the options of openness or secrecy, it could also be suggested that there is a third option, namely to delay making a decision at all. This is a cautious, uncertain approach, saying in effect, 'Let's wait and see what happens in the future'. Various comments by parents show that leaving this decision until later means they end up sharing information for the first time with their children or offspring when they are older. This does present some additional challenges, and many parents have said that it has been important to have discussions with counsellors about this.

Because the parents featured in this book have all made the decision to be open, their comments tend to reflect the advantages they see in taking this option. For some of these parents, there was always confidence and an undoubted acceptance that they would be open about the nature of their family-building.

> *We knew that we would talk to our parents, even before beginning the treatment and that we wouldn't try to hide it. And we also talked to some friends and we also knew that we would talk to our children.* Bettina

> *Leonie had always wanted to tell, so it wasn't anything that came on us slowly or something significant that happened; it was just something that we'd always wanted to do.* Warren

> *Neither of us really talked about secrecy or openness but there was clearly an unspoken assumption between us that we were going to be open.* Olivia

> *We were both of the opinion that we would tell Desmond. We decided that before beginning the programme. And we both agreed that we would tell some people.* Grant

> *If we were going to choose this way, then I felt it was our absolute obligation to take the responsibility for living it, not just steal it somehow secretly – it just seems crazy.* Greg

> *It is absolutely impossible to keep it as a secret for our whole lives, so this point was quite clear from the beginning, we would tell the children and tell some other people.* Sven

For others, the decision to share information with their child came as an emerging thought.

> *We were open with our friends and we thought, 'Why couldn't we*

be open with our child?' No-one influenced us, except ourselves. That was the decision we made. Female, Melbourne Focus Group

A central aspect of being able to make an informed decision is the need to first gain as much information as possible. Information comes from lots of different sources – written material, support groups, other parents, and professionals, such as doctors, nurses and counsellors – but it is sifting through and discussing the different information that is going to be crucial.

When evaluating the information from all available sources, it is prudent to be somewhat cautious, particularly of professionals who are strongly advising you one way or the other, i.e. to pursue openness or secrecy. It may be useful to ask people who are giving such advice why they are so strongly of that opinion and also to ask what recognition they are giving to the need for individuals and couples to work through the issues in their own way.

They were trying very hard to counsel being open but I just said that we would deal with that when we fall pregnant. It was not that we didn't want to tell our child but we just wanted to forget all of this and savour these few months. When we have the baby, we'll sort that out. Female, Sydney Focus Group

I'd ask the professionals to sit down with a sheet of A4 paper and in neat handwriting, write down the justification for keeping secrecy, then read it and believe it. I don't think they could. Male, London Focus Group

When there are two partners involved in using DI, the central issue is whether or not the issues have been worked through together. Is the communication between both partners open and honest? If there isn't an ability to communicate openly and honestly in your relationship, then how likely is it that open and honest communication will be able to take place with any children?

Be confident and proud of your family and even though it feels threatening to talk about some of those things that might threaten the relationship, in fact that relationship is always going to be the same anyway. Female, Sydney Focus Group

It is also important to recognise that when there are two partners involved, it is only natural for there to be some conflicts arising from differences of opinions. No two individuals are going to agree on everything.

> *I wanted to tell them and my wife didn't want to tell them and that was a very big issue that took quite a long time to work through.* Male, Sydney Focus Group

> *[My ex-wife and I] had reached an agreement that we would never tell him. And while it wasn't upsetting her, it was upsetting the relationship that might have been between him and his mother. I felt that it was really important stuff and it took me quite a few years to work through that and actually get to the stage where I felt, 'I've just got to put what she said out of my head and concentrate on the boy and let him know what's what because I think it's just going to be a mess if I don't'.* Male, Sydney Focus Group

I recall working with a couple where the female partner was very concerned that because other members of the family knew about the nature of their daughter's conception, that they would pass this information on to their daughter, either accidentally or as a result of malice. She was very anxious to avoid this happening and believed it was essential that her daughter should learn the important information concerning their family from the people she trusted and loved most of all. The woman's partner disagreed, however, and felt their daughter didn't need to know. Their conflicting opinions naturally caused considerable tension between the two of them – a tension that almost certainly would have been picked up by their teenage daughter, although she probably wouldn't have known what was causing it.

Deciding on whether to adopt an open approach is a very important decision and it is necessary to take time to consider all the information. While one or both partners may desire to move quickly through decision-making and on to having a baby, this should, if at all possible, be resisted until both partners have explored and agreed about the basic issues. Part of that exploration will relate to the values and priorities that each partner has. "What value do I place on openness and honesty? And why perhaps is this more, or less, important to me than to my partner? How do our beliefs fit together and if these are different, how do we come to an agreement?"

It is important here to remember the discussion in Chapter Two about how with heterosexual couples, the thinking and discussion may differ between the two partners, due to the fact that men and women may experience infertility differently and deal differently with problems in general. However, although partners may find it difficult to know how to express their expectations and beliefs to each other in a way that is readily understood and accepted, there is a great need to always aim for clear and honest communication together, and ultimately reach the point of an equal commitment to a jointly-made decision.

Some couples have told me how the process of arriving at the decision to use DI and to be open about this was the most valuable part of their relationship. They say they have faced one of the largest threats they are ever likely to face in their lives together and as a result of working through the issues together, they have become closer and added strength to their partnership. As one person told me, 'I understand my partner now in a way I never understood him in the first few years of our marriage'.

If a couple feel they are 'stuck' in their consideration of DI and openness and can't come to a joint decision, it is wise to seek professional assistance from a counsellor, social worker or a psychologist. Such people are trained and knowledgeable in helping people discover what has contributed to the 'stuck' position and what can be done to move on.

There are usually teams of specialised professionals in assisted human reproduction clinics and it is to be hoped that they will be understanding and supportive as they assist you to clarify your thoughts and feelings. Unfortunately, not all counsellors operate at the same professional levels, however, so if you feel you are not being understood and not being able to freely express your thoughts and feelings, it is important to raise this with the counsellor and if the situation does not change, to consider seeking another counsellor. This is easy to say and sometimes very difficult to do because if, for example, you are having counselling before conception, there is the fear or anxiety that by questioning a person, you may be deprived of the ability to access the DI treatment. If you do find yourself in a situation like this, support groups can become extremely important in providing assistance in dealing with the clinic about your concerns.

Much of the discussion in this chapter with regard to making the decision to be open is relevant to heterosexual couples. For many lesbian couples and single women who use DI to build their families, the situation concerning openness can be very different. Studies show that most lesbian couples and single women indicate a high degree of commitment to openness right from the start. The first reason for this is that some explanation about the nature of the conception will be necessary and the use of DI may be seen as a more sociably acceptable means of family building, than intercourse with a male who is not a partner.

There is, however, another equally important factor for openness amongst single women and lesbian couples. In my discussions with those who have utilised, or are considering utilising DI, there is a high level of confidence. After careful consideration of the issues and implications, they have opted for DI with no feelings of shame or uncertainty. This has been in contrast to some heterosexual couples, who, because of a perceived stigma, have opted to be secretive. Perhaps it is because for heterosexual couples using DI, there is the possibility of being able to 'pretend' the child is the genetic offspring of both parents, whereas no such pretence is possible for single women or lesbian couples.

> *That's the thing about DI, it has been easy to pretend because when you go through a pregnancy, it doesn't actually occur to people that it could be anything else than your child.* Female, Sydney Focus Group

> *It's easier in some ways for us because there is no man here. We can't not tell; there's never been a question about it.* Andrea

It needs to be recognised that in the past, the number of parents who had shared (or would-be parents who intended to share) the family's DI origins with their children was limited. Studies in Sweden, USA and the UK all show this.[5,6,7] However, this situation is changing as more and more parents around the world decide that they don't need to feel ashamed about utilising DI to build their family and as a result, they don't need to hide behind the cloak of secrecy that has so long been characteristic of DI use.

They want to be open and honest with their children and, as appropriate, with others. Parents who have adopted the open approach have found it to be beneficial for themselves, their children and family relationships.

> *I can say that the way we've done it was the right way for us because they've accepted it and they are two well-adjusted young adults. They are comfortable with their situation. Nigel even says, 'If the same thing happens to me, Mum, I'll go through it. I can understand why you did it and I would do it'.* Evelyn

> *I think we have very confident children who know how much we love them. They know how much we wanted them; they really are each other's best friends and I think that they feel very confident in belonging to our family and the extended family.* Ali

The high level of comfort in families who have chosen to be open can also be reflected in the light hearted comments that get bandied about.

> *When I got pregnant with our fourth child, who is the biological child of both of us, we sat the kids down and told them that Mum was going to have another baby and actually this one is from Dad. And one of them said, 'Well Dad, you've played the biggest trick on us! You told us your body was broken and there's nothing wrong with it!' That's what it's like in our family; it's open and they can talk about it when they want to.* Female, Melbourne Focus Group

In the London Focus Group, one father said his children tease each other with comments like 'get back in your test tube', while at the Sydney Focus Group, one woman recounted the story of when a mother was at a support group meeting, her teenage daughter jokingly said to her father, 'It's your fault she's got to go out because if you were able to have sperm, she wouldn't be involved with it; she would be at home.'

> *If it's open and there is bantering, it's probably extremely healthy because it's showing there is a degree of comfort with it, as you would probably suppress saying those things if you weren't comfortable.*

Male, Sydney Focus Group

In conclusion, there are two large and challenging issues people considering DI need to face. Firstly, is this the right way for us to build a family? And secondly, if it is the right way, what decisions will we make concerning being open and honest about our choice?

6 The journey from treatment to birth

Most of this book so far covers what can be described as the preparation phase for building a family with the use of DI, i.e. arriving at the need to seek assistance, the impacts of choosing DI, and exploring the benefits of open communication. This chapter moves on to look at events after the preparation: the experiences of couples during treatment, pregnancy and the birth of the longed-for child. Parents also share their thoughts about the donor at this stage of their journey and some of their feelings about subsequent pregnancies. As before, the themes of confidence, support and communication are to the fore.

Having made the decision to utilise DI, the expectation is that it will lead to the desired child and family, but although the success rates are high, it needs to be recognised that for some people the treatment may not be successful. This naturally is a devastating experience and feelings of disappointment and grief are likely to be intense. In such circumstances, the pain and distress of the early stages of discovering infertility is likely to resurface.

It also needs to be recognised that some would-be parents may commit to the treatment and go through the initial consultations and procedures, but then decide not to proceed with the first insemination after all. Others may decide to discontinue after one or two inseminations, while I am also aware of couples who have conceived but then terminated the pregnancy. For all of these people, it seems that, on reflection, issues emerged that made them realise the decision to use DI was not the right one for them. My hope is that the information in this book encourages as much thinking, discussion and reflection as possible before treatment begins, thus avoiding the additional distress of later deciding to withdraw from the DI programme. Having said that, it is also important to realise that making a new decision or changing one's mind is acceptable whenever it feels appropriate.

It is to be hoped that the professionals involved will assist in the full preparation of the individual or couple. This will include details of the medical treatment and procedures, with everything being fully explained in written form as well as at a verbal level. This is a time when many prospective parents need a lot of reassurance, as they can feel vulnerable and acutely aware of the 'power' of professionals. Illustrating this, a female participant in a group discussion with couples who had used DI described how she became very anxious about her vulnerability in dealing with the 'powerful' professionals. She said, 'If he had told me to go and stand on my head in the corner for a day, I would have done so.' To which, another member of the group said, 'I did!'

In comparison with other treatments, DI is a very unusual form of medical intervention: although the cause of infertility (in a heterosexual partnership) is located within the male, it is in fact the female partner who receives the treatment.

> *My experience with Romana at the time was that for you having to go through the donor insemination programme was a bit of a slap in the face – that you felt you were a vibrant, healthy young woman and that you shouldn't have to go through this.* Grant

> *Feeling angry that it is you who is going to have to go through treatment when the fertility difficulty is not yours, is a very normal part of the process of coming to terms with what is happening to you both.* Letter from Olivia to Would-be DI Mums

Coming to terms with using DI also includes the ability to accept another man's involvement, a factor that is crucial if the couple are to feel comfortable about going through the treatment process.

> *I had to accept the consequences that I couldn't do it for myself and someone else would.* Greg

> *Men can be very angry and/or upset by the insemination process if they haven't had the opportunity to think through their feelings about infertility and the reality of using donor insemination, before treatment begins.* Letter from Olivia to Would-be DI Mums

It is not just the male in a heterosexual couple who has to accept a third party's involvement, however; the female also has to come to terms with the fact that the semen has been provided by a man other than her partner. Some women find it easier to deny the reality of the 'other man' and instead focus on insemination as only being a medical procedure.

> *I was just thinking of this as not a human being, just some liquid in a test tube. I didn't ever think that there was a male connected to it.* Female, Melbourne Focus Group

> *I just didn't entertain the thought that there was another man involved. I had blocked it out. There was no man, we're talking about semen; we're talking about test tubes here. So I didn't even think about it until further down the track.* Female, Melbourne Focus Group

> *Many women find the idea (and sometimes the experience) of another man's sperm being put inside them really weird. I have heard some women say that it felt like adultery, although it wasn't like that for me. Adultery involves intimate contact with another person and this is unquestionably a clinical procedure.* Letter from Olivia to Would-be DI Mums

Many of the women who feel uncomfortable about the insemination process say that it makes them feel personally violated or that it stirs up feelings of being party to an immoral act.

> *I remember the first time that I was inseminated, I actually felt like I had been raped. I felt quite violated and I got in the shower because I wanted to get clean.* Female, Melbourne Focus Group

I felt quite immoral having another man's semen inseminated into my body. I used to feel quite unclean after. But I had to grit my teeth and knew that the outcome would outweigh the disadvantages. I kept those feelings to myself; I didn't even discuss that with Laurie. I shut him out of the experience to a degree. I was very inwardly-thinking. Evelyn

By keeping feelings to yourself, there is always a tendency for them to become even more significant than they would otherwise be. However, by sharing them with someone close, preferably your partner, there is the opportunity to clarify your thoughts and perhaps hear other perspectives or viewpoints.

Open communication between partners is also one way of keeping DI as much a shared experience as possible. Another way is by ensuring the male partner is as actively involved in the treatment process as possible, or as desirable.

Some couples like to go to treatment sessions together. For others, the insemination process feels so much like 'just another clinic appointment' that the man either sits in the waiting room or doesn't attend at all. We're all different. What is important is that whatever way you play it, both of you agree. Letter from Olivia to Would-be DI Mums

Although the man is not a partner in the biological aspects of the treatment, he is undoubtedly a partner in the psychosocial sense. He has of course been intimately involved in dealing with the issues and making the decisions surrounding the use of DI, and he is also an integral part of the ongoing building of their family together. Yet it is common that during treatment, the focus is primarily on the female, as she is the one who is being inseminated.

Sometimes you feel like a passenger. You could literally be sitting around, having breakfast, and my wife would say, 'I'm going to go off and get sperm this morning' and you are going to work. When we had to abandon her eggs, in my mind there was a difference

and there seemed to be a more even balance in the power. We were both having problems then, it wasn't just me. Male, Melbourne Focus Group.

I didn't ever feel that I had more power. The position of insemination made me really feel powerless. Female, Melbourne Focus Group

Because he cannot fulfil his traditional role, a male can often feel like a bystander in the whole process. This can lead to feelings of discomfort at the time of insemination, although the need for the female partner to have him present can be very strong.

I remember feeling uncomfortable being in the doctor's office when she was inseminated. I didn't want to be around; I did it because she wanted me to be there. Greg

I can remember on the first DI, I was holding her hand and I wanted to let go but I didn't. I can remember thinking that I mustn't let go but there was another bloke happening there. Male, Melbourne Focus Group

Warren's been there for all the inseminations for our kids. It was really important for me to have Warren there. Leonie

When partners view their role as a supporter, carer and nurturer of each other and they have an equal commitment to family building, they are both sharing in the treatment process, albeit in different ways.

I wanted to be with her from the first day, the first second. I wanted to see her and be with her when she was pregnant and see what was going on with her and the child. I wanted to be with her when the child was born so everything was as normal as possible. Sven

When couples journey towards family building, their feelings of it being an equally shared experience are likely to be enhanced if the health professionals involved also recognise this need. Most progressive clinics ensure that both partners are fully involved, by having them attend appointments together and also by encouraging the male partner, or the female partner in a lesbian couple, to be present at the insemination. Both partners can look at the sperm through a microscope and in some cases, if the couple wishes and there is no medical reason for not doing so, the woman's partner can even carry out the insemination under supervision. When medical professionals recognise that the opportunity to do this may be important and significant to a couple, they make a very helpful contribution to the couple's well-being.

It is natural that a number of different thoughts are likely to occur during treatment. One of the most prominent, of course, is whether the insemination is going to lead to a pregnancy.

> *First of all, we had to go down and choose the donor, then you go through the process of having straws and then of course, it's not just like paying your money and you get a baby. You have to first of all get pregnant and that often takes several goes.* Grant

> *After counselling, we made the informed decision to use donor sperm. We were apprehensive with the first treatment. After its failure, we realised we were on the program for the right reasons because we were just as devastated at this loss as we had been with our own gametes.* Female, Melbourne Focus Group

The expectation is of course that a pregnancy will occur, but when this doesn't happen within a reasonable period, some would-be parents have to face the question of, 'How many times do we keep trying before considering other alternatives?' Many people have written about the tension of deciding if and when to stop, as well as the implications of doing so. Although the couples who feature in this book all have children now, some of them did not conceive easily.

> *It took a long time [to conceive the second time] and we nearly gave up. We talked about that. We nearly stopped at one child – it was really horrible at one stage.* Leonie

> *In the very beginning, I used to set goals for myself. 'I'd like to be pregnant by Thanksgiving. I'll be pregnant by Christmas time.*

> *I'd like to be pregnant by Easter.' I became really angry that this was not going the way that I had planned and I took one summer off. When I started back with the DI programme in the fall, I decided I was not going to plan so far in advance. I was just going to break it into smaller pieces and say, 'I'm going to do this for three months and then I'll make a decision whether I want to continue doing it'. The more times I realised I wasn't pregnant, the thought of 'I could do this for another whole year' was way too big.* Ali

In a German newspaper article a few years ago, Valeria Stockey said she found the drive back from the clinic was worse than the drive there because of 'the inner tension over whether it had really worked this time'.[1] On the other hand, her husband Uli felt driving to the clinic was worse. He said, "My perspective was 'Well, Uli, we are only driving there because of you,' and that was quite a burden."

While hope and the expectation of a pregnancy are clearly dominant thoughts during treatment, the range of other feelings can be varied, including anxieties about things going wrong.

> *I guess there is a fear of them getting the straws mixed up and you ending up with a baby of some other racial origin, or something like that.* Warren

> *Prior to becoming pregnant, I had very strong dreams about carrying a monster inside me. What would this child be like? I didn't in my conscious life but clearly the anxieties were there and I did dream quite a lot in that way. But as soon as I was pregnant, they went away.* Olivia

In the case of a lesbian couple or a single woman going through the treatment process, sometimes there is an added anxiety that the professionals may have certain moral views and as a result, treat them in a different way from heterosexual couples.

What couples do immediately after the insemination can be quite important. Many couples I have spoken to have gone to have a quiet cup of coffee – just wanting to be together and to share the intimacy of their feelings for each other.

For all would-be parents, when an insemination has been successful and conception has occurred, the long journey towards parenthood passes an important milestone. As with the insemination process, pregnancy is a time for both partners to be considered as having equal involvement.

> *The doctor knew our history and I used to go along with Debbie to the doctor and I used the stethoscope and, 'This is the heartbeat' and all sorts of things like that and he deliberately got me very involved and it was great.* Male, Melbourne Focus Group

The vast majority of people will naturally feel elated and excited once they find they are expecting a baby. They are ready to enjoy the experience of pregnancy.

> *I loved being pregnant. I enjoyed every minute of it. It was just a recipe book pregnancy and delivery and I just couldn't wait to do it again.* Ali

However, mixed together with the happiness of the pregnancy, there may also be lingering feelings of denial, shame or anxiety. This makes many people eager to leave the nature of the conception behind and to move on.

> *When I was doing the treatment, I didn't want to tell people. I told my closest friends and my family but I wanted to pretend it wasn't really happening. I wanted my pregnancy to be just like all the other women around me but I always thought that my pregnancy was less perfect than theirs. The treatment was done; it was traumatic, I was pregnant and I just wanted to pretend that it was 'normal' so I didn't want to have to explain to people what I had done.* Romana

While the desire to normalise the pregnancy is natural, it is not beneficial for parents to 'pretend' in order to deceive themselves. Without being able to accept the reality of the conception, parents may have difficulties dealing with some of the important long term issues that arise for parents of children conceived via DI.

When first sharing the news of pregnancy with their male partner, some women express feelings of concern or anxiety, perhaps anticipating that his reactions will be different from their own.

> *When I ran to tell Grant in his office that I was pregnant and I couldn't get it out because I was crying, he said, 'It's okay, we'll try again next month'. He thought I was crying because I had got my period! I remember through all the blur, watching his eyes to see what his reaction was to this news. Would he have a positive reaction or would there be some hesitancy or wariness? I wanted a normal reaction. I wanted him just to be happy and he was. I remember being a bit worried or a bit concerned that maybe he was hoping that it wouldn't work. I was worried to see that expression in his face of, 'Oh my God, what have I done?' It wasn't there but I remember watching for the reaction.* Romana

There may be men, however, who react differently from what could be expected in more traditional situations. Previous doubts and anxieties may resurface or perhaps pregnancy raises issues that haven't previously been fully explored.

> *He told me that when I was just pregnant, some friends said to him, 'I heard you're pregnant'. He thought to himself, 'She's pregnant'. It wasn't, 'We are pregnant as a family'. He didn't have that pride thing, male turkey feather thing, passing out cigars, and he wasn't very interested in listening to the baby's heartbeat. But I felt sure that he was whole-hearted about wanting the pregnancy and I didn't have any doubts that once the baby was born, he would embrace it.* Susan

> *I can't recall specifics about it. I think I had to grapple with the idea that her pregnancy had nothing to do with me and that the kids I was about to have were not going to be genetically related to me and I had to process that in some way.* Greg

> *You're always worrying about whether the baby, the child, will love you and whether they will think less of you or reject you because you're not their biological father.* Warren

Sven highlights the importance of clarifying your thinking before the pregnancy occurs. The use of DI seemed to be irrelevant to him once he and Bettina had conceived.

> *Once you have said yes to it and your wife is pregnant and you see how the baby is growing, other things are not of importance. But you have to be convinced in advance – before you do it. You cannot say, 'We will do it and wait and see what happens'.* Sven

Some men may suddenly question the whole process of becoming a father, but it is important to note that this can be a typical reaction for any prospective parent, irrespective of how the child has been conceived.

> *I thought, 'What have I got myself into?' But then, I would have felt that way anyway, if the kids had been naturally conceived.* Male, Melbourne Focus Group

Many men have little or no anxiety or apprehension. As a result of their confidence in their relationship and their decision to use DI, they are in a position to enjoy the pregnancy, and to anticipate the birth and the notion of becoming a family.

> *I was just very excited when Olivia fell pregnant and remained pretty excited all the way through, even more so when William was born. It was just the most exciting and compelling time; going to antenatal classes and feeling incredibly proud of her. It was all very focused on the positive.* Walter

> *One of the things about having your first child is that you don't know what you're getting yourself into and on my part anyway, it was very much an adventure. It was exciting and interesting and something I never had really thought about doing. And there we were, having a child, and goodness knows what was going to happen.* Grant

Pregnancy is also a time when thoughts concerning the donor are likely to occur. Such thoughts are natural and to be expected, although they will vary widely in nature and intensity for different people.

For some, he is a very real person whom they think about and attribute qualities to. For others he is a shadowy figure to whom they feel grateful but really don't want to think too much about. Others find it difficult to acknowledge his contribution at all. Letter from Olivia to Would-be DI Mums

I used to think about the donor. I could never visualise what he looked like; he was just a man. Leonie

As far as the donor, I just felt gratitude. I just thought over and over again, 'We are so lucky'. I never really thought what he looked like. I just didn't care. At that time, there was no background information available and I thought that was a good thing. Now I don't think that. Ali

I didn't have a vision of the person or of a personality or a spirit or a soul or whatever you call it that makes the very humanness of that person and nor indeed a physical picture of that person. The way I looked at it was that we are very lucky that we have accessed this and that he must be a really nice bloke because otherwise he wouldn't do it and we wouldn't be in the situation where we have a beautiful daughter now. Bridget

The above comments suggest that a lack of information about the donor makes him very difficult to visualise. This doesn't seem to be a problem for these parents, however, as their feelings are mainly focused on gratitude for what he did, rather than focusing on who he is or what he looks like. Other parents see the lack of information as something positive.

I felt this was very easy to handle because I didn't know much about the donor. I just had a problem and I had somebody who wanted to solve this problem. Maybe if you get certain information, you start to think about things you would never have thought about before. Sven

I didn't want to know who the donor was. That was part of my ambivalence about the whole process. Having children is wonderful but I didn't want to know anything about the donor himself. I had

> *this primal thing about rivalry; a kind of jealousy thing. A person who I don't know had this intimate relationship with my wife, whose offspring was with her. It seemed fundamentally a biological reaction and this was slightly uncomfortable.* Greg

Others may simply view the donor as not playing a major role and therefore give him little thought during pregnancy.

> I *can't honestly say that I thought too much about the donors while Leonie was pregnant.* Warren

> *When Bridget was pregnant, I didn't really think about the donor or what he looked like or what impact he would have.* Andrea

> *I felt very confident with the doctor who chose [the donor]. He described who gave the sperm and he said often they are students and so I didn't ask very much. I thought, in the end, it's not so important who it is; the main contribution comes from us, after the birth.* Bettina

As with pregnancy, there is likely to be a wide variety of thoughts and feelings that occur at the time of the birth. Some women may still be experiencing feelings of needing to protect their partner, which makes them more sensitive to their own actions during labour.

> *I ask every woman I meet this question, 'How did you behave in the labour? Did you yell, swear and scream at your husband?' It's always the DI mums that don't say something to their husbands. I remember being really conscious during the labour of not wanting to yell at Grant. Women don't get annoyed at their husband during the delivery. And that is because they can't. It's that protection again. The guy came to the party. He offers to do DI. You are not going to start yelling at him during labour. No way. I wish people would talk about this because they would find out that the men can handle it. And if they can't, they get help to deal with it.* Romana

Romana's emphasis on talking about experiences and issues is of central importance. Many people have said on reflection that if they had had more preparation and discussed issues more openly, some of the uncertainties they experienced after their child's birth could have been avoided.

One of the most common concerns people express to me in counselling sessions during pregnancy is how they are worried that they may find it difficult to bond with their child after it is born. Some parents do experience difficulties and bonding may not come immediately.

> *It took me quite a while, probably a year, to bond before I'd feel comfortable with him and love him. Maybe part of me was saying, 'Is this really my kid or is it someone else's?' Talking to other people sort of felt good but I guess that I could have done more prior and that would have helped me. [Things changed with] having Stuart there all the time and seeing him growing and developing, and me probably growing too, as I became more experienced as a father.* Male, Melbourne Focus Group

Other parents find that the presence of their child is an acute reminder that DI was utilised, and this can cause some conflicting emotions surrounding their ability to bond completely.

> *When Des was born, he didn't look like anybody I knew. There was love there but there was also a part in the back of my brain that when I looked at him, I didn't recognise him. I realised that the donor issue was not going to go away; that it was there to stay and that I would face it very time I saw him. So then I had to realise if I was going to be the best mother, I had to get on top of these feelings.* Romana

For some parents, it could be that the gender of their child plays a role in the way they bond.

> *My first child was a girl and I never had any problems but when I had a boy, every time I changed his nappy, it was a constant reminder of another man. For six months I never bonded properly with him. My love for him hit me one afternoon like a tidal wave.*

I felt guilty once I started loving him and then I would hold him at night and wouldn't want to put him to bed because someone would take him away from me now, through cot death, because I had just started to love him. Female, Melbourne Focus Group

For many other parents, however, any fears about bonding are unfounded and they experience no difficulties bonding with their child.

I was happy that she was pregnant and I wanted to see the child in her tummy grow, so I accompanied her sometimes to the medical ultrasound screenings. If you are able to identify yourself with the child while your wife is pregnant, [bonding] is no problem for you. Sven

I wanted to know the sex but she didn't want to. I thought I would have had nine months of being able to visualise in a male kind of way this little baby growing, so that I could bond with him more. Then he came out and they cleaned him and looking back, I don't think it made any difference. Male, Melbourne Focus Group

By the end of the pregnancy, I was pretty excited and didn't have really any concerns or reservations. I was ready to have a child and I was with Susan when she was in labour and I caught him when he popped out and the first night when we were home, he slept on my chest. I was pretty much smitten. Greg

You have this child in your arms for the first time. It is your child. I only thought, 'Oh a new life, a new person, a new human being! Sven

Certainly no feeling of 'it's not really mine'. For me, there's never been that feeling. Male, Melbourne Focus Group

The following quotes illustrate Warren's positive response, which seems to be typical of many men after the birth of their child. However, it could also be that his response was enhanced by the way in which Leonie wanted to ensure the arrival of each of their children was a truly shared experience.

The gift I gave Warren is that he was to have first cuddle of all three

> *children. It's really interesting how they give the baby straight to the mother and I said, 'No, give it to my husband please'. They were our children and why shouldn't he have the first cuddle? A lot of Dads miss out on that. Perhaps I also thought it might have helped the bonding between child and Dad. I remember when somebody came to visit us in the hospital and said, 'You need a crowbar to get that baby out of Warren's arms!' It was just magical.* Leonie

> *It was a real feeling of excitement. Here was this new person just arrived in the world and you look into their eyes and think, 'That's amazing'. All you can do is cuddle them and it's really a wonderful feeling. I never for one moment felt that she wasn't my child.* Warren

As with any parent of a newborn baby, there are overwhelming feelings of nurturing, dependency and, of course, the desire to know the child is healthy.

> *I was counting the fingers and toes and making sure that everything was right.* Male, Melbourne Focus Group

> *After the birth, everything is so important. You ask, 'Is the child healthy? Is everything okay?' You don't have time to think of these philosophical things.* Bettina

> *I need a day. After that, I'm relaxing about it – it's healthy and it's breathing and I'm hugging it and then I start to love it.* Male, Melbourne Focus Group

Some people find the feelings for their new baby overshadow any doubts about DI. The anticipation, enthusiasm and excitement they feel about the future of their family mean the nature of the conception ceases to be such an important factor.

> *The instant he was born, something clicked and I saw this flash of a little life that was depending on me in so many ways. I knew I had to be there for this child and from that point on, and then when you develop a personal relationship with the child, the genetic issues become pretty irrelevant.* Greg

A wide range of reactions can obviously be experienced upon the birth of a child, and while some parents bond immediately, for others the bonding may emerge over time. This is of course true for any new parents, regardless of whether the baby was conceived by DI or in a more traditional way.

> *Genes don't tell us who to love. For some genetic parents, learning to love a baby takes awhile for one or other of them. DI parents are no different.* Walter's letter to would-be DI Dads

Up until now we have been talking primarily about the arrival of the first child but of course many parents desire to have more than one child. There can be differing points of view as to the importance of both children being conceived by the use of the same donor.

> *At the time I felt that it would have been nice if it was the same donor, so they would have been full brother and sister but I look back now and it hasn't made any difference with them.* Evelyn

> *I don't think back on it and think I would prefer them to be children of the same donor. I think I was, and still am in a sense, grateful that those decisions were taken away and were not our decisions.* Walter

> *When we had Bryony, they lost the sperm in transfer when we moved and we really got upset about that because we wanted children all from the same donor.* Female, Melbourne Focus Group

Some parents may conceive a subsequent child without the assistance of DI, and as a result, they may possibly experience different feelings towards their children initially.

> *There is just pure and unadulterated love for both of them. But when Max was born, for me he was instantly familiar. He looked like family. So I got to have the birth in a way that I wanted, and it was really healing in that respect. But that doesn't take anything away from Desmond because I would never have become a mother if it wasn't for Desmond, so I always say to them that they have both*

> *given me something really, really special.* Romana

Having two children conceived in different ways can raise some unexpected issues for parents, including the way others may view this.

> *When we had conceived our second child [naturally], people would say, 'Good on you mate'. It made us feel like people thought there was a difference between a DI child and a 'real' child. When the baby was born, they were all saying that he looks like Stephen. Bryony came up to me very quietly and said that she looked like Daddy too. She had listened to everybody. It just happened and we hadn't realised that it was going to. I felt really sad and angry that they were saying things like that but they didn't mean to do it. I spoke to them and they were quite surprised. They adore Bryony and were worried they had hurt her. We said, 'There are some things that you have to be careful about because the children have feelings' and I didn't want that to happen again.* Female, Melbourne Focus Group

This clearly shows how sometimes we don't think about what we say, how our words impact on others, or the meaning they may attach to our words. As well as parents being conscious of the possibility of this happening, they also need to take the initiative and prepare friends or relatives for dealing with certain situations, particularly when children within the same family have been conceived differently. (This is discussed further in Chapter Eight.)

In all cultures, the arrival of a wanted child is normally greeted by the parents and others with great enthusiasm and excitement. There are often certain rituals or celebrations that are associated with the birth, including some which are primarily for men. 'Wetting the baby's head' and 'shouting drinks' for people are common ways of celebrating. But what happens to the rituals and the excitement when the child has been conceived by DI? Is it still appropriate to celebrate? Are the rituals undertaken in the same way? Do other people feel the same way about it? These are some of the questions that may need to be considered around the birth of your baby, and the answers will often depend on your own feelings of acceptance and those of the people who have been supporting you during your journey through the diagnosis, treatment and pregnancy stages.

The fundamental aim of individuals and couples using DI is to build a family which is based on love and a positive acceptance, but arriving at such a position is something that only results from undertaking the preparatory work, working hard at exploring the issues together, and gaining support from those who understand your decisions and share your joy.

> *Going through it together was a unifying thing. Contrary to feelings that conceiving a child naturally was easier, the fact that we were having to do this was making it a project, rather than something that was just going to happen by chance. We took the initiative and we could make it happen.* Male, London Focus Group

> *We celebrate our 20th anniversary this year and we have learned that it doesn't matter what hurdles have been thrown at us. We have just said, 'We'll just take this'. Coming down here for DI and accomplishing that first pregnancy told us, 'It doesn't matter what comes your way. We are going to do this and we are going to do it together.'* Ali

> *It's part of the growth we gained as a couple going through this. We had to make an extra strong effort in parenting, so not only does it tie us closer but it ties our family closer.* Tom

7 Talking with your child about your family creation

That's probably one of the biggest struggles of going through the DI programme – how to tell your kids and when to tell your kids. Tom

Many of the parents I have met with, or who have shared their feelings in consumer group newsletters and consumer group meetings, echo Tom's view. Some parents feel the notion of sharing information about DI with their children is so overwhelming that they have either decided not to, or they are just avoiding making a decision about it at all, and have instead adopted the 'wait-and-see' approach.

In her presentation of research findings to a conference in December 2000, Clare Murray from City University in London, England, noted the difficulties some parents face in knowing how to talk with their children.

> The time and methods of disclosure was also a problem for many of these parents: when and how to tell the child may have contributed to the parents' decision not to tell the child. One DI mother said: 'Well I don't know at what sort of stage you tell them? They couldn't understand it when they were small and if you told them when they were 11 or 12 they'd start worrying about their father. I think it could cause them real problems. Maybe you could tell them when they are 20 or something? But by that stage it becomes a terrible shock.'[1]

It needs to be acknowledged that sharing information is certainly challenging, perhaps mainly because parents do not know how to do it. Normally when confronted with a new situation, we gain ideas on how to deal with it by falling back on our own or other people's experiences, but of course in years gone by, very few parents were talking openly with their children, let alone sharing their experiences of how they went about it. In other words, there have been no scripts available for parents to follow.

> *It's still very difficult to get special information on how to tell the child because just a few people are willing to talk about it. If you go to official institutions, they say, 'Well we've got experience with adoptions but for DI, we do not have as much experience', so it's difficult to prepare yourself by getting informed.* Sven

The desire to be able to learn from other parents is shown very clearly in an interesting study carried out in New Zealand by Anna Rumball and Vivienne Adair.

From speaking with parents who had already shared information with their children, the researchers gained a valuable insight into parents' needs.

> [There is] a need by many parents to be informed of methods of disclosure used by other couples. Such factors include ways to broach the subject, specific examples of terms and language used by other families at the child's various stages of development and the actual dynamics of disclosure/discussion. Furthermore, parents reported a need to talk about this with others, and it was noted that with who, was less important than the support that was actually provided.[2]

In addition, Rumball and Adair reported that 90% of the parents who were telephoned asked the researchers questions about other parents' experiences of telling their children. They wanted to know what information had been shared, and at what age the children had been told.

The need for this type of information has also been noted by Aline Zoldbrod and Sharon Covington.

> [T]he primary desire of couples considering DI and parents who have not yet disclosed to their child is for more detailed information. Parents would like guidance on how and when to tell, delivered in a nondogmatic, nonbiased fashion... In addition, parents want accounts from other parents who have moved slowly toward openness in a way that maintained as much privacy as possible in the wider world.[3]

In 1998, Leonie Hewitt presented a paper at a forum in South Australia, describing her and Warren's experience of telling their children about their donor conception. A decade prior to that, when they were preparing to talk with their five-year-old daughter, they too had hoped to learn from other parents who had already shared information with their children.

> We went along to a support group and we met people who had donor kids but they weren't telling anybody. I rang every clinic in New South Wales to ask if they knew of another recipient couple who had told their child about their conception but they didn't know of another family who had told their children. Then I spoke with the counsellor at Prince Henry's hospital in Melbourne and she said such a significant thing to me. 'I know another family who's told their two boys and she's even taken them on a tour of the clinic and shown them where the straws of semen were stored'. And I thought, 'She's pretty cool!' We rang this woman and she helped us and I didn't feel so alone. Up until then, I thought I was the only fruitcake in the world who wanted to tell their kids! I'd never met another person who'd done it.[4]

The strong need by parents to have practical information and support was also confirmed by Clare Murray when she concluded her presentation of research findings.

> Perhaps it might be more productive to move the 'telling debate' on from simply whether to tell or not, to looking at ways of providing parents with practical, positive and helpful information about the telling process, such as when and how to tell the children.[5]

Not only do parents seek guidance on talking with their children, many also see the ability to share experiences as an ongoing need. This was highlighted in the conclusion of the proceedings of a series of workshop/forums held in Australia.

> [Donor families] want further opportunities to talk together about what they are doing, to share ideas and strategies, and to tell each other what is happening within their families.[6]

One of the major strengths of this book is how the parents, who are so much a central part of it, recount their experiences, views and approaches regarding the sharing of information with their children. Their hope is to assist other parents who may struggle with knowing how to talk with their children. It is also worth remembering, however, that although other people's experiences can be extremely helpful in providing ideas, ultimately, as an individual or couple, you need to make your own decisions on how to share information with your children. There is no standard or 'right' method, and the decisions you make will be a reflection of your own beliefs and comfort level, as well as the knowledge of what your children are ready to comprehend.

As we move through this chapter, we will first look at gaining an understanding of how children view themselves and their family, given that we need to place ourselves in their shoes to understand their level of thinking and their emotional needs. We will then look at how parents can prepare themselves for the sharing of information.

Originally, I had intended to follow that with details on the more practical aspects of what, when and how to share information, and to include parents' comments within that framework. However, it proved almost impossible to separate these areas, as they are all intertwined. Instead, I have included *Stories of Sharing*, which are conversations edited from the verbal accounts by the parents who have contributed to the book.

Their stories reinforce that there are many different ways of sharing information, but that it is always a process that takes place over time and has many twists and turns. I think we are very privileged to be able to hear these personal stories, which are engaging, moving, informative and inspiring. The parents are more than happy to share their experiences because they want to pass on the potential benefits to others – something that many of them were not fortunate enough to have themselves.

In addition to the parents I interviewed especially for the book, there is another couple, Irene and Peter Ryll, who I would have loved to have been able to interview, but they live in a part of Canada that I have been unable to visit. On the two occasions I have met Irene at Canadian conferences, I have been impressed and moved by what she has told me about her and Peter's experiences of sharing information with their three children. Over the years, I have also been privileged to receive email messages from Irene, in which she recounts conversations with their children. She and Peter have very kindly consented to my reproducing some of these and they follow the 'Stories of Sharing'.

Finally, I will conclude the chapter by reviewing the thoughts, experiences and outcomes that have been highlighted by the parents' stories.

We begin then with a consideration of children, their needs, and their levels of understanding.

It is helpful to consider children and their ongoing development in a holistic manner. While their physical growth is easy to detect, less obvious are changes within the other equally important areas of emotional and intellectual (cognitive) growth. Yet, just as we provide food and liquid to aid physical growth, so too do we need to provide stimulation and information for the mind, and love and security for the emotions.

There is an appropriate time for parents to introduce solid food into a child's diet if it is to be beneficial, and in a similar way, there is an appropriate time to introduce certain information for the child's mind if it is to be understood. In contrast, love is not something that is introduced gradually; it can be, and needs to be, given all the time. It is so crucial for children's psychosocial development to know they are loved and to experience the emotions that emanate from this – feeling secure, wanted and valued within their family. Bonding and attachments are formed during the first five years of their life and sometimes beyond, and at this stage children see their family as THE family. This is where they belong.

Children's sense of security impacts on the way they view themselves, their families, and others they interact with, which in turn impacts on how they behave. Therefore, loving your children is the greatest gift a parent can give. By ensuring children feel valued and a vital part of the family, you are building a strong foundation for them to develop as healthy and well-adjusted individuals. You also provide a secure emotional base on which to introduce information about your family building, and which will have a positive influence on their ability to receive and process that information.

> *When you think about why you want to have children in the first place, to me it's always about love and wanting. In the story I told Desmond as a child, it was that we loved each other so much that we wanted more in that relationship.* Romana

When we give information about family-building, we are first and foremost sharing facts, i.e. what happened, where it happened, when it happened etc. But the associated feelings you have in regard to those facts, such as your level of comfort, discomfort or anxiety, are also of great significance. Regardless of whether you actually explain your feelings, children are very sensitive to the emotional messages that accompany verbal communication, and also, as we have already seen, are intuitive as to whether information is being avoided or withheld from them. Therefore, it is important to feel comfortable about what you are saying to your children and to trust in the love and bonding that exists within your family.

Sharing information with your children is a process, not a one-off event. The story will be told many times and will be gradually added to, as their interest and their ability to understand information develops. As Rumball and Adair said, "As the child grows, so does the story".[2]

Children's responses to the information you are giving them will naturally depend on their comprehension and interest level. It could even be that they have no reaction at all, because although the information is significant to the parents, it may well be of little relevance to a child at that particular point in time.

> *My five-year-old wanted to listen in to what I was reading to my nine-year-old but she just got bored and went out of the room because she didn't understand it. That was okay. It's about tuning into where they are at the time. I do think it's a continual story.* Female, London Focus Group

> *Initially, we used to tell him and got very little response for quite a long time. Then when he finally understood it around the age of 12 or 13, he saw that there was permission to talk about it. If you'd only mentioned it once or twice, although you might have seemingly said, 'We haven't got secrecy', you have given another message that really there is a little bit of a secret and yes, it is a bit uncomfortable. What happened with my son is that once he understood it, he got quite easy to talk to about it because he had been brought up with it.* Female, London Focus Group

By putting ourselves in our children's shoes, we have a better understanding of what is important to them. We can recognise what they need to develop a good sense of security. Parents need to learn how to communicate with them at an appropriate level. Best of all, by building a strong foundation of love, parents and children grow together as a healthy and well-functioning family.

Having considered the child's perspective, we now turn to parents.

Talking with your children about your family's beginnings is not the most comfortable thing for many parents to do, but it can be made easier by thinking carefully about it beforehand and laying the groundwork for the way in which you will share information.

The most important preparation is to ensure you have a good level of self-confidence in the decisions you have made and a high comfort level about using non-traditional ways of building a family. In the preparation groups Petra Thorn and I offer couples in Germany, it is very obvious that the couples who are confident in their decision to use DI are also confident about talking with their children and with other people.

I have already suggested that most of the work for dealing with the emotional issues and gaining confidence needs to be done prior to entering a DI programme. However, the birth of your children, and later, talking with them about your family's beginnings, may reactivate certain anxieties and concerns.

> *Unless the parents have got it sorted out, it's going to be very difficult for the children. I think that if the parents have come to terms with it and are comfortable with it, then it's going to really help the children to feel comfortable too – just in terms of what's communicated to them and how good they are going to feel about it.* Male, Sydney Focus Group

Part of your confidence in talking with your child will stem from being able to place yourself in the 'here and now'. By this, I mean it is important not to let the events of the past continue to impact on the way you feel at present. In Chapter Two we talked about the losses people face when coming to terms with not being able to have the children they thought they would have, and how it is important to be able to acknowledge this in order to move on. This does not necessarily mean that the feeling of loss has gone away, but if there is too much enduring frustration and sadness, this may interfere with your ability to be in the here and now. As a result, communication with your children may be less effective and may ultimately have a negative impact on your relationship with them. Children demand a great deal from parents, and you will find it easier and more effective to parent them if you are not preoccupied with issues from the past.

When preparing to share information, an interesting issue emerges as to whose needs are being met and how important it is to focus on the children's needs first and your own needs second. In many ways, this is what parenting with maturity is all about. As it has been said, mature people are able to give more love than they need to receive.

Unfortunately in some instances, the need for parents to share information in order to relieve or reduce their own anxiety is so great that the child can almost be 'used' to receive the news. I remember one mother making it very clear to me that she just 'had to' talk about it with her child, but she brought up the subject so often that the child began to 'turn off' whenever the issue was raised. This is an example of how a parent's need to share information can override the child's need to receive it.

When preparing to share information with their children, one of the first things parents may consider is whether to raise the subject as a special 'talk' or whether to introduce information gradually. One of the advantages of choosing to have a special 'talk' is that parents have more control over deciding how to share their story. They can plan when and where to impart this information and prepare for the conversation a little more actively by sharing ideas and views beforehand.

Other parents decide to share information gradually, often taking advantage of other events or experiences to introduce the concept of their family building. As an example, parents can use television programmes that talk about babies, infertility or adoption to start educating their child about the different ways in which families can be formed and how some people's desire for a child cannot always be easily met. This is, in effect, preparing your child as well as yourself.

> *It's the same as other parents who aim to be practical with their children, talking about reproduction and relationships. You look for the hook to hang it on. You build the story with the hooks that are around and if the child is ready and interested, then they will ask more.* Female, London Focus Group

> *Use natural opportunities such as TV programmes, friends' pregnancies, etc. to repeat this sort of information and after a few weeks or months, add, 'And this is how you were made' or, 'And this is what Mummy/Daddy and I did when we wanted to have you'.* Letter from Olivia to would-be DI Mums

Whichever way parents decide to talk with their children, most have found it very beneficial to practise what they are going to say, to become comfortable using the words and phrases. Some parents practise between themselves or friends and family members, while others may choose to explore options with a counsellor. A number of parents begin talking with their children when they are still babies, to have the chance to hear the words out loud and to imagine what it will be like sharing that information when the child is older.

When there are two parents involved, it is beneficial for them to both be seen as equal partners when talking with their child, particularly if they are sharing the entire story as a first-time 'telling'. It adds to the child's security that this is a story about the whole family and that parents are united in their approach and confidence.

> *I think both parents have to be there and it just needs to have a positive, loving way about it.* Warren

Even if the subject arises unexpectedly and only one parent begins the sharing of information, it is still important and possible for parents to adopt a joint approach. This will emerge when the parents have good communication about their aims and expectations in relation to information sharing.

It is not only important that parents are united in what they say to their children but also with the emotions behind the words and how the message is conveyed. It is not going to be very helpful for children if one parent feels confident and is ready to start sharing information, while the other is lacking confidence and feels a certain amount of discomfort. Again, children are likely to pick up on this.

> *If you had the parents not communicating well and giving different messages to the children, that could be very confusing for the kids.* Grant

While acknowledging that it is possible, and even advisable, to prepare for talking with your children, it also needs to be recognised that there are some questions that can never be prepared for. Underlying a parent's reaction to unexpected questions, however, is again the degree of confidence that parents feel.

> *Even if they have caught us off guard, we never let that show. We always come across as being, 'Oh well, we're fully prepared for this question!'* Ali

One father has told me about the time he and his young son were in the bath together and the son, knowing of his father's infertility, reached over and picked up his father's penis, asking, 'What is wrong with this, Dad?' Although it wasn't a question the father expected, the conversations he and his wife had already had with their son meant that he felt confident in providing an explanation, without feeling embarrassed or uncomfortable. The question was treated very naturally.

To summarise, three issues emerge as being important in terms of parental preparation. Firstly, preparation does need to be undertaken. Secondly, both parents, individually and as a partnership, need to be as confident and secure as possible in being able to deal with the 'here and now' issue. Thirdly, there needs to be a recognition that if the parents feel comfortable about handling this information, then so too will the children.

Stories of Sharing

We move now to the excerpts of how the parents shared information with their children. Each of their stories is different and covers a variety of different factors, such as how they prepared, what they said, when they said it, how they felt about it, their children's reactions, how they refer to the donor, and their thoughts in hindsight.

Olivia and Walter:

W: My recollection of it is reading a straightforward children's story book about how babies are made – seeds from the daddy, eggs from the mummy and when we got to that page, I used to pause and say, 'And some daddies don't have enough seeds, so they borrow them from another daddy'. And because it was a pause and because I was obviously not reading from the page, that became a little routine. You obviously read the story time and time again, along with half a dozen other stories, and it was not difficult for me and he was just listening to the story. And it wasn't too difficult to move from that, to saying, 'And that's what we did with you. I didn't have enough seeds, so we borrowed some from another daddy.' I think we may have been doing that when he was about four or five. I really can't remember whether Olivia and I talked about it [beforehand] or whether I just started doing it but I couldn't just read this story and not qualify it in some way. I don't think William would possibly remember that book or all this business about borrowing seeds. It's just so much a part of him.

O: Walter used to take responsibility to read that particular story. And I would look for opportunities to hang other little bits of information on – if somebody else was pregnant or something else came up on television. Unfortunately I just can't remember the language we used with William very much. I slightly remember more about Susannah. And it seems that we told Susannah because it was already a subject that was on the agenda in the household, so as the second child she came into it probably rather earlier than we started with William. I can remember having a conversation with her in the bath, when we were talking about the nice man who had given us some of his seeds so that she could be made. And it became very clear from what she was saying that she thought I had met the nice man and might even have had sex with him. And I remember thinking, 'Oh my gosh!' You really have to be careful with young children because they will with their limited experience and understanding of the world, put two and two together and make five and a half. So you always need to check out what it is they understand and know.

W: The other bit of misconveying I remember that you mentioned at one point was that Susannah had certainly got the impression that this man must have engaged in some major self-sacrifice. That giving away his seeds probably deprived him of the chance of having a child. This nice man who had given us his seeds – it's an idea which is natural to us who know that you've got many seeds.

O: And that men are making them all the time. But small children don't know that. I remember the day that the book *My Story* arrived by post. By that time William was eight and Susannah would have been five and I remember that you left it upstairs on our bed and the kids were on there and they unwrapped it and William sat on the bed and read it out loud to Susannah. And it was in the middle of getting ready for school and we said, 'That's interesting, isn't it? Do you remember this is what we've talked about?' And on the way to school that morning – and this has happened two or three times, and I've heard other families say this, the kids were sitting behind me, so there wasn't eye-to-eye contact – but William asked a million questions. He said, 'Is it really right what that book says, that I don't come from daddy's seeds? It was somebody else?' And I said, 'Yes'. I can't remember the other questions he asked, unfortunately, it is too long ago now, but he did ask quite a lot of questions that day.

W: I think what it showed was that he was always aware, though it had probably not been reinforced recently, and that even though he was eight and he was reading a children's story book designed for four or five year olds, this was actually a way he could absorb the information in a definite way. And that's why we think it is such a splendid book. We've heard stories of people giving it to their parents because that's another way of conveying information.

O: I think it came at exactly the right time. At eight, children have moved on in their thinking and development and so it suddenly all clicked into place for him at that point. Whereas, although Susannah could read the book, I'm not sure it actually properly clicked into place for her at that point, simply because her understanding hadn't got to the point where it was possible.

W: I don't remember him asking questions of me but I remember you reporting on various occasions that he had asked something or you had found an opportunity to say something. You'd mention later on in the evening, 'By the way, on the way to school this morning, William said such and such'. Something indicating that he had understood something.

O: And very often, these conversations seemed to take place in the car, which I thought was really interesting, without the eye contact.

W: Looking back, I don't think we would have done anything differently but if we'd had access to *My Story* earlier, we would've used it. It would have been much easier than having to use a book which wasn't quite designed for the purpose. But I think broadly, we would have gone about it in much the same way. I don't think we've got any major regrets or thinking there were perhaps opportunities or moments that we regret not having said something.

The one thing that I'm pretty certain about is that they didn't realise until really quite recently that they were from different donors. They never asked that, so we never particularly mentioned it. That is something that we ought to have. But when they were little and we were explaining it all, we didn't necessarily say anything about having to borrow from a different daddy. So either they twigged onto that or they never even thought it was terribly interesting to ask. It could've been something they could've played on very easily.

O: I've certainly never heard, and I'm sure Susannah would have reported to me, if William had said anything about, 'We're only half-siblings anyway, you know, thank God I'm not your full brother!'

W: No, it's never been the case. Never that. You think it might have been something they would have been curious about but I feel comforted that it's just not that important for them.

O: The donor issue doesn't seem to enter into [teasing], at all.

W: And being three years apart, I'd be very surprised if they talked seriously to each other about it when they were younger.

Leonie and Warren:

W: I don't think there is any set time or age [to talk with your children] – the younger the better. But they also have to be ready at some level to be able to take on the knowledge you are giving them.

L: We told Geraldine at five but, in the years before she turned five, we talked about it between each other – about the positives of telling and the negatives. We used to talk about it with our friends. We did have some help from a friend, who gave us some forms of words to use. We looked at those and we used some of the words. Warren and I were like two actors. We had written a script and we rehearsed our lines.

W: I know I was very apprehensive. You just don't know what the reaction is going to be to this news. I think that's probably because you're putting an adult's perception on it. If someone told me now, it would be a huge blow, but because she was so young and she didn't understand the full implications of it, it wasn't such a big deal at that age. It was a lot of ill-founded apprehension, because you think, "Oh well, is she going to say, 'You're not my real Daddy!" These are the sorts of things that go through your mind. How would you cope with your child saying that to you? But there was none of that.

We brought her in here and sat her on the couch between us and made sure that [her younger brother] Kieron was in bed. First of all we had to explain a little bit about how babies were born, so we gave her a basic version of the facts of life and then we went on to say, 'Well, you weren't born, or conceived, quite like that'. We explained that I didn't have healthy sperm so I wasn't able to make Mummy pregnant and then we had to get some sperm from a man who did have healthy sperm. 'And that's how you were born.'

She obviously wouldn't have understood the full implications of what all that meant, but she just seemed to feel, 'Oh that was very nice of that man to do that'. And that was it – she seemed to just accept it, there wasn't a big drama about it.

L: When you told Geraldine that you didn't have healthy sperm, she said to you, 'But Daddy we should take you to the doctor to make you better.' One of us said that we had been to many doctors and they can't make Daddy's sperm better.

We told her that she could talk to us about it at any time. 'You can always discuss this with us – at any time you like, ever, ever. You don't have to ask permission.'

We also had some friends who had an adopted child and we talked about them – how this is another way of forming a family.

About three weeks later, we were driving along in the car and she said to me, 'You know, Mum, when I get married I'm going to have ten children. I hope my husband has healthy sperm so I can have ten children'. She raised that herself. There was a trigger there and she suddenly thought of it.

Whenever they've said something, we've always tried to write it down. (Reading) Geraldine to Mummy early November 1989: 'It doesn't matter that Daddy doesn't have healthy sperm, it just matters that he enjoys children and loves them.'

We waited a little bit longer to tell Kieron, he was eight. I think I was a bit concerned about telling a male child because I wondered, would he think that he would be infertile like his Dad? Would that

L: raise some anxiety for Kieron? And it may have for all I know. We haven't asked him that one.

W: I don't think he was so much interested in babies when he was Geraldine's age, and that may have been a factor why we held off with him for a bit longer. I felt that he wasn't really at a stage where telling him about how babies were born was appropriate when he was five or six. But Geraldine was always talking about babies, always playing babies, she was baby-mad.

L: We told him that he is able to speak to us any time about it, and told him that Geraldine knew and he could talk to her. Of the three [children], he's asked the most fascinating questions. At eight, he was asking, 'Was it the same man?' Who would have thought a child of eight would have asked that question. Even some adults don't ask you that question.

(Reading). June '96, this is Kieron: 'How does the man get the sperm out? Does he press a button? If it only takes one sperm to get to the egg, why can't all the other sperm help push it up?'

We said to him, 'We think it's important to tell you this and it's your right to know how you were born. Some people say we shouldn't tell you Kieron, and that you don't need to know.' 'But it's my business.'

We asked Kieron, 'What did the DI support group mean?' He said it was to support people who had babies. We went on to explain the difference. 'Why do you think it's important to have a support group?' 'So I don't think I'm the only one in the world.' We said, 'There are lots of children in the support group just like you.'

In regards to Daddy's sperm he said, 'I think you should give them swimming lessons, Dad.'

W: They stir each other up about the characteristics they have. There is a lot of joking about it and there are times when we go to the clinic and we talk about it then, but I don't think there are a lot of other times when they talk about it.

L: I think they do but we're just not privy to it. From telling three children, I've learned that we still have work to do as parents and we have to be the instigators of the subject. If we wait for the children to bring the subject up we might wait until they are adults and they may never bring it up. We should discuss it as a family. 'Have you got any thoughts that you want to talk about?' And I feel that Warren should probably be the instigator of that, because they may not raise it because they don't want to hurt his feelings. But if Warren seems to raise it, if we both seem to raise it, that's going to send a message to the kids that it's okay to discuss this with Mum and Dad, because they're bringing it up.

Laurie and Evelyn:

E: Knowing that the little country town was absolutely rife with gossip, it became a matter of having to tell the children, it was only a matter of 'when' and not 'if'. We agonised over what would be the best time to part with the news to them, and we did not want to leave it any later than when Nigel was going into secondary school and starting to get into puberty.

We decided we would tell them both together so they could talk it over with one another and have each other for support.

Part of it was knowing where to begin, who to ask because we didn't want to do any damage that couldn't be repaired. We went to a counsellor and had a visit together and then she had a separate visit with each one of us. We had some role playing, practising the correct words and things that we shouldn't include and things that we shouldn't say. We had thought that we would make it a bit of a celebration but she told us not to go out to tell them. She said, 'If you go out to a restaurant, or wherever you take them, and you then tell them there, they've got nowhere to go. Tell them at home where they can go to their bedroom, or go to wherever they've got their own space, their own surroundings.'

L: Evelyn prepared them very well for it. Something would come up on the news or on the TV about IVF or anything like that. And she'd talk it out with the kids.

E: We'd say what special little babies they were and how loved they were by their parents, how lucky their parents were to have these little babies and how desperate they must have been to go through what they were going through. Because it was on the news, they sat down and watched it with me and they just accepted it.

We gave them the book *How I Began* to read and I guess that's where they got the basic birds and the bees and where they understood how Mother Nature worked. And then we were able to follow up with, 'Well, it wasn't quite that way for us.'

Laurie and I spent a lot of time discussing it between each other. We agonised over it and, as the day got closer, we got more tense – knowing that we were going to tell them, when we really weren't quite sure what the reaction was going to be. Had it been a negative reaction, we knew that we would have serious problems. I definitely wasn't sleeping well because it was on my mind all the time.

L: My memory is a bit hazy about how I felt at that particular stage. I know I was fearing rejection.

E: [The night we told them], we finished our evening dinner and brought them into the lounge room and said that there was something we had to tell them. It was something they needed to know. Nigel said, 'I know what you're going to tell me, I'm adopted aren't I?' So maybe from those [earlier discussions] Nigel might have got that idea. He knew that Lauren wasn't adopted because, even though he was only two years and four months, he can remember when I had Lauren and brought her back to the house.

We just told them about their conception and said, 'Have you got any questions?' And Nigel looked out the window and saw [his friend]. 'Oh he's playing footie, I must go out and play with him.' So he went off out. Laurie and I looked at one another and I said, 'I don't know whether it's hit home, what the consequences are,' until the next night, when I said to them, 'Right, kids. We're going out for a celebration tonight, your choice, where are we going?' Nigel said,

'We don't need to go out for a celebration for what you told us last night, nothing's changed. Dad's my Dad and always will be." And he put his arms around Laurie. So he certainly perfectly well did understand what the consequences were.

It couldn't have been more perfect – the words he chose – if he'd rehearsed it. It was exactly what Laurie needed to hear at that stage because what concerned me leading up to the telling was Laurie. Any opposition he had to telling the kids was, 'How are they going to treat me from now on?' That was something that had been in our minds right from the word go about the telling. How will they react? How will they feel towards Laurie as their father from now on in? That was really big. But I was really confident that there would be no reason for rejection because Laurie had been a wonderful father to them.

And Nigel couldn't have chosen anything better to say. It was just a lovely moment. I think it definitely cemented the reality of the love within our family. We knew then that they are loving children and we knew that there was nothing artificial in our family. It ended the nagging doubt that Laurie had; the fear of rejection. The fear had been erased with just a couple of words.

L: Every time Evelyn tells that story, tears come to my eyes.

E: The main ingredient through your relationship is to do things in a loving way. Make sure that they know that you both love them. Explain to them that they were deliberately conceived and much wanted. Just tell them that you're there any time they have any questions about whatever they're feeling, and that you will answer them honestly.

Andrea and Bridget:

B: I think that we started to talk to her when she had no way of understanding, to practise, to say the words. At that stage it was, 'Mummy and Rara (that's what Ellie called Andrea) had to go to hospital in order to create you, as a baby'. Then we would give examples in her life to compare, such as, Uncle Andrew and Auntie Annie, who hadn't needed to do that because Uncle Andrew had the seeds. But we don't have the seeds, as Rara doesn't have the seeds. As she's got older, she has much more understanding obviously, than she did at 18 months, which I think is probably around the age we first started saying that. A lot of it, if we're honest in looking back, was not lead by us, it was lead by her. So when she started to show a desire to have information or chat about it, then we would go into it.

A: And it was very drip-feeding because, she was only 18 months old.

B: It was very small. It really started to take shape when she was about two.

A: Out of the blue, she'd say, 'Where's my Daddy?' And we'd say, 'Well you don't actually have a Daddy because at the moment, your parents, the people who look after you are Mummy and Rara.' And the very beginning of it was trying to establish her place in the world in a real global sense because she really wanted to know where she fitted into this picture. [One of her friends] has got a Mummy and a Daddy but his Daddy is black and his Mummy is white, so that was a difference. [Another friend] has got a Mummy but no Daddy. So that was a difference. And then you've got people like the twins, because then we've got, 'Where's my sister?' So this was all in the same sort of questioning, all the time. 'Well if I haven't got a Daddy, where's my sister?' 'Well actually you don't have a sister.' It's about where she is in the world. So that was the main thing for about four months, from about two, which is for her, when it started to take shape.

B: When she first started [asking questions], it quite took me by surprise. I didn't expect to have such a simple question that was going to require a simple response to come so early. I'd, in my adult mind as adults do, thought I might be having just a bit more of a discussion. It's hard as adults, even though we actually theorise that we will always say things at a children's level, I think it is actually very difficult for an adult to do that in practice.

A: I also think that the questions that you expect are not, 'Where's my Daddy' but, 'Where did I come from?' but that's not what she wants to know.

B: On a couple of occasions in Sainsbury's, 'Is he my Daddy?' 'No Darling, he's not your Daddy.' But we would always answer the questions; we'd been very clear about that. We'd always answer and to answer there and then, not, 'We'll talk about it later' because that's just absurd to a two year old. To answer them honestly but simply. And what we found is that they basically just become interwoven as part of our everyday, week-to-week, month-to-month conversations. It is being very much shaped by her, which is not actually what I expected. I would've expected to be more responsible for giving information, where in actual fact, she has lead us into her need for information at the time that she wants it.

We have facilitated some of that as well, by situations we have been in as a family. A lot of that has been lead by the attempted conception of another child. We took her along to the hospital. 'This is the clinic we've come to and these are the doctors, this is the nurse and these are the people who help us to make a family.' So we talk about family in that sense, in a very broad sense.

A: Previously, she wasn't in a position where she said, 'I understand fully' or in any knowing way, what was happening. She came with us to our last insemination and we'd agreed this would be a really good springboard now because we'd paved a bit of the way with the fact that she knows that she doesn't have a Daddy, or there isn't a Daddy there, and that Mummy and Rara are now trying to make another baby, in the same way she was made. She had some kind of understanding, so it was in some ways a lot easier to be able to take her along and show her. That was an experience in itself.

B: Because of course now she is more able to articulate her thoughts and feelings, she didn't like some of it. She wasn't very sure about what was happening to Mummy. She was a little bit fearful.

A: And she couldn't see exactly what was going on, she was with me and we were talking about it and talking to the nurse.

B: I think it might be important to backtrack a bit, with last year, I actually had two miscarriages. One was a probable ectopic pregnancy and I was quite unwell with the very slow miscarriage and was very weepy and there was a lot of upset and distress in the house. She had an understanding of what was happening and the fact that Mummy had been trying to have another baby but it had not worked out and that Mummy and Rara were feeling very sad about that.

A: So when we went to the hospital on this last attempt, it was very much prepared for then and now there have been other babies on the way for other people. 'You might like to have a little baby brother or a baby sister.' 'Oh yes, I'll have a baby sister'. She was quite clear about that! 'To be able to do that, we need to try and get Mummy to grow another baby in her tummy.' 'How will we do that?' 'We go to the hospital. We have to just see if we can grow another baby in Mummy's tummy.' And this was all the build up to actually going to the clinic that day.

B: So we've talked about what's happening in the treatment process but we've also talked about it not working as well and having to try. Maybe it will and maybe it won't.

A: You can't just grow a baby in your tummy; you need to do certain things. And that's when we got to eggs and seeds. And she was upset about the fact that what was the nurse doing to Mummy's bottom? And then we were able to say, 'Well she's got some seed and she's going to put it inside Mummy's tummy. The only way to put it in Mummy's tummy is in through her bottom.' She didn't like that much because obviously the way things go into her tummy is through her mouth. So that was a little bit confusing. 'What's she doing now?' Mummy was fine, Mummy was just lying there and that was okay. 'Well what's the seed going to do?' 'Well hopefully, the seed is going to make an egg grow and when an egg grows, what grows then?' 'Baby'. And then the baby will grow in Mummy's tummy.' 'Right.' So that's where she's at with it at the moment. Then we have the issue of boys and girls and we're able to introduce the fact that you need a boy and a girl to make a baby. 'The seeds come from the boys and the eggs come from the girls and then the baby grows in the girl's tummy.' Which really are all very simple things.

B: Also I think that our dialogue with her is an acknowledged risk. We try some phrases out and then some of them don't work or they don't sit with her and then we try something slightly different. We're building on it all the time. We learn all the time. So it's quite a dynamic thing and we just see it as developing with her and with our skills in telling. Also, we're actually very used to living with difference because we are a lesbian couple and we are open and therefore confront difference all the time and face the challenges that come with that. And they are sometimes uncomfortable and they are sometimes difficult but we live with it.

B: We are in a fortunate position because she has led us and we have learnt a lot from her. She has shown us the way and how to phrase things. I think that's a lot of the hang-up, isn't it, with grown-ups. How do you say 'intercourse'?

A: We've tried very hard not to say to Ellie, 'You're very special', excusing where she is in the world because she's got two female parents. I think it just puts up barriers and it creates no end of problems.

B: Burdensome as well, for the child. It's a lot to bear for a little one. We talk to her about us and our family, as a couple and how we love each other and how we love her and how she's part of all this.

A: And that it is about the family, it's not about her, it's not about me or Mummy or anybody, it's actually about families. It's all centred around this wider theme, never centred on her and I think that's got to be the way to go.

Marie:

M: When I conceived my son, Lee, it didn't matter [about telling him], that wasn't the issue. When the baby is little, it is all happy, he is with his Mum and his Dad but it's only when they get older, that you think about this child having a life.

I read an article in the paper when he was about nine or ten and it was then that I wanted to do something about it but I didn't know where to turn. No one knew and I was scared of telling a stranger in case they would tell him. Eventually I did speak to a counsellor, who was a lifesaver; she was so good and really encouraged me to tell, and how to do it.

I must say that it was the hardest thing I ever did in my life, telling my son, because he was 11, coming up to 12. I wanted it to be over because it's such a big thing, and there was this build up and I was writing notes and reading and thinking about it. The anticipation made it very difficult. There were my feelings as well because you can't tell something like that without having feelings.

My husband loved his son so much and at this stage he had moved out of the home and was living abroad, so I said to him that he should come to London and it was then that we'd tell him. We had a whole script on it, rehearsed what we would say and we did it together and it was the best that we could do in the situation.

When we told him, we were sitting on the settee at the side of him. We told him how much we loved him and why we wanted him so much and that he was treasured. He didn't say anything and then he started to cry. It was so sad really. You want to say the right words and you want it to be exactly right but it's hard. I guess that it was the shock because of the age he was – if he had been three or four, or any age younger than 11, it would have been easier.

We went out for a meal after and we were hugging and holding his hands. I certainly had a bit of a release from the pressure but he didn't mention it that much. The next day he said, 'Do you think [my best friend] is like this as well?' I said, 'No' and he asked me if his own brother knew. And I said, 'Yes', because I had told him at this stage. The reason that I told him was because Lee might mention it to him because he's pretty close to his brother and looks up to him and I didn't want it to cause a problem. But Lee didn't seem to say much about it after that.

He seemed to be okay and there didn't seem to be any change in him but then, after a couple of weeks I said, 'Would you like to talk about the DI?' He said, 'No' and he said, 'I wish you hadn't told me that'. Since then really I've tried to say things to him, such as, if I was going to the DI Network meeting I would ask him if he would like to come and he always says, 'No'. There are lots of children there that he would be able to meet that are his age but he always says that he is busy and that he doesn't want to go there. He has probably buried it and it's very hard for me to open it up. He doesn't want to hear anything about it but my dearest wish is that we could open it up and talk about it. It is difficult and I must say, for me, it worries me a lot, it's always there.

I wish I had told him earlier, maybe at two or three. It would've been so nice if it hadn't been all locked away. I think that is my biggest regret, not having told him when he was younger. I think that a child has a right to know. Lee asked why it took so long to tell him and I said that the doctor had told us not to tell and also, I had been very ill for a couple of years. He seemed to understand that I was so glad that I had told him.

At the moment he is a bit isolated and I feel that I'm stuck; that I can't move forward with him because I can't make him talk. I do think that it will come, but it is difficult. He is 15 now, so maybe when he is 17 or 18 he might have all these questions and want to know if he looks like his Dad.

Tom and Ali:

T: We agreed that they needed to know.

A: But we didn't know how to handle it. We didn't know whether we should sit them all down and say, 'This is our story, this is what happened' or whether we should just wait. We couldn't resolve that so we just left it and once we listened to what the kids were saying, the doors opened.

Right from the very beginning, Eric was involved in coming down here, "Well, we want to have another baby and the doctors and nurses down at London need to help us because we can't do this on our own". We tried to explain it in very simple terms, give them only the information that they were asking for. I always felt that we shouldn't mess it up with too much detail.

And then there were a few little opportunities. With Carly for instance, she came home from kindergarten one day, I believe it was when she was four, and told me that her friend had told her where babies come from. And that there was a sperm and an egg involved and was this really true? And I said, 'Yes it is true, Carly'. I said, 'The lady has the egg and the man has the sperm.' I asked her if her friend had told her how it got in there and she said, 'The man's penis has to go into the lady'. I thought, 'I could leave it there but I'm not going to', and I chose my words very carefully and said, 'You know that's usually' – I tried to avoid the word 'normally' – 'that's usually how men and women make babies but sometimes, there are men or women who can't have babies. They don't make sperm, they don't make eggs, and then they need help from the doctors and nurses'. And I went on to tell her that Dad is like that, Dad doesn't have any sperm, so we go down to London when we want to have a baby and there is somebody called a donor and he donates his sperm to make babies. And she said, 'Really' and I said, 'Yeah, that's how you and Eric and Adam were born', and she said, 'Oh!' And that was it, she turned and walked away. That was all she needed at the time.

It has not really been an issue since she was four and now she's nine. There have been a few other times where I've listened to what she was saying and taken the opportunity to always show our family's point of view. Any time she's ever talked about babies and sperm and eggs, I always, always, think here's another opportunity to reinforce that not all children are created that way and that sometimes help is required and that help is there and how grateful we are to the donors and it's really all they've needed to know. We're always trying to keep our ears open for the times when we can say those things.

I remember one specific incident where it really forced us to have to speak more to our older son, Eric, than we already had. Tom had taken all three children to register our daughter for a dance class and a woman sitting at the counter happened to be our neighbour's mother and she looked at Carly and she said, 'Oh, you look just like your Mum.' And she looked at Adam (who could be Tom when he was a little boy) and she said, 'And you are the spitting image of your Dad.' And she looked at Eric and said, 'Well you don't look like anybody, where do you fit in?'

He was just devastated. He was angry, really angry. 'Why don't I look like Dad, why does everybody say that Adam always looks like Dad?' And that was our opportunity that we had been waiting for. We were, at that time, thinking, 'Do we bring it up? Should we wait until he brings it up?' And it was a relief actually. As sad as I felt for Eric, that it had come about this way, it opened the door for us to give him just that little bit more information and talk to him about genes in your makeup and that children could be conceived the 'normal way' and still end up looking more like one parent than the other. And it's just the luck of the draw; it's not that way simply because Eric has been conceived through DI.

I remember going to bed that night and saying, 'Wasn't that a relief?' I felt like a weight had been lifted off my shoulders. I think he was probably in grade four or grade five and we were really spending a lot of time wondering, 'Well, what if they never ask? What if they wait until they're 14 and then they ask? And why would they ask? I mean what on earth is going to make them come and say to us – this is kind of our naiveté in the whole thing – what would make them come and say to us, 'Could you tell me what donor insemination is?'

We would talk about, 'Well we need to do something. I think we need to bring it up with them.' But we didn't know how to do that! So we were just very grateful, even though it hurt Eric terribly because of that comment, it was probably a good thing because it was just the perfect opportunity.

T: The timing wasn't the best but we knew we couldn't wait until they were teenagers.

A: I think we did what came naturally. We knew what we needed to tell them and we just knew they had to know.

T: And we knew they didn't need to know every single detail. They needed to know the basics.

A: They had seen a couple of children's books about DI which I read to them but it was like a regular storybook and I would do the Mum thing, 'Now do you understand what that means? Let me explain a little bit more to you,' and they couldn't really have cared less. It was, 'That's a weird bedtime story but okay, if we have to read that book, we'll read it,' and it was never brought up again. But they were too busy. They were just busy in the life of being children and it wasn't important to them.

I don't think they actually speak to each other about donor conception. I think what we are hearing more of is Eric may comment to Adam, 'Oh, your hair is really dark,' or whatever, and Adam might say, 'Oh, I get that from Dad'. And that's my time to say, 'Pardon?' and then it's like a lightbulb goes on and they both go, 'Oh, yeah!!' They keep forgetting and we have to keep reminding them. But I don't think they really ever talk. I've never heard any conversation about the actual donor insemination process. I just think it's not really a big deal for them.

People seem to spend a lot of time really, really fretting about talking with their children. And we did too. But once we saw how things were going to unfold and saw what worked for us, we felt so much more comfortable with that. They couldn't catch us off guard because we were prepared, even though we didn't know exactly what the question was going to be, when it was going to come and what we were going to say. We felt confident in saying, 'Just answer their questions. Keep it simple; don't give them too much information. Listen to what the question is and just answer that particular question.'

T: There have been times where I haven't been around that Ali's been asked questions. She was in the car one time and got a bunch of questions from – Adam I think it was at that point – and so, you don't say, 'Well I'm going to wait until Dad and I can talk to you!'

A: I have said to all of them, 'If at any time you have any more questions or there is anything that's kind of worrying you, just come and ask me and Eric said, 'I don't really care. It's no big deal.'

T: We also reinforce that by making sure that we have new information and as much information available to them as they may need – if they ask other questions in the future about background history.

A: Which they haven't. And from what I hear from Eric, he really is not interested in that.

T: We've asked them, 'Do you ever want more information, would you want to know?' And they haven't come back that they want to know.

A: When we are talking about it, it's very casual conversation. But I think we also have waited for these times when the door opens just a little bit more and we can feed a little bit more information through and because we don't make a big deal of it, because we're not secretive about our trips to London or anything, it's just something that they have grown up with, they don't think it is weird or unusual.

T: It's natural to them. It's not in the forefront in their mind; it's just another part of their growing-up process.

Bettina and Sven:

B: I read a book on adoption and it described the problems children have when they learn at 16 or 18 and that it is always bad for them. There was no story in which it was good that they learned about their adoption at 20. So I knew, for me, I would tell.

S: We never made a big secret of it.

B: I always felt that if my son asks me, 'Where do I come from, Mama; do I come from my father's sperm?' I wouldn't lie, I knew this. We could not agree on the age when we wanted to tell it to our children. I said at about three or four years of age and when Sven heard this he said, 'You are crazy – you can't tell a four-year-old child these things!' And I said, 'Yes', because of the examples from the book of adoption – how they did this. But we had to discuss it a little bit.

S: This discussion took place just before Peter was almost four years and not at the stage where we made a decision to use DI.

B: I tried to convince Sven that four years was the right age and that I would try to explain to him that we had been sad and wanted a baby, and our feelings. I imagined the words I would choose for him so that he could understand our situation.

The book on adoption said the child should never believe it has been any other way. If a child is six or seven years and then you say, 'He's not your father', you have been lying to the child, so it should be there from the beginning.

S: When Bettina said, 'Peter asked some questions about where babies come from', and that was at the age of four, she said, 'We now have to tell him'. Then I realised, 'Well, I said, four years ago, yes, I will tell my child, but at that stage I thought I had 10 or 12 years time to get used to it, to get the right answers, and now he's four and I need some answers immediately'. But I thought that it might be the right time afterall because, at the age of 12 they start to get difficult. I always expected that this relationship between my children and me might cause some problems when they were teenagers because it is a difficult age. Maybe if you don't agree with them and they are angry they might say something which might hurt you. So I said, 'Okay, they should know everything just before they get to be real teenagers and not afterwards, because this might lead to a more intensive conflict situation'. Now I think it's better to tell the children as soon as possible, even if they do not know exactly what's going on, so they feel there is something different in connection with how they were conceived.

B: And I think it's important for the parents because they are afraid of this moment, when do they tell the children? But I think it's not the right way [to leave it until the children are older] because the children feel there is something strange and the parents shouldn't wait until this point where they are nervous and excited. I was nervous and excited even when he was four years old. I was afraid of his reaction.

S: I think the worst case is if we say in advance, 'Well, we will tell our children,' and then you wait one year, wait one more year and say, 'Our son is now 15, do you think we should tell him? Or, he hasn't realised anything, let's wait one more year. Okay, now he's 18. It's never the right moment.

B: It came up with Peter in the evening at six or seven o'clock. I had spent the afternoon reading and talking with the children. He was four years old and he had to have a circumcision, so we talked a lot about the male penis and then we told him that Sven had had an operation when he was 10 on his testicles. I knew I would use this later to explain about donor insemination. Some days later I showed him a book with photos of a baby in a mother's tummy and there were also pictures of sperm and eggs. I told him something about how life begins and about men and women and sperm. He asked about babies and how they got into the mother's tummy and all those questions. I know he did not really understand what a sperm and egg were but I explained that it took these things to make a baby. I then explained that when we wanted to have a baby we were very sad because the doctor told us my husband has been ill and has been operated on too late and there couldn't be any sperm to make a baby.

But the doctor said he could help us – he could give us the sperm of another man. So we were happy and we went there and the doctor put the sperm into my tummy and then a baby – you – were born.

And then, two years later, we were so happy with having the baby, we wanted another baby. We went back to the doctor and he again asked this man if he could give us his sperm and so Katherine could grow in my tummy. I talked with him quickly – I was nervous. He only asked, 'Mummy, but this man – can't he now have any more babies?' He was preoccupied with the worry that this man couldn't have any other babies because he gave his sperm to us. This was his first question. Okay, he didn't understand the genetics and that he is not from the genes of Sven. Perhaps when he is 10 he will realise and understand but it makes no difference now.

S: Bettina said to me, 'Well, today I told him. You should talk with him again, so that he knows it isn't just my story, it's our story.' I don't know how we started the conversation but in the end it was some kind of reconfirmation. He said, 'Well, Mummy told me this and that,' and I said 'Oh yes, that's true'. So I started this conversation but in the end I got the feeling that it was some kind of reconfirmation for him of what Bettina had told him some hours before.

B: I was relieved afterwards because I thought it would be difficult and he would ask, 'Who is this man and can I meet him,' but of course, he didn't ask it.

S: Not at this stage.

B: If he does, then it's no problem. We can try to find him. But I also had a worry that he might say, 'Why didn't you tell me before?' or something like that.

S: The risk of having to answer difficult questions is on the minimum level if you do it at the age of three or four or five, so it's really easier.

B: And it's important to say it's not only that you talk once to your child and tell him this. You have to talk every year or every two years – it's a process.

S: I think for at least three months afterwards he sometimes talked about this but since then it has never been talked about any more. At the moment it seems, for him, to be quite natural, the most natural thing in the world.

B: He knows we go to a meeting where other couples want to have a baby and can't, and we tell them that we asked another man and a doctor, who helped us.

The easiest way [to bring up the subject] is when children start to talk about babies or, if a friend is having a baby, you could talk about how babies are made and about sperm and eggs. I think when they are four or five they start asking. For a four-year-old child, it is only important to know, 'Which tummy have I been growing in?'

S: Even Katherine, she is now three and a half, and of course she asks questions. Maybe Peter will tell it to her with his words.

B: Perhaps it is better he is with us at that moment. I don't know. Perhaps we will wait another year with Katherine. But I think it would be a strange situation, we will create a strange atmosphere, if we were to say, 'Oh, Katherine, now we have to talk to you alone'. That wouldn't be good; it should be as natural as possible. Katherine was with us when I talked to Peter, she was two years old. So perhaps she already knows everything! I don't know.

S: I believe people should tell their children as early as possible. The difficult question is, 'How?'

B: With easy words and only the basic information. There is no need to try to explain the medical treatment.

S: The basic information that something is different, but this 'something different' is normal and we can talk about it at any time and anywhere. Just offer that to the child.

Romana and Grant:

G: Having made the decision early to tell Desmond made things very easy for us. And where I see some of our friends having trouble is where they've decided to tell their kids but they've let it go a few years. Some of our friends tell their kids when they're nine or ten. I can see that it's hard for the parents to do it, they're worried; they're not sure how to do it.

R: And also, one woman said a very smart thing: 'A social worker told me to tell my children around the age of seven but that means that I can't tell anybody else because somebody might tell my child before me.' So I said to her, 'That's right. And then you're also missing a whole avenue of support.'

G: If you make the decision early, then you're telling the kids before they know what conception is. It's quite easy.

R: It allows parents to become comfortable with using the words of explanation before the child starts asking difficult questions. Children can understand that their parents are open to communicate about the topic and a child understands at an early age that he or she has permission to talk about his conception. People say, 'But how would they understand what the word *sperm* means?' And I say, 'Well how do you think they understand what the word *mother* means, until you use it?' Why do we assume they can learn *mother* but not *sperm*? Sure, Des didn't know what sperm was at the age of six months but I got to say *donor*, I got to say *donor sperm* and I got lots of practice.

I brought it up from the minute I met him. I told him the story as a bedtime story. 'Once upon a time we were two happy people.' And that's the story he asks for, 'Tell me the story of how I made you a mother.' And Grant's version is, 'Tell me the story of how I made you a father'.

G: I make a point of telling it to him, periodically. When he was young, for the first few years, I'd make a point of having a conversation about it on his birthday. That way I knew I had not let one year go by without a discussion about it. At different ages they understand things on completely different levels. I'm not sure exactly what he picked up but he'd been to donor conception meetings, seen other donor children, we've had a number of conversations, and I remember there was a time where I asked him what a donor child was and he told me it was the firstborn, that's what donor meant.

I clarified him on that point; pointed out that there are other donor families where they were all donor kids. And so he worked that out in his mind. Then about six months later, I heard him telling Maxwell that he wasn't the donor kid because he was the second born. And I reminded him that this wasn't the right definition and he said, 'Oh yeah, I've got that. I remember that.' So he still wasn't clear in his mind exactly what it was but he definitely had some pigeonhole in his mind that donor children weren't quite as numerous. They were around, we'd bump into people and they would have a donor kid, so he knew that there were other donor kids around. But they weren't in every family.

R: And we'd always talk about this. Once I joined a support group, it was really easy because I got to say, 'I'm going to donor children's meetings,' but up until then, we would drive past the Royal Women's Hospital and I would say, 'Oh that's where we got the sperm to make you and that's the hospital where you were born'. His photo album contained the DI nurse in it too. I tried to find avenues of bringing it up in everyday conversations to let him know that it was okay.

G: It's become so much more concrete now that the donor is on the scene.

R: Yes, the questions are fast and furious.

G: Before that, I guess he was just coming to terms with our usage of the words, what that meant for him and these other families.

R: I remember telling Desmond that he was special, but then, an adopted woman said what that feels like from the adopted person's perspective. She said, 'No, no, no. You don't want to be special; you just want to be like everybody else." And also she complained that her mother used to say to her, 'You're God's gift to me. You're just a gift.' She said, 'If you make it like they are a gift, then they feel like they owe you something. And they don't.' I immediately realised that he didn't want to be special and he didn't want to be 'wanted' or 'chosen' or any of those things; he just wants to be family. So I stopped doing all that.

My advice to other parents is to start early, in infancy, pre-language, and just use the words in normal conversation like, 'We're going to a donor children's party,' 'This is the hospital where we got the sperm'. That's where you begin I think. And then the child will start asking questions and you go and discuss them with your partner and bring back the answers. Often Desmond would ask a question, [Grant and I] would talk about it and then two days later I'd say, "Desmond, do you remember when you asked that really good question the other day? Well, I was thinking about it and ..." And then I would give him another response.

G: In terms of telling the children, we would try and treat it as a matter-of-fact without making too much fuss about it and try and talk about it as honestly as we could. If that meant using words that they couldn't understand, then that was better than trying to make up explanations which weren't correct. It was very important to me that we stick to the truth. I hate euphemisms.

You can talk about genes and they don't know what that means but they pick up something from the gist of the conversation. I noticed even with 'blood'. I mentioned to Desmond that he and I didn't have the same blood and I stopped doing that because blood tends to scare a lot of kids. But we hit on the hands, that when he grew up, he would not have the same hands as me. I think that's when he first really understood.

R: And teeth too, remember the thing about teeth?

G: That's right, if I was going to give advice to parents, about trying to communicate what it means to the child, I would talk about physical similarities, as opposed to the physical processes that brought about their conception. Not that they shouldn't stray away from it but in terms of things that the children can understand. What our boys understood profoundly, first, was the physical side – he knew my hands were different from his hands. It puts the whole question on a very mundane and practical level. We're not talking about life or death, or things about whether you are 'mine' or belong to somebody else or anything else; we are talking about simple things like physical characteristics.

R: But he is to this day trying to work out the connections. At age four he was still asking, 'Is the person who gave us the sperm a man or a woman?' And that was after hearing the egg and sperm stories since the beginning of time. It does take them a long time but I think people should persevere and I also think that people need to give children permission to ask questions. We have to not be afraid to hear the questions.

Susan and Greg:

S: I was really active with Resolve when Rowan was young, so he would be sitting on my lap and I would be taking a call about donor insemination. He was very verbal when he was young and I knew he was taking in what I was saying, so we would talk a little bit sometimes, when he was old enough to have some sort of comprehension – maybe aged two or three. I can't remember the first time or the first concept of it, but basically when he was very little, we had kids' books with a mum cow and a baby cow and we just talked about how for there to be a baby, you need a mummy and a daddy and how the dad part wasn't working, it was broken so we got some help. Kids don't grasp all the concepts but they could understand that they had a mummy and daddy and something being broken and needing fixing and getting some help.

G: I can remember talking about these issues and getting the feeling that maybe the kids were just a little too young to take much of this in.

S: Yeah, maybe Eli was. It seemed like we ended up talking to Rowan earlier than we might have, just because I was so active with Resolve at the time. It was the situation that I couldn't take a phone call and say, 'Hold on, I'll go put the baby in the playpen somewhere and talk to you in secret'. It didn't work out that way. Probably we wouldn't have brought it up until they were a little bit older but at about three, kids do understand about babies and at that time, we brought in the idea a little bit. I don't think they grasped it much until they were maybe about four or five but it just became part of what they understood about themselves, which made it so much easier when we came to talking about it. Even if they aren't grasping it fully, it still becomes just a part of the way that life is.

When we elaborated on the explanation when they were older, as they understood a little bit more, we always communicated that this donor had given the sperm just so that we could have a baby and how very much we wanted them and how very grateful we were that this had happened. They have lost having a genetic father but on the other hand, they do understand that they were very wanted.

G: Obviously we feel that they are special but some parents are so proud of their kids that they have to tell the world how special they are. We recognise that as being probably not the best approach for the sake of the child. If anything I think we've played down the special nature of it and just said this is how we did it and that there are other ways to do it. We needed to do it this way because I am infertile and we are so thrilled that we have you kids.

I don't talk much with them and I sometimes wonder if we talk enough – as they grow older and they can understand more. I don't go out of my way to talk about it anymore because I feel like we have laid the groundwork and they don't bring it up very often.

S: I have conversations with them in the car. Just the other day when we were driving into town, somehow it came up and Eli said something about, 'I have two Dads'. We were talking about it a little bit and then they were talking to each other. It was just a natural sort of conversation; it wasn't a big deal. They were defining a father. It was a semantic discussion between real father, biological father and genetic father. Eli will sometimes say, 'My real Dad', thinking about the biological father. The other day I said, 'You mean your genetic father' and he said, 'That's the word'. He has settled on genetic father as a good way to talk of the donor. Otherwise, I don't know how much they talk about it to each other because I don't actually think they think much about it.

G: I don't really think about it that much anymore and I haven't seen evidence that we need to have a discussion about this again. If something came up, if they said something that suggested that we needed to talk more about it then I would certainly do it.

S: I will occasionally bring it up if it fits into the conversation and occasionally they'll say something but that's because we've laid the groundwork over quite a long time. It seems the way that we talked about it when they were young worked out fine. We just gave them a little bit of information that they could understand; the concept of sperm and egg. It was not a big deal and we didn't make it into having a big talk, it was just something that didn't have a lot of force behind it. There wasn't that scary energy of, 'This is time for a heavy talk'. We just brought it in and at certain points there was a particular reaction from the boys. I remember Rowan at one point said, 'Why couldn't I have been born like everybody else?' He was about five or six. And Eli at one point last year, when he was about eight, said something to Greg when he was angry.

G: He said something like, 'You're not my Dad'. I just talked to him about how in fact I was his real Dad because I was the father to him, I was raising him. It was true that he had a genetic father but that I was the Dad he had from day to day and every day. I wasn't too concerned about it and didn't take it too seriously, but I didn't want him to make it a habitual way of thinking. I felt a little bit hurt, which is interesting, because generally speaking I don't feel in the least bit emotionally vulnerable around the kids.

S: Maybe we brought up the concept of a 'biological father' but I know that when I have mentioned that to the boys that I am always talking about the donor. It's the kids that have then started making sense about it and trying to think about it and have ended up talking about fathers. They start trying to work out the ideas of fatherhood and where all these fathers belong.

I told them there's biologically the sperm that helped make you when it joined with my egg but the person who wanted you to be born and took care of me when I was pregnant and was there from the moment you were born and takes care of you all the time, that's what your father is, that's a real father. That's what I tried to really help them understand.

G: For a child, the father who cares for them is really what father means and this other stuff about genetic father or biological father is really a pretty artificial construct to them. Father doesn't mean genetics to them. Father means someone who raises them, it means me. I can recall struggling with the terminology in the beginning, so I think I probably introduced the word 'father' without ever intending to, just because I was struggling.

S: It seemed to me that we were able to use the word 'father' in a way to mean the biological aspect. I would say that he donated genetic material so you could exist.

It's a matter of reinforcing the concept of the father who cares for you and loves you and is with you all the time and functions as your bona fide father, versus the man who maybe fathered you in the literal sense.

After getting a little bit of information they both at some point, maybe about six, really had to fit this into their burgeoning world view and deal with their ideas of their selves. It was hard, there was a little bit of abrasive stuff happening but not anything drastic or frightening. And all I could think of was that I couldn't imagine springing this on a 17-year-old.

G: I can imagine that there could come a time when they are teenagers, when suddenly it will become an important issue for them again. We will have to sit down and talk about it again in more depth and try to help them understand on some level where they are having difficulty, but there has been very little evidence so far that they have been uncomfortable with the situation.

Emails from Irene and Peter Ryll:

I thought I'd share the first comments about DI from our children – Adam (5) and Megan (3½). I'm writing all of this down in a journal for our family before I forget exactly what was said, by whom and when. I think this will be a pretty special journal to share with the children as we grow as a family.

We've read a couple of books, *My Story* and *Mommy Did I Grow in Your Tummy?* to the kids on and off but there wasn't really a lot of interest at the time with the kids being quite young. So we felt we would start off simple and let them take the lead. Sharing this last book with the kids has led us to have talks about the baby in mommy's 'tummy' (we tried uterus, but tummy won out with the kids for now) and how an egg from a woman and sperm from a man can make a baby. We have a couple of books with the amazing photography by Lennart Nilsson, one of them written specifically for kids by Sheila Kitzinger, with his photos. This was very helpful to us.

So we would add in bits of our story about not being able to make a baby together, being very sad about this and going to the doctor to try to make a baby. We mentioned that we were able to use the sperm from a man who gave it to the doctor so that people like their mommy and daddy could make a baby. We mentioned how happy we were that this man did this and that our wonderful children were here with us now. They never commented on this at the time.

One and a half weeks ago Megan pulled out the DI books and asked me to read them to her. Adam was playing and sat down after a bit and asked if it was okay if I started again from the beginning. Megan said okay.

While I was reading the part about the sperm donors and mentioned again that was how mommy and daddy were able to have you, Adam asked me if I had a picture of our donor. I told him no, that we didn't, and we didn't know very much about him. I asked Adam why he wanted a picture of him and he said he just wanted to know what he looked like. I finished reading the books and then thought, 'Okay, I'll try to take this one step further and see where it leads us'.

I asked them both if they could say something to their donor, what would they say? Adam piped up that he would ask him if he could draw a picture of him. I asked him why and he said he wanted to know what he looked like and to make sure he wasn't a vampire or something like that. Adam has quite an imagination and at around that time was talking about vampires.

Then Megan said in her sweet little voice with her eyelashes fluttering, 'I'd tell him that I love him.' When I asked her why, she said that she loved him because he gave us some sperm and helped us make a baby and she loved babies. What a very special memory this is for me!!

And where was Peter during all of this? He was working on the computer and came out shortly afterwards. I told him that we read the stories and about my question to the kids and asked him to ask the kids what they said. They basically told him the same thing. We both thought it went very well, considering it was our first 'conversation' and that was the end of talking about DI or donors that night.

* * * * *

Adam, out of the blue, has just mentioned when Daddy's sperm couldn't make a baby, we used the sperm from another man's collection and the doctor put it inside my tummy and it made a baby! I said, 'Yes, that's how we were able to have all of you."! I chuckled to myself at his choice of the word 'collection' (he's into collecting stuff right now) and thought to myself, 'Okay, this is sinking in'.

I wonder how this would go over if out of the blue he mentions this to his playschool class etc. With Peter or myself not being there to support him and explain this, it could be most interesting or disastrous! So perhaps now is the time to mention that this is our 'special' family story and we usually only talk about it with our family. I don't want him to think there is something wrong but perhaps this is a time to plant the seed of privacy. Or would that just encourage the opposite? I know there is no book on the right way to approach all of this. People need to take their cues from the children and what they themselves feel comfortable with. Of course we want to present this as positively as possible and I hope that we have so far. I'm glad I haven't been asked how the doctor gets the sperm, or how it usually gets into the mommy yet, but I'm sure it will come up out of the blue sometime soon. I'll have to practice this one!

* * * * *

Adam (5) was just working on making a Mother's Day card and couldn't wait to give it to me. He had drawn people on the front, inside and on the back of the card, along with hearts! I gave him a big hug and asked him who the people were.

On the inside were three people, one is himself, one is me with his two sisters in my tummy, and the other one is Daddy. On the back, he tells me is another one of me with babies in my tummy.

Then I asked him who was the one on the front and he says, 'He's the guy who gave you sperm'. You can imagine I wasn't quite expecting this. Then I told him how special this man was and that he gave us the greatest gift his mommy and daddy could ever have – all of our kids – and we had a big hug. That was all he would say about the drawing and I didn't want to press him further. This is the first time Adam has mentioned our donor since our talk [six months ago].

* * * * *

Adam is 7½ now and doesn't ask questions about his origins on his own. I will bring it up once in a while to see what he does remember and give him an opportunity to ask questions. Megan will bring it up more and likes to still read the DI children books, though we haven't done that in a while. Amy who is now three is starting to hear the story, but she's still rather young. She does ask me frequently how God makes people. I tell her that God made people able to make babies and that seems to satisfy the question. Megan recently asked me how the donor gives the sperm to the doctor. I told her the doctor gives the donor a cup and tells him how to put the sperm in it. Give me a break – she has only just turned six years old! I'm not ready to explain masturbation yet but I better start because that question is coming!

* * * * *

The last time Adam and I spoke about his origins was several months back when he actually brought it up on his own. He said to me that he must have half my genes because I argued with my parents and so does he. Then he said, 'I wonder if the other man argued with his parents too'. I asked him who he meant and he said the man who made him with his sperm. We talked a bit more and I felt pretty good that he had an understanding of his origins and remembered.

When we talk to the kids about our donor, we use that term to describe him – a man, a donor who gave us his sperm to help us have a family. I think using the term 'biological father' right now with the kids might be confusing to them, and so will build on that as they grow. This feels comfortable for us right now. Peter and I have no problem recognizing that the donor is our children's biological father, nor using that terminology, but it's not our first choice.

* * * * *

Last week I asked him if he remembered the story of how Mommy and Daddy became pregnant with him and how we became a family. He said, 'My Dad's sperm didn't work, so he was made from the sperm of his other father, his 'real' father'. I shuddered inside, thinking, 'Oh, my goodness, how did he come to say that?' We have never used the term 'real father' and it's probably the term that bothers me the most. I explained to him that his Dad is his 'real father' and that the word 'real' isn't the word we would use to describe the man who helped us. I explained he was our sperm donor; he isn't a 'real father'. Would that mean that his Dad was an 'unreal' father? He agreed that it wouldn't and I told him the story again about how we went to the doctor and he suggested using the sperm from a donor who wanted to help couples like us have a family.

Today, I asked Adam if he remembered talking with me about his origins last week. He said, 'Yes' and I asked him if he could tell me the story. He said, 'My Dad's sperm couldn't make a baby with my egg so we used the sperm from another man who wanted to help us.' I asked Adam what he calls the other man and he replied, 'A friend'. I said, 'Why would you call him that?' 'Because he helped us and that's what friends do.' I told him that because we don't know him and never will, we can't really call him a friend, and that's why we call him a donor. I then asked Adam if it was okay to call him a donor. Adam said, 'I know we don't know him but if someone was in a building that was burning and someone from another floor helped him, even if he didn't know him, he would still be a friend because he helped him. Because that's what friends do, they help people.' My God, I love this boy and these are very special conversations. My son, though he is only seven years old, has taught me something today about how he views his donor.

* * * * *

I asked Megan if there was something else she would want to know. She said that she would like to know why he gave away a sperm to make a baby. I asked her why it was important for her to know this. She said it was important because then she would be able to tell her children and they could pass it on to tell their children and everyone would know why.

These kids just blow us away. They seem to know so much already for their young ages, more than most adults and we're amazed. Peter said it's moments like these that make him emotional and make him feel like we're a family. Does this man not sound wonderful himself?

Learning from These Stories

As you will no doubt agree, the personal stories are very powerful. Some will make you smile, some will bring a tear to your eye, but all provide a valuable insight into the different ways parents have shared information with their children and the different ways in which the children have responded. To complete this chapter, I will summarise the key points that have emerged from the stories and what we can learn from them.

Parents

Reinforcing the notion of parental preparation, many of the stories show that parents have found value in preparing for the sharing of information with their children. This is seen on both a practical and an emotional level. The practical level is characterised by the way parents gained advice and guidance from others (professionals or other parents), rehearsed the words together, or talked with their children long before they were old enough to understand. This communication enables parents to try out ideas of what they want to say and to hear the words out loud.

Preparation on a practical level also plays a part on an emotional level, by helping parents deal with the anxieties and tensions that are still likely to occur to a certain degree, even with preparation. You will have noted the relief many parents felt once the information had been shared.

It is also clear that if there are two parents, being unified in their approach and their level of commitment to openness is likely to be beneficial for them and their children. It reinforces the fact that it is a family story – 'our story' – rather than a story solely about the child.

> *I like the idea of talking about, 'This is how our family was created'. It's about having a relationship that's built around this and it's not just the child that is a product. It is an inclusive way of talking about it.* Female, Sydney Focus Group

Clearly there is no one right way to share information – there are advantages and disadvantages in introducing the topic at an early age, in having a special 'talk', and in waiting for offspring to initiate the subject. It seems likely that in the initial stages of information sharing it is parents who lead the discussion, but that ongoing conversations often arise when parents pick up on their offspring's comments and questions. In other words, they have a desire or a readiness to know and understand more.

Questions

Parents need to recognise that if they are being open and encouraging communication about information sharing, there will of course be questions. These questions, as parents have indicated, can come at a much earlier age than expected and are likely to come at very interesting and perhaps potentially embarrassing times. There is therefore clearly a need for parents to be prepared for the questions to emerge at any time and in any form!

Being able to be open in conversations with your children and to handle questions in a way that does not reflect embarrassment or distress is very significant. Children quickly learn whether this is a sensitive and difficult area that causes some distress and therefore is not a subject to be raised again, or whether they are free to ask questions and continue the dialogue.

> *Our child will just talk about it lots. He'll just pop up the subject when we are dropping him off at school.* Male, Melbourne Focus Group

Answering your child's questions immediately, even if it is somewhere such as a busy supermarket, is clearly seen by some of our parents as being very positive, whereas others feel more comfortable discussing the question with their partner first and then returning with a carefully considered reply. This is all part of a parent's responsiveness to their child's needs, albeit in different ways. Regardless of how they respond, the parents who have shared their stories with us find it important to encourage their children to ask questions and to ensure they know that their parents are open to discussion about their family building whenever the children desire it.

Reactions

Children and offspring will, as we have seen, react in many different ways to the information that is shared with them. Most have a need for time to digest and process the information, particularly if they are older, and then to return later for further explanations from their parents.

The level of comprehension that children have to the information you are giving them will of course vary according to their age.

> *When I asked her (age six), 'What makes a father?' she said, 'It's*

the person who you come from'. I said, 'Do you remember how we said that in our family it took three people for you to be born, that Dad didn't have any sperm so this other man gave us the sperm to help create you? She said, 'Oh yes'. And I said, 'Maybe you look a little bit like him.' And she said, 'I don't look like him, I'm a girl!' She had a bit of a think about it but doesn't make the connection. Female, Sydney Focus Group

When I got pregnant, their teachers at school would come up to me and say, 'I hear you are pregnant with an embryo'. It just became their language and what they understood. I used to wonder if they knew that it could happen naturally and then one of them told me how her teacher got pregnant. 'But not like you, Mum. They actually did it themselves – naturally, with sperm.' They did understand. Female, Melbourne Focus Group

She's five and some things are starting to re-emerge. What is her response going to be because it doesn't really seem to have sunk in. She's read 'My Story' many times and she's asked questions about it but I am not sure, even now, if she puts herself in it. So we're coming to the point where presumably we will have to start again to see what sort of a comprehension she is capable of having in relation to this. Male, London Focus Group

The potential for a negative reaction will always be there. Teenagers, in particular, want to conform and avoid being different from their peers. It is natural that they may go through a stage of wanting to bury the information, viewing it as something which is unpleasant, uncomfortable and not to be talked about. Interestingly, this reaction is likely to occur during adolescent years, regardless of whether they are learning about it for the first time or if they have grown up with the knowledge.

It is quite normal for teenagers not to want to talk about their DI origins for a few years. Being just like your mates is really important at this time. Letter from Olivia to would-be DI Mums

> *My eldest one initially didn't believe me. He thought I was making it up. Then he was quite upset. The youngest one, I don't even think was taking it in and I don't really think that he has taken it in now. Every time I bring it up, he says that he doesn't want to hear about it. That's probably due to telling them when they are nearly adults.* Female, Sydney Focus Group

> *Sometimes he does not like all the fuss over it. I think he prefers to put it right to the back of his mind – the fact that he was ever conceived by DI.* Evelyn

> *Our son became particularly touchy between about 12 and 15, which came as a little bit of a shock to me. I thought, 'Where is he getting this message from, that he wants to be private about it?' But he seemed to let go of it after 15 or 16.* Female, London Focus Group

> *A negative reaction makes you feel particularly guilty. I had not spoken to him for a long time and then I spoke to him and he was negative and said that he didn't want me talking about it to anyone and then I felt awful.* Female, London Focus Group

> *Part of being a responsible parent is knowing when to let go and allow them to own that information. As William went into teenage years, he wanted to be quieter and quieter about it. It's a transitional time for them anyway and it's perfectly normal but certainly he has now moved beyond that, where he is very easy to talk to about it and has recently told friends and is again happy for us to talk about it publicly.* Olivia

One of the anxieties that many parents talk about is that there will be an accusation of, 'you are not my real father'.

> *Now she's five, I think, 'Is this going to come up in the inevitable rows?' People always say, 'Yes, of course it will, but so will all sorts of other things'. In some way, it will be used against you. 'You're not my Dad. I don't even like you etc.' But it's not worth getting worked up, as you work out each stage as best you can.* Male, London Focus Group

It is wise for parents to see this kind of challenge as part of normal behaviour from children who are growing up and to be prepared for a variety of reactions regarding your family building.

> *The problem we get more is from our second child, who is by definition 'an accident'. It wasn't a planned pregnancy because we didn't think I could make her pregnant, so he will actually throw at us, 'I'm just an accident. You never wanted me.' And that's an intriguing thing! He demonstrates that if kids want to have a go at you, they will. It doesn't matter if they are a DI child, an adopted child, or a natural child with one leg, two legs or three legs. They all find something to have a go at you about.* Male, London Focus Group

Terminology and confusing language

There were several instances of parents using language that they thought children would clearly understand but the children were in fact quite confused and uncertain. It is useful to remember that the language that makes sense to us is not necessarily the language that makes sense to others, especially when talking about sex and reproduction with children.

> *Language has been a very important consideration. We don't like using words that could invoke imagery of events and relationships that never existed. Phrases like 'real parents, adoptee mother, test tube baby, donor daddy' are all emotive phrases with powerful imagery associated with them. We think that this imagery can confuse kids conceived with IVF and donor by giving them a false perception of their own existence. We choose words that make the kids feel that we are their parents, they are brothers and sisters and we are a family.* Female, Melbourne Focus Group

It is helpful to be aware that words like 'seeds' and 'eggs' can be confusing to some children. They usually think of eggs as being something used for baking and seeds as something that is planted in the ground, so it will no doubt be necessary to explain further the meanings of these terms to younger children.

The terms 'donor Dad', 'biological father', 'genetic father' and 'real father' also have the potential to be confusing or to convey meanings to a child that parents do not intend. This highlights the need to be very clear and unambiguous with the terms you choose to use. Some parents feel quite comfortable using the terms 'genetic father' or 'biological father', while others are equally certain that it is a word they would never use to describe the donor.

> *He is only a donor. Father is a caring person, the person who looks after the child and the donor has not done anything and never intended to.* Male, Sydney Focus Group

> *If you want donors to feel comfortable with openness, referring to them as 'father' is not going to make them feel comfortable. That confuses their role. It is not what they intended to be.* Female, Sydney Focus Group

> *He's no father. Using the word 'father' is just insulting the one who is really doing the work.* Male, Sydney Focus Group

> *We use the word 'donor'. We don't use the word 'father' at all. I'm very clear of that because 'father' as far as I'm concerned is a socially-constructed role and has nothing to do with genetics.* Olivia

> *We use the term 'the donor'. I can't see any other term that I could use for him at this stage. If people refer to him as the 'biological father', that's okay. I don't live in any false paradise that he doesn't exist. He's there and we are ever grateful that he is, or that he was. We can't ignore that he did a very important part of the procedure. But Nigel and Lauren don't talk about their 'biological father'; they just refer to him as 'the donor'.* Evelyn

> *We talk about 'social father' and 'biological father'. I think it's quite simple to explain to children, due to the fact that a lot of parents are divorced nowadays and you have the same situation. You have the biological father and if the child or children were very young*

when the couple divorced, you might also have the social father. One person might be both the social and biological father but they might also be different people. On the other hand, 'biological father' doesn't say the whole truth because it could also mean that you have had another man before we married. Sven

I choose the word 'man'. 'The doctor asked another man'. And I tried not to use the word 'father' because it would be too confusing for a four-year-old boy. If they are older they can understand the real difference but it would be better to say 'sperm donor'. Bettina

Genevieve used to say 'biological father' but now she calls him by name. She could never say the word 'biological' properly but she said 'father'. Geraldine and Kieron refer to the donor as 'the donor'. Leonie

I remember the first time that Grant used the words 'biological father'. Desmond was two and a half and he turned to Grant one day at dinner and said, 'Are you my real father?' Grant said, 'Yes, I am. Because you've got two – you've got me and you've got your biological father.' I remember being horrified. I said, 'No, no, no. You're going to confuse him. You can't use 'father'; use 'donor' and Grant said, 'No, society uses 'biological father'. That's what he is.' Next thing you know, he's using 'donor Dad'. We had big lively discussions about that. I finally capitulated because he was right. That's what society called it, whether we liked it or not. Romana

Another term that has been highlighted as possibly being contentious is 'special'. All children are of course special to their family but in the area of DI, my own view is that it is the family who is special, not the child. We also need to be very aware that many children, at certain times in their development, have a desire to be the same as everybody else, rather than to be seen as 'special' or 'different'.

I don't like to use the word 'special'. I like to say he's an ordinary kid and we are an ordinary family and these are our issues as a family. I

> *don't want him to feel special. He's just like any other child.* Female, Melbourne Focus Group

It is obvious that different people use different words when sharing information, choosing terminology that feels comfortable and appropriate to them. As with many topics, a unique family language usually emerges – one that parents initiate and therefore have a considerable impact on, but which often evolves when parents listen to the language their children use to make sense of their family and the relationships within it.

Using connections

Many of our parents talk about the aids that they had in relation to story telling, both physical items and natural opportunities. These include books that are now becoming available (some of which are extremely good), items on the radio or television, the pregnancies of, or adoptions by, friends and family members, or seeing the hospital or clinic where the conception occurred. Clearly the connections are going to differ according to the ages of the offspring but they can be very useful for facilitating conversation.

> *We had a book called, 'How Families are Made'. It had all these different children in it and they all had different stories. It was a really nice thing about how families are made.* Female, London Focus Group

> *I needed to touch on facts and managed to find this book that mentioned DI and there was another part on assisted conception. I read him a couple of bits and he read a couple of bits. I thought then that I would leave it at that and he would bring it up again if he needed to talk about it.* Female, London Focus Group

Another opportunity to raise the subject of DI is when parents are attempting to conceive a sibling for their child. One parent did however make an interesting observation about taking her older child to the insemination.

> *I felt a bit funny about it. I wondered if it was a bit too much. I wouldn't let Stuart watch me have sex with his Dad and I really thought that the children don't have to know everything.* Female, Melbourne Focus Group

Recording your family history

Some parents have a box or scrapbook that holds all kinds of memorabilia related to the conception and birth of their children, while others keep a record in the form of a story book, which children usually want to be told over and over again. Alternatively, as with Leonie and Warren, and Irene and Peter, some parents keep a note of particular comments and conversations with their children, while others have implied to me that they wish they had!

> *My recollection of it all is not that brilliant. You should tell other couples that they should keep diaries about all this, Ken, because you do forget!* Walter

One of the things that professional people in the field of counselling and social work often use is called a genogram. A genogram is a way of creating a pictorial map of the relationships of different people (similar to a family tree) – grandparents, down to mother and father, mother's and father's brothers and sisters, their children – and it seems to me that in the case of families who have used DI, such a genogram can be a very useful way of how everyone belongs to a much larger family. It allows for the fact that there is also the donor, who is present in terms of having made a contribution to the family but not present in the sense of being actively involved with it. (The donor's place in the family is discussed fully in Chapter Nine.)

The message of love

It is important to acknowledge that while families built with the assistance of DI are different, the difference is not a negative thing and it is far outweighed by the similarities shared with all other families. One of the most important of these is of course the love parents have for their children.

Adults build families when they have made the choice to share their lives with children, loving and caring for them. The underlying message of the parents' love is that the children were, and are, very wanted, and by growing up in such a loving environment, children feel secure and strong.

A nice way of thinking of the message of love is that it is two-way. As parents wish for and love that child, in a sense the child gives them a gift by making them a mother or a father and loving them as such.

> *It's much more about our infertility. It's not just the sort of narrow thing of an egg and a sperm. I say how I wanted a child and now we have a child and she is my daughter forever and how that is very important to me.* Female, London Focus Group

It is interesting to see, in many of the stories, how love also plays a part in the responses of the children when learning about their beginnings. Some made loving comments to their parents, while others wanted to buy a present for the donor, i.e. to offer a gift of love and gratitude to him. These are truly positive responses.

Conversely, when we look at the title of a professional paper written some years ago, *How to tell your child that he or she is not your biological child*,[7] I'm sure that most readers will agree that this kind of approach has a potentially negative and damaging impact. Although the paper contains a lot of helpful guidance for parents, the title focuses on what the family has missed out on, rather than reinforcing the positives of what they do have. If, instead, you accentuate that you are all part of the family and that every member of the family is loved and valued, you communicate the very strong message of love to your children.

In concluding this most crucial chapter, I trust that the experiences of the parents I have spoken with will be of immense help to you. Their recollections and reflections will undoubtedly provide you with practical advice and inspiration, while also helping you to build confidence in exploring your own approach of sharing with your children how love led to the creation of your family.

8 Talking to others about your family

When children 'pick up' from their parents that they are hearing important information, especially if it is about themselves, it is only natural that they will want to pass on their new knowledge to people who are special, trusted and important to them. Therefore, by sharing information with your children about your family's DI beginnings, it is almost certain that they will want to tell others. This can be disconcerting for parents, even if they have already been open with friends or family members, because parents don't have a lot of control over whom their children talk to, and how these people might respond.

> *If you tell your child the truth, you have to expect the next day that he talks to your neighbour or to other children at kindergarten or on the street to his friend, and you have to be prepared. You need to know how you would like to react.* Bettina

One of the things that can reduce anxiety over who their children talk to is for parents themselves to share information with appropriate people, especially once the children have received that knowledge. Parents then gain the opportunity to prepare others and seek their assistance in the way they respond to their children, particularly as it is likely to be a topic that many people will not have encountered before. This avoids the possibility of responses to the children such as, 'Oh that can't be true'; 'That's not how things happen'; or 'I've never heard of such a thing'.

Another benefit of ensuring all significant people in their children's world know about the use of DI is that parents avoid the need to try and place limitations on who their children talk to.

> *You can't tell it to your child and say, 'No, don't tell your grandparents'. And when the child is five years old, he says, 'Well, did you ever see my father?' or something like that.* Sven *If you tell your child, you have to tell everybody else.* Bettina

> *One week after I told him, he talked on the phone with his aunt and he told her the whole story. I couldn't believe he repeated it that way. I realised it is for him as if we had told him he had the kidney of another person or some kind of body part to help him, to help us.* Bettina *We asked her, 'Did you understand what he explained to you?' and she said, 'Yes, I think it was explained very well'.* Sven

Although parents relinquish a certain amount of control over who their children talk to, they can still discuss with them the appropriateness of talking to people outside of the immediate family – particularly other children.

> *We explained that it wasn't something that she couldn't talk about, except that she was learning about how babies were made at a lot younger age than most children and it's not something that you can go and talk to your friends about because their parents could get annoyed at you telling them how babies are born. Those parents want to tell them in their own time and stage – when they think it's right for them to be told.* Leonie

> *They've all asked, 'Can I talk to Eric or Adam or Carly?' And I say, 'Sure, we think it's a good idea to talk amongst yourselves but not necessarily to your friends because they may not quite understand it the way that you do'.* Ali

This is a good example of how the issue of "secrecy versus privacy" can arise. The notion of secrecy of course relates to withholding information, and implies that these matters are shameful and not to be talked about.

Privacy, however, is associated more with recognising this information is family-oriented and is only shared with those who are special or who need to know. In my experience of talking with many parents, the notion of privacy is one that is easily understood by children or offspring, and is fully accepted within the majority of families. The key to this is allowing children to have the opportunity of exploring with you what is appropriate to say and to whom, and also helping them to make decisions about setting their own boundaries in regard to information sharing, especially as they grow older.

> *As they have developed and wanted to know more, we have just said, 'Okay, but we don't go and tell everybody that because it's private stuff'. I think they've just got a sense of family trust; that it's within the family and we'll talk about it but it's not public knowledge in the school ground. We never actually said that they can't talk about it but they have decided there are safe environments of where they want to talk about it. They made that decision. We haven't had to do it.* Female, Melbourne Focus Group

Parents may question whether they should be preparing their children for possible negative reactions from others, or if it is better just to see if in fact something untoward is said and then be there to provide support. I remember only too clearly a situation in my own family, when one of our twin daughters came home from school and told her mother that some friends had said that she and her sister weren't adopted. When this was explored, we found that our daughter was looking for reassurance about her adoption because her friends believed adopted children were stolen out of prams!

To actually try to prepare a child for unexpected responses may well be setting up the situation in such a way that the child decides not to proceed – in other words, the fear of being misunderstood, teased or rejected may stop them from being open and honest. As with many other areas in life, children are going to learn from a great variety of experiences and some of that learning will be painful and some will be pleasurable. Overall, I feel that it is more appropriate to allow offspring to find their own way and to always be there for them when they come back to talk about their experiences.

Desmond didn't want us to tell his people at school. I respected that. His concern was that he would be teased because it's different and in the end, he was right. He did get teased a bit [after our story appeared in the paper]. What I didn't know about children before I had them is that they are very conservative. They hate difference. He wanted his 15 minutes of being in the newspaper but now he wanted to just go back to being an ordinary boy. [The teasing] went on for a few days and I said to him, 'Look, nothing's changed except that people know a little bit more about you. And that's a good thing.' Romana *He'd forgotten it in a few days time.* Grant

While parents cannot prepare themselves and their offspring for every contingency, it is certain that by sharing information with their children about their conception, the children will at some stage talk to others about it. Without a doubt, some of these people will be less tolerant of DI because it is not 'the norm', and others will be supportive and understanding.

This is, of course, also true of the people parents talk to – some will respond more positively than others. To gauge the type of reaction they could expect to receive, some parents have talked about 'testing the waters'. For instance, they may initiate discussions surrounding a news item relating to assisted human reproduction, IVF, surrogacy or DI. While the comments from others may not reflect their actual response to your own situation, they do give an indication of their understanding and attitudes concerning the general issues.

It is of course immensely helpful to recognise in advance the people who will be understanding and supportive of your choices. The likelihood is that you would first discover these people during your infertility journey and that you would share the subsequent journey of building your family with DI with these same key people. Although everyone differs as to when they feel the need to share information with others, as we saw in Chapter Two it is often when they are experiencing difficulties conceiving, or when treatment is being undertaken, that people begin talking with others, with the goal of seeking support.

We went to see an uncle to tell him about what we were going to do. He said he would support us whatever we did. Female, Melbourne Focus Group

When we were in treatment, we talked about it; we told people close to us what we were doing. There was a couple of people, friends and parents and family. Which is a good thing to do. Romana

I conceived on my first insemination so we weren't in treatment for a long time. Whereas, I have spoken to a number of people who have been in treatment for a very long time, and women in particular feel a great need to talk and gain support from other female friends and relatives, and are likely to tell at that point. Olivia

While the support most commonly sought from family and friends is of an emotional nature, it may also be needed on a more practical level.

There's the other side of things where people need to talk to their parents because they need the money and financial support to go through treatment. Walter

As well as receiving support, another benefit of talking with others is that their appreciation of the difficulties you have experienced means they can share with you at a deeper level the special joy of pregnancy and the subsequent birth of your longed-for child.

It doesn't just involve the relationship between Ali and I. It involves our whole family and it really brings out the players that are there to support us. We didn't have one family member or one friend who wasn't there for us or wouldn't give 150%. We were very fortunate to have a family that we could tell. Tom

All of my brothers and sisters, spread as far and wide as they are, they've all been okay. They all were very supportive around the time Bridget was pregnant. Andrea

Only the cousins and Laurie's sister and brother-in-law knew. They came that week [Nigel was born] and brought presents for him. They just accepted it and thought it was a good idea. There were never any negatives from them. Evelyn

Some couples decide that the best way for them to announce their decision to use DI is by taking unilateral action, in other words, telling others about it once the 'deed has been done'. It is sometimes easier for people, who do not want or need to share information during treatment, to do so once pregnancy is achieved.

> *I would suggest for people who have felt nervous about telling anybody else that you don't have to rush out and tell people straightaway. When you've actually got some news to tell people, that's the moment when you need to decide what you're going to say. There's not a great deal of point in saying anything beforehand. We gave [my parents] the bad news and the good news. The bad news was that this is going to be a DI baby and the good news was that Olivia is pregnant and we were going to get married. My parents had already been through my older brother's adoption of his child and were very, very positive because the main thing for them was that there was going to be a grandchild and the genetic stuff was entirely secondary.* Walter

> *We didn't discuss it with them in advance. In fact, we had done it already. We said, 'Well that's the situation, that's the solution, that's what we decided. If you want to have grandchildren, you have to accept it or leave it.' And everybody did accept it and were really happy and it has never become again a big point in discussions with the grandparents.* Sven

While this approach will suit some people, others may find that a lack of openness with those who are close to them leads to the added pressure of maintaining a secret.

> *While we were having treatment, I found it quite stressful being in a waiting room with people and never being able to talk to anybody. I couldn't contain this stuff. I needed to talk to somebody about it, so I picked the nurses. And there was the stress of having to go to work, having to get up early during the treatment, and that shouldn't be minimised. And we weren't telling people then and I wanted to be shouting at the rooftops.* Leonie

Some people may have been told about the difficulties in conceiving, and may have become aware of the clinic visits and the pressure and tension of waiting each month to see whether there might be a pregnancy, but they may not necessarily know about the decision to use DI. For a couple to then become pregnant, these people are likely to ask questions, or alternatively, if friends or relatives perceive this is a sensitive topic, they may avoid talking directly to the couple but perhaps discuss things amongst themselves.

For many parents, regardless of when they share information with others, there is an uncertainty about how people will react, but often the fear of a negative response is unfounded.

> *When we told everybody, it was* everybody. *I went around to every member of the family and told them how they were conceived. I wanted my kids to be able to go everywhere without any fear. I never took my children with me when I told them because if they did reject them, then I didn't want my kids to see that rejection. But they were not rejected. Everybody loves the kids for what they are. In some ways it worked out better because the kids already had a relationship with the family members, so it didn't matter. And they understood more about why we had been acting strange for the last few years.* Female, Melbourne Focus Group

Other parents may not be as fortunate in having such positive and supportive reactions. It is not uncommon for some family members or friends to have difficulty in adjusting to the news of how you achieved your family building – perhaps in much the same way you might have had to make adjustments in your own thinking when considering using DI.

> *When we went to get the DI, David's mother was quite good, looking after the other two children. But when he was born, she wouldn't hold him.* Female, Melbourne Focus Group

> *My parents were a little bit uneasy. My mother couldn't quite integrate it and for years she would forget that DI conceived the boys. Now she is used to the idea.* Susan

I told my Aunt, who was 90 at the time. She just couldn't work it out. I know she thinks of him as not being ours. Female, Melbourne Focus Group

Our parents were a little bit astonished but they said, 'Okay, if you want to do it this way, do it'. Bettina

As you would expect, it can take time for some people to get used to the idea of family building with the use of DI. In the same way parents have had to face the issues, other people may have uncertainties about what this means to the family tree, or they may feel a sense of loss of the genetic child that might have otherwise been. Their feelings may be ongoing or only arise at certain times.

My father and his wife acknowledge Ellie as Number 13 on the grandchildren list and treat her as they treat every other one of their grandchildren. The only difference that has started to emerge is the family trait business. My father has said once, maybe twice, 'Oh, she'd be different if she was a Prout'. That stung a bit for me. She is a Prout. And he said, 'Well you know what I mean'. And actually what he means is gene pools, biology, that's what he's talking about. Andrea

It may be helpful to remind grandparents that even when their grandchildren are genetically related to them, they can exhibit far more characteristics of the 'other side' of the family and almost appear unrelated to themselves.

When people don't fully understand the issues of DI or know how to deal with them, they can sometimes make inappropriate comments or perhaps avoid commenting at all.

Someone said once about the real parents and I had to say, 'Well we are the real parents'. Language and trying to educate people is important. You need to be clear about using the word 'donor'. Female, Melbourne Focus Group

> *I told my Mum and it has never been mentioned again. They know about it and they are happy to know but they don't have to mention it.* Female, London Focus Group

A lack of full, open communication with friends or family may lead to instances when parents feel it is necessary to broach the subject and help those close to them come to a better understanding.

> *Terry's father knows about his infertility but didn't want to know the background of Hamish's conception. I said, 'Well I am going to tell you and I want you to listen'. We wanted him to understand what difficult things we had gone through to have that child.* Female, Melbourne Focus Group

The ability to talk openly with others stems from parents having a high level of confidence about their choices surrounding their family building. Many parents feel that even if other people have difficulty with these choices, it is important to still act on their own confidence, and leave others to make adjustments to their feelings of acceptance in their own time.

> *I think that the most important thing is that the couple have made a clear decision and even if someone – their parents – do not agree, they should do what they think is right.* Sven

> *People who aren't okay about it, it's their problem and I wasn't willing to compromise. If they didn't want to have anything to do with us as a family, then that was their choice, but this never happened.* Greg

There is also the notion of 'normalising' DI and your family, which is the process of coming to understand and be less fearful or anxious of events which have previously been perceived as being different. By talking with your child and with other people, you are normalising your family building in your own mind, while also helping them to be able to normalise it as well.

In addition, openness gives you the opportunity to educate others, which ultimately helps to encourage social acceptance and eliminate prejudices and misinformation. The goal is to have recognition within the community that while DI is different, the difference does not mean it is better or worse. It is just different.

> *Most people are positive, most people are curious and want to ask questions and I educate them. I remind the fertile world that while they may be fertile, they need to know about infertility because any of their children could be infertile and they need to know how to support their children or their children's partners. And you may be fertile today but you could be infertile tomorrow because of a virus or cancer of the testes or whatever.* Leonie

> *Within seconds, our neighbours [aged 78 and 71] said, 'Well how did she do it (get pregnant)?' And we just told them in very simple terms because they don't need the nitty-gritty. And they said, 'That's wonderful'. And of course everybody got to hear – not that they all wanted to know how we did it. In fact, it wasn't until Ellie was born, that people would say, 'So how did you do it then?' And that was fine.* Andrea

People will react in any number of different ways to the information you share with them, and this is usually a reflection of their level of understanding. Even when there have previously been uncertainties, anxieties or a lack of complete understanding by others, it is still possible for children to break through these barriers and be accepted.

> *When the child has arrived, everything is changed. Even if they did not want it this way, where there is a baby, everybody is happy and perhaps they forget the problems they had.* Bettina

As with talking to your children, talking with other people means the extent to which information is then passed on moves beyond the control of the parents. Other people will naturally make their own decisions about what to do with the information you have given them, but parents may also want to discuss what their expectations are, and what they feel is appropriate, with regard to remove the sharing of your information.

> *We've said it's up to our brothers and sisters to tell their offspring about these things. It's not our responsibility to jump in. If our niece asks any questions and she needs an explanation, we will be more than happy to talk to her about it at that time.* Tom

Another issue some parents will face is what to do if their children don't yet know about their conception, but other people do. By choosing to wait until children are older before sharing information with them, you may be creating difficulties as to how the people who do know about your family building manage that information in the meantime. If we look at it from a parental point of view, there is a need to share information with others in order to gain support. At the same time, however, it would clearly not be helpful if these people then passed on the information to a child who did not yet know. It is important that children receive information as significant as their DI conception from the most loved people in their lives – their parents. It is wise therefore, if you are sharing information with others before sharing it with your children, that you tell these people of your intention to unfold the story with your children as they grow and develop. You may also like to add that rather than having other people raising the subject with your children, your hope and expectation is that they will respond appropriately when your children raise the subject themselves.

How and when parents share information with others will differ as to whether the person you are speaking with is part of your 'inner' network or part of your 'outer' network. For some people, the centre of the inner network is their family; for others it could be friends; or as in most cases, it will be a combination of both. In each instance, the inner network is characterised by people whose love and support are strong, significant factors in the relationship and, because of this, there is a hope and expectation that they will offer understanding, acceptance and endorsement of your decision to build your family with the help of DI. Some people will offer this spontaneously but there may be others who need your guidance as to what you need from them, and how best they can support you and your family.

> *Although everyone knows, including family, no-one ever talks to my children about it. They say things to me. I have said to my*

> *Mum, 'Why don't you say something to them about it. Bring it up with them.' I want my children to be able to talk to anyone about it.* Female, Melbourne Focus Group

Finding themselves in an educative role can place an added burden on parents, but it is important to remember that DI is potentially a very new topic for many people and they may have a great need for more information and clarification, as well as a chance to discuss any uncertainties they may have. As a result of discussions, they may then be in a much stronger position to provide support and understanding.

> *I felt like I owed a very good friend of mine an explanation. I told her the whole story and she said, 'I can't believe this! I've watched how you are with your children and often thought there's a quality there but I could never put my finger on why I would feel you mothered differently.' And I said, 'Well, these children are my gifts.' And she said, 'Now I understand. I'm honoured that you could tell me.' It was a very positive reaction. She made me feel we had done something remarkable. Because it's been such a long time since we told anybody, I felt really proud. I would never have kept it from her from the point of view of it being a secret; it's just the privacy issue.* Ali

If there is a belief that love is what keeps friends and families together, then it is hoped that these people will focus on what is best for you. However, not all parents will feel safe sharing with their entire inner network, especially with people they suspect will have strong moral views regarding the rightness or wrongness of DI.

> *I never told any of my family. My sisters are moralists. I never shared it with them, which caught up with us in the end when they found out from the town gossip. One brother-in-law was disappointed because I didn't tell him myself. My other sister and her husband were so angry and didn't talk to me. That is my regret, that I did not tell my family.* Evelyn

I was asked several years ago to write a commentary on a papal encyclical (a statement from the Church of Rome), which described what was acceptable and what was not acceptable concerning reproductive technologies. In summary, the statement took a condemnatory approach to the new developments, saying they were contrary to the Church's position. In my commentary, I explained that the Roman Catholic Church had no alternative but to adopt such a position, given its history and its longstanding views. I did however conclude the article by saying that it seemed strange to me that a Church that believed children were a gift from God should place limits on the way in which God would give his gifts.

Potentially, people with very strong moral or religious viewpoints may find it difficult to accept DI as a legitimate way of building a family. On the other hand, it may not be wise to automatically assume that just because people do have these beliefs, they will not accept the use of DI.

> *I told my Aunt Opal who was very conservative and very religious and she had no problem with it at all. She said, 'I'm sure it's going to be the most loved baby,' and I realised at that point that I would tell people because you would be making some pretty heavy assumptions about people rejecting you and not being supportive. I think the fear thing prevents people from even risking telling people, when maybe it would really be okay.* Greg

An interesting aspect of talking with other people, especially those in the inner network, is the consideration of the needs of those with whom the information is being shared. We have already covered some of the reasons why parents share information but the responses they receive very often depend on the needs of those who are listening. Comments and questions from other people can be related to their need for clarity, for understanding, or perhaps for expressing their moral viewpoint. Many people – especially at first – are likely to be more focused on their own needs, working out what this information means to them and how it affects their lives, before being able to look at understanding your needs and how they can best support you.

An example of how people relate information to their own situation occurred in an interview I once had with a New Zealand gynaecologist as part of a study. In our discussion about his views of donors, he became very thoughtful when he discovered the Christchurch programme at the time used medical students as donors. He finally commented, 'I suppose I could be a grandfather because my son is a medical student in Christchurch'. He had in fact been practising DI for some years but it was as if it had suddenly taken on an entirely new meaning – a personal meaning – when he thought of the implications as a father of a potential donor.

We turn now to support groups. While support group members are not necessarily part of the natural inner network in terms of love and commitment, they are certainly part of the inner network in terms of the openness they encourage and the support they provide. So many couples talk about the value they have received in being able to share with others at an intimate and personal level, knowing there will not be naïve or inappropriate comments or questions. The support is significant because group members have all been through, or are going through, similar experiences and therefore can have a deeper level of understanding than perhaps friends and family members who haven't had to face these issues personally.

> *We [parents] talk about things but grandparents don't have any training about how to react. We go to groups and talk about it but they don't.* Female, Melbourne Focus Group

This comment suggests that grandparents could benefit from support groups too – gaining a greater understanding of the issues, feeling more comfortable in discussing them and also learning how they can best support the parents.

Parents who are able to attend meetings on a regular basis will find support groups especially beneficial, but even if they can't attend meetings, parents will also gain understanding and support from being able to read about other people's experiences through the consumer group newsletters. Even more so, parents who for various reasons are not open with their family and friends, have often told me how support groups fulfil their need to talk and provide their only avenue of support.

A few years ago, when I was facilitating general infertility support group programmes for the Christchurch Infertility Society, it was interesting to see how an obvious pattern emerged as couples supported each other in working through the issues of infertility. There were four sessions in the programme and the groups were normally limited to ten people. I always operated with a female co-leader, thus replicating, as it were, another couple in the group. This was beneficial for the male and female participants, in that they often said that both perspectives were in evidence.

During the first session, the discussion invariably revolved around each individual's personal experience of infertility. Both males and females talked about how it was for them, including the pain and distress. The second session, without any guidance from the leaders, looked more at the relationship between the partners, while in the third session, couples focused on how to talk with relatives and friends, and their feelings of being different from others. The focus in the fourth session was invariably on the professionals – their adequacies and inadequacies, the jubilations and frustrations they caused, and how people could get the best out of them.

What intrigued me about these group programmes was that most of the people who came to them ended up moving into leadership roles, e.g. chair, deputy chair, treasurer, secretary, or a committee member of the society. It was as if having had their needs met within the group, they were able to start to look beyond their own circumstances and towards the needs of other people – they felt confident about contributing to and for others.

I feel a parallel process operates when parenting children conceived by DI. Parents need to first meet their own needs and deal with the issues regarding infertility and family building via DI, and then they are better able to move into a position of supporting their children, seeking to meet their children's needs, and beyond that to thinking of those in the networks and to the wider communities of which they are a part.

We now turn to the outer networks, beginning with school teachers, who often talk about how parents can have no secrets as their children come to school and talk openly about all sorts of issues!

> *There is a phrase in German, 'Kindermund'.* Sven. *Yes, the children always say the truth.* Bettina

Knowing how frank some children can be, many parents find it prudent to prepare teachers, with the intent of avoiding any unexpected or unhelpful reactions towards their children. This can be particularly important with the growing emphasis on exploring genetics and genealogy at school, with children often being expected to complete family trees.

> *We told each class teacher, because if it actually came up, the teacher should not appear shocked and disbelieving.* Female, London Focus Group

Other parents – perhaps when their children are older or more private about their own information – find it appropriate to talk to teachers on a 'need to know' basis.

> *I had cause to tell a teacher when he was set an exercise on reproduction and assisted reproduction methods and he just couldn't write it. He was just completely blocked and was getting a lot of flak from the teacher. I rang her up and talked to her about it and she was extremely pleased to know.* Female, London Focus Group

How teachers handle sensitive matters in the classroom can be extremely important in supporting your child's feelings about DI, but there is no way of knowing how teachers are likely to react unless you have taken the time to discuss it with them. While this could be seen as a protective measure, it can also be seen as proactively educating teachers, so their greater awareness can in turn help towards the understanding of others, including the other children in their class.

Talking to your child's teacher should not to be seen as turning DI into a large issue; it is similar, in a sense, to telling a teacher about a child's health condition or family situation. It is a detail about the child's background that may have an impact on how the teacher deals with, or responds to, issues that emerge in the classroom.

> *When our daughter was nine, she did mention it. The teacher helped her explain to the class and they then carried on with the lesson. Our daughter continues to talk about her DI origins in school. Our*

> *son doesn't, although he did say recently (aged 17) that he had told some close friends.* Letter from Olivia to would-be DI Mums

Another significant person in your outer network will be the family doctor. Most family doctors are likely to know of the DI conception because they are often the first port of call when people are experiencing difficulties conceiving, and they are also the ones who usually refer couples for treatment. If, however, the family doctor has not been involved and is not part of the information network, there may well be questions asked at some stage about your child's genetic history. While some parents may feel perfectly comfortable about discussing this, other parents may find it an awkward situation to deal with, particularly if their child is with them when such questions are asked. It is therefore advisable to ensure your family doctor, or indeed any doctor who sees your child, is familiar with your family situation.

> *We were asked two days after Peter was born, 'Are there any known hereditary problems in your family?' We told the story and said, 'We don't know. I am not the biological father of this child.' And the young doctor was very upset and embarrassed. He said, 'I didn't want to know that.* Sven

> *But we were relieved that we could talk about it this easily because it was important. It's more embarrassing for the other people, I think. And if you try to speak very confidently, then it's not a problem. But you have to try. The first time it's embarrassing but the second time you say it, it is not so embarrassing anymore.* Bettina

When it comes to acquaintances, parents seem to find it more appropriate to decide on whether or not to share information at the time of the conversation, rather than coming to any pre-arranged decisions. This could depend on many different factors, including the nature of the relationship, the rapport with the acquaintance, how you perceive they will respond and whether or not it is necessary for them to have the information at this particular time. However, even though the appropriateness of sharing information with different people will sometimes require an impromptu decision, it is still a good idea for parents to have some discussion as to how to manage such situations, before they occur.

> *When the boys were younger, people would make certain comments, even if they weren't really close to us. If they were people who I cared about and was in an authentic encounter with, sometimes we would bring it up at that point but it wasn't like I had to wave a flag and say my kids were conceived using DI.* Susan

> *She said, 'Your kids don't look anything like you, what does your husband look like?' It was one of those situations where I was wondering, 'Will I or won't I talk about it?' So I did. I said, 'Actually, I have donor kids.' She was a bit taken back because she didn't ask me much. She just didn't quite know what it all meant, she was trying to piece it all together.* Female, Sydney Focus Group

> *If it comes up, it comes up. There are still times now when it will come up and I will tell and get quite a compassionate response. But if I thought that it would threaten that relationship, I would probably back off and not tell them.* Male, Sydney Focus Group

While children are young, it is of course the parents who make decisions about the sharing of family history details. Eventually, however, decisions about talking with others will naturally progress from parents to their offspring. It is often said that the offspring become the 'owners' of that information, with the right to decide with whom they wish to share it.

> *The older they get, and not just at a fixed age point but in their own maturity, the more you feel they can cope with the downs. You can leave them to make their own decisions and do their own telling, but for quite a while you are the parent and you do it for them.* Female, London Focus Group

> *It's her information, she owns it and it's up to her how she shares it.* Bridget

> *As Desmond got older, I became more conscious that it was his right to tell his friends if he wanted to. I became more careful of not telling the parents of his school friends.* Grant

These comments suggest parents need to have sensitivity towards their growing child's needs and an awareness of their ability to take control of information sharing.

> *The decision of really going public also was tied up with the fact that Bryony at 'Show and Tell' at school told everybody that she was special because she was born from donor insemination. And that was the first time it came out publicly and the teacher came up to me that night and said, 'I've had some interesting news today'. And she told me. I was so glad that I had dealt with those issues of not keeping it a secret because if that had happened and I was still trying to keep it a secret, it would have been devastating. It was Bryony being so open about it that made us really think that if she's okay to stand up and tell everybody, then that's a good thing.* Female, Melbourne Focus Group

> *Someone said to Hamish, his friend's mother, 'You look so much like your Mum; it's unbelievable how much you look like her,' but didn't know Hamish was conceived through donor sperm. And Hamish was nudging me in the arm, saying, 'Can I tell, can I tell?' I said, 'It's up to you' and he went to tell and got cold feet and said, 'Can you help me?' So we started to talk. The friend's mother said it was fantastic and said how great his Dad is. 'I know your Dad and he's the best Dad you could have wished for.' And Hamish said, 'Yeah, and that's why I look so much like my Mum'.* Female, Melbourne Focus Group

The positive response in the above comment was particularly affirming and valuable to both the mother and son. It also reflects the ultimate goal in this whole area, which is for parents to know that their offspring are comfortable and confident enough about their family history to be able share this information with others, as appropriate.

I'm just really happy that she can talk to other people about it. She doesn't feel that she has to keep it a secret – that she's ashamed of it – and that's really good. Leonie

Having looked at the notion of offspring 'owning' their own information and parents being sensitive to the needs of their children regarding the sharing of that information, it follows that offspring also need to respect the needs of their siblings in regard to information sharing.

We will be saying to them, 'You can talk about your own things but be very careful about talking about your brother and sister because that is their knowledge and that is for them to talk about'. Male, Melbourne Focus Group

One of the opportunities emerging from greater information sharing is that, in the same way that parents talk to other parents of children conceived by DI, their offspring are also beginning to talk with each other. To help facilitate this, the Donor Conception Support Group in Australia and some regional support groups in New Zealand hold events such as picnics, where parents and their children can get together socially. Reactions to these can of course be varied. Some parents see this as beneficial for their children and their family as these events give their children the opportunity to meet, and be able to relate to, other children who were conceived in the same way as they were. Other parents express concern that the opposite might be true.

Since we became involved with the group, our son has said to me that he has some sense of belonging with these children. Female, Sydney Focus Group

It's really valuable to say you are like someone else or that you have been created in the same sort of way. They have got a reference outside themselves. It's something to know that 'I'm not a freak, I'm not the only one, I'm normal too'. Male, Sydney Focus Group

The children also have other people that they can talk to now, outside of the family, and trust them. Female, Sydney Focus Group

> *We haven't brought them to any of the picnics organised with other donor families because I don't want them to feel, 'Why are we going down to this picnic with all these kids we've never met before?' I think that would make them feel there was something different about them.* Ali

Many adult offspring who know of their beginnings have also linked up via support groups and Internet groups, so support is available not just at the parental level but also for offspring of all ages.

Looking into the future, it is highly probable that the need will arise for parents and offspring to share information with a further set of people – the offspring's partner and any children who result from that partnership. Information regarding your family building will be significant for them, too.

> *I am expecting that when he gets older and starts becoming serious with a girl he wants to marry, we would explain it to the girlfriend. I am sure we will be asked all these similar questions again. She will probably have curiosity about the family tree. I think it's necessary to keep it open and be able to answer as many questions as you can.* Male, Sydney Focus Group

This chapter has, in effect, focused on the family and its relationships with others. We have moved from consideration of parents and children as individuals to seeing the unit of the family with all members being involved in deciding what information they will share with others. Such a move is based on the confidence and security of the parents.

9 The semen provider and your family

My sense of gratitude to the donors is profound. I don't think about the donors much, but when I do, I am moved to tears because I wouldn't have these children if it weren't for the gift that the donors gave me. To never acknowledge that seems, to me, so ungrateful at some level. Susan

We only have families built with the assistance of DI because there are men prepared to provide their semen. One of these men (or possibly two or more) has undoubtedly played a major contributing part towards your own family, but how do you view this man? What feelings do you have towards him? What might be the nature of your relationship, if any, with him? Most importantly, how will your children/offspring view him? These are all challenging questions to consider, so challenging in fact, that some parents might prefer not to consider them.

It's really a strange feeling. We've been able to have three beautiful children, from strangers we don't know. Our children are the most precious assets in our marriage and yet we don't know anything about the people who helped us have them. Leonie

Our boy made a family tree this year and wasn't really sure what to do about his biological father. We talked to him and decided that as we don't have very much information, we should choose the father

that we know. He accepted that readily, but at nine, he had already started thinking. Female, Melbourne Focus Group

I like to reiterate that we're the family. The donor is there but we are the family. Romana

Evelyn also sees a humorous side surrounding the existence of a donor.

He's always the scapegoat. We always say the bad points are from the donor. They never come from the mother! Evelyn

Being a semen donor is never going to be the most popular activity for men and in fact, only a small percentage of men do donate sperm. The minimal number of donors has been attributed to many factors, the most common being that men do not want to be identified to any offspring in the future.

The ignorance is out in the community about the people who want to have rights to contact the donor. The first thing they say is, 'They'll want his property'. And I say, 'It's the last thing on their mind. It's the contact they want, not what he's got in material possessions.' But that's the ignorance of people. Evelyn

Many people initially see things from the donor's perspective but this book, with its theme of sharing information, is of course a challenge to anonymity, based on the fact that the needs and well-being of offspring and families have a greater priority than the needs of semen providers and doctors.

In the era of secrecy and non-disclosure, it was possible to place the semen provider in a 'locked closet', which rarely had to be acknowledged, let alone opened. In the emerging culture of information sharing and openness, the closet has become a 'room', the door of which can be opened – at least in some countries – and this has many implications for both your family and the donor's family. An increasing number of offspring want access to the 'room', although of course, others do not want or need this.

There could be two camps that DI offspring could go into. They could

> *say, 'I want to know who this donor is because I don't feel I have all the information about myself until I find out', or they could say, 'I don't want to know about this because I am perfectly happy with the family I have got and I don't want to be destabilised by seeking information about some other person.* Male, London Focus Group

This comment raises a number of issues. The fact that there are 'two camps' – one for those who want information with possible contact, and one for those who don't – is accurate.

> *Our second child is wanting to find out information and our first child doesn't want to know – it's just not important, she has her life, she's happy, she's in a happy family and she is whole.* Female, Melbourne Focus Group

Those who do seek information frequently mention that their major reason is to assist them with their genetic history-gathering. In other words, like many adopted people, the information helps them complete their identity picture and answer the question, 'Who am I?' Interest in the donor, and sometimes the desire to meet him, is particularly likely to occur during adolescence, when the whole process of identity formation is very important.

> *When they are 16 and have strange ideas, they think everybody in another family is better. They may think it is like that with the biological father but they will overcome these feelings and they will realise he is not better. I don't think they will leave home and say, 'I want to live with my real father'.* Bettina

If one reason for offspring not seeking information is, as suggested earlier, 'because I am perfectly happy with the family I have got', it could be seen as implying that those who do seek information are not perfectly happy with their families. This has certainly not been the experience though of the parents I have spoken with, whose offspring have sought or are seeking information. In fact, these parents encourage and support their offspring to do so.

An outstanding video has recently been produced by the Donor

Conception Network in the United Kingdom, entitled *A Different Story*. It is a beautiful and moving record of seven offspring, ranging in age from seven to 21, who talk of their views and experiences surrounding their DI conception, including information concerning their donor. The young people in the video all talk of their happy and healthy families but also have a natural curiosity about the half of their genetic background that is unknown and inaccessible to them. Being interested in having information about their donor is not an indication that they are dissatisfied with their family and are searching for another one. In fact, I have never yet met a person conceived as a result of DI who has talked about looking for a father, or a replacement father. On the contrary, donor offspring are always quite certain of who their parents are.

When thinking about the semen provider and accessing information about him, there are two different approaches, or models, that can operate. I have developed the following two diagrammatic models to convey these different approaches.

In the closed model, the semen provider occupies a position as an outsider, separate from the family. He might almost be seen by some as

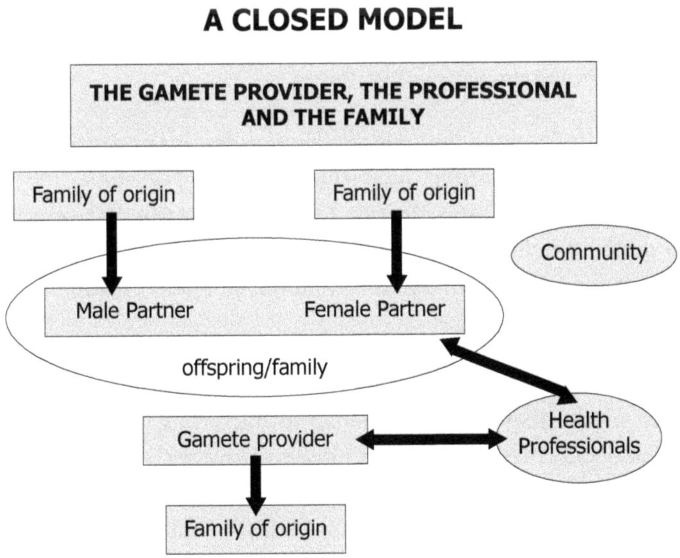

being non-existent. Access to him or information about him is managed by the professionals, many of whom ensure the room is locked and that they hold the only key. This closed model, with the semen provider (and his own family) firmly distanced from the recipient family, is something that many people feel comfortable with.

> *There is one person who is not a member of the family and that is the donor. I don't think he would ever be part of our family, even if we met him or knew who he was.* Male, London Focus Group

In other families, there is anguish for the parents, who find themselves unable to meet their offspring's desire for information regarding their semen provider. These parents want their children to be able to have access to that information, should they desire it.

> *If I was doing it again I would be far more particular with the donor and the information they would be willing to provide to us, maybe not identifying information, but as much as we feel that we need to satisfy the child's needs. We would go into it much more thoroughly.* Female, Sydney Focus Group

> *If we had the possibility, I would choose a donor programme that wasn't absolutely anonymous.* Susan

> *Our son is trying to find out information but is not getting much. He's always known from the start that we would do our best to find out about the donor for him but it might not happen. We were open and honest right from the start. The donor is only one small part of our strong family unit.* Female, Melbourne Focus Group

In the open model, it is acknowledged that the semen provider does indeed exist and has contributed significantly to the formation of the family. The open model also allows for the family, including the offspring as they mature, to decide on the nature of linkages, if any, with the semen provider. The family could decide that it is not necessary to make any connection, or alternatively, they may choose to obtain non-identifying information e.g. interests, family, vocation, medical history etc.; they may desire the

AN OPEN MODEL

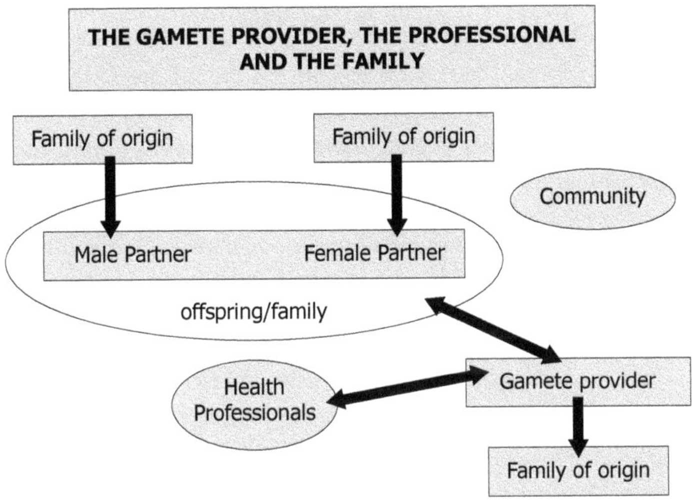

opportunity for written communication via a third party; or they could request access to identifying information which may lead to meeting the donor.

In this open model, the decision-making rests with those who are most involved and whom the outcomes will ultimately affect, rather than others making decisions on their behalf. Recognising the rights and needs of offspring and their families to make their own decisions, a growing number of governments around the world are moving towards the open system. The opportunity of having a choice about accessing information is something many parents strongly support – usually seeing it as more of a right for their children than themselves.

> *To me, the need to know about the donor is not really important at all. I don't have any great desire to know anything about the donor but what I do want is for the children to be able to get access to that information if they want it. If the opportunity arose to have a meeting, I suppose I would welcome that but it's not a priority in my life for my own personal benefit. It is a priority for my children*

> *to know about it.* Warren

> *The offspring should have access to information when they can understand what they will be told and understand why they're doing it, why they're seeking this information. I don't know that I have a right to Lauren's information. I think the number one are the offspring, maybe grandchildren are the next because they're affected too.* Evelyn

> *These children are living, breathing, unique, special individuals and I want them to have the right and the opportunity to know their full history.* Leonie

> *I think medical information is interesting, in case you need it. I don't want to have it, but I want it stored in a certain place where I can say, 'You can get the required information there'. As a last resort, maybe they also know where this man is.* Sven

> *We have non-identifying information. It's about eye colour, hair colour, height, professional background and interests. It was asked for, it wasn't automatic. At the time I didn't necessarily want more information but I think I might now, because of Ellie and her awareness, and her awareness as she gets older and the questions that she will ask. I think what is quite apparent is the lack of information.* Bridget

In most countries, information about semen providers is very limited or not available at all. Clinic staff members make the decisions about 'matching' donors and couples, and all information is controlled by the professionals, as in the closed model.

With the new and emerging culture of information sharing, however, some clinics are doing things differently. In New Zealand, for example, the practice in fertility clinics is for semen providers to complete extensive information sheets about themselves, which include details concerning:

- physical characteristics – eyes, hair, complexion, height, weight

- education – level attained, favourite subjects
- occupation and interests – current and past jobs, future plans, sporting and music activities
- health – allergies, vision, smoking and drinking habits
- personal comments – reasons for becoming a donor, partner's comments, thoughts on future contact
- family health history – parents and grandparents physical characteristics and age/cause of death

Those seeking to use DI are then offered full written profiles of several semen providers and are able to choose which semen provider they would like to use. The information they see is non-identifying, although semen providers will have already agreed to identity release to future offspring should they want this, once they are over the age of 18. The legislation soon to be enacted in New Zealand will formalise the right of offspring conceived after a certain date in the future to access information, and will also ensure a standard and secure national method of keeping this information on record.

Would-be parents report varying reactions about choosing a semen provider from the profiles. Most are enthusiastic about being able to make the decision themselves, rather than having it made for them, but some are apprehensive about accepting responsibility for the decision. One consequence of operating within this open model is that those seeking to use DI are confronted with a more concrete picture of the person who is providing the semen – in other words, the more they know about him, the more real his existence becomes. Many report that this is helpful in that it reinforces the reality of DI for them and helps them avoid the 'pretend notion' e.g. this is not important.

Anecdotal evidence suggests that would-be parents choose a semen provider for various reasons. One couple said, "We liked the humour in the completed profile", while another made reference to the genuineness and warmth that was evident in what the semen provider had written.

I suspect that few readers of this book will be able to have the opportunity of choosing a semen provider. However, this option was not available in New Zealand 20 years ago either, so policies and practices do change, and often quite quickly. It takes people, either on their own or in collaboration with others (e.g. through consumer organisations), to ask and advocate for change for the things they believe to be important.

Of course, the availability of the patient decision-making option is also determined by whether there are enough semen providers available for a choice to be made. There is no doubt that every country and every clinic would like to have more semen providers, particularly in situations where those seeking DI have to wait for long periods of time because of a shortage of men coming forward.

In the vast majority of cases worldwide, the semen provider is not known to the parents and will also never be known to the offspring. He has been described as the "silent partner" by the Donor Conception Network,[1] while I have talked about the notion of "the stranger in our midst". Both of these phrases highlight the contradictory nature of the connection with semen providers – there is distance as described by the words "silent" and "stranger", yet there is closeness in terms of "partner" and "in our midst". This unusual combination can be very confusing for families.

Feelings of closeness can be a reflection of the loving relationship parents have with their children, as well as the fact that the semen provider has a genetic connection present within their family. Having been unable to fulfil their strong desire to have a child without assistance, parents will naturally be grateful to the man who enabled them to reach this goal in an alternative way. Many parents describe the opportunity to use DI as a 'gift', but it also needs to be recognised that in acknowledging their appreciation, it is very difficult for parents to separate the gift of semen from the man who provided that gift.

> *Anytime I've ever said anything about the donor, I have always said, 'You know, we are so lucky that there are people like that who would do this so that people like us can have children. We are so lucky that there are donors who are willing to do this'.* Ali

> *I can't wait for the day when I meet the donors. I want to say, 'Thank you' and shake their hand. They are a living breathing human being with faults and positive traits, just like me. They're not a figment of my imagination. These people are important in our lives. They*

> *may not think they are but we wouldn't have our children without these three men.* Leonie

Parents of children conceived by DI often tell me that in valuing the semen provider's contribution, they also want their children to understand their gratitude. In many of the *Stories of Sharing* in Chapter Seven, the imagery conveyed is of the semen provider as a caring person, who assisted and helped the family. It is an image that children and older offspring respond to very positively. For example, Leonie and Warren, who conveyed their appreciation to their daughter, said how she wanted to thank the "kind man" who had donated sperm.

> *She thought for a moment and then she said, 'We should buy that man a present!* Leonie

As offspring grow and develop, they also come to understand that if it had not been for the semen provider, then they would not be in existence. One adult offspring whose story appeared in the British Medical Journal said:

> To the donors out there, I would like to say thank you. I owe my life to one of you. I wish I could know more about you. I wish you could be proud of my achievements and me. You gave me the opportunity of life and I have tried to live it to the full in return. [2]

Not all families have such positive feelings towards their semen provider, however. Many parents I have worked with perceive the semen provider to be a potential threat. They are very appreciative of what he has given but also fear that he may interfere in their family's life. They imagine that being faced with his actual existence could be disruptive or painful, even while acknowledging that information about him is important to their children.

> *I think it is easy to live without any real conceptualisation of the donor. And I think it is slightly disturbing to think of the donor, to envisage a real man, who might play a real part.* Walter

As with feelings of appreciation, if parents feel confused, uncertain and threatened by the semen provider's existence, they are likely to convey and transfer these feelings to their children. For this reason, it is beneficial for the well-being and security of their children for parents to have fully considered and come to terms with the issues surrounding the semen provider and his contribution to their family.

At a 1995 forum in Melbourne, Australia, Karen talked about some of the uncertainties and anxieties would-be parents have about donors.

> Sometimes you think of the silliest questions, but you do think them. Do they accept ugly donors? I've never met a donor. Why do they donate? Will they be looking for the offspring? The donor is an unknown factor.[3]

Bettina echoes the desire and need for parents to understand more about why men become semen providers.

> *I think it's important that everybody who wants to can have the information on how the donors are chosen. Who is this person? Why is he doing this? More information, so people are sure it's not somebody from around the corner who wants to earn money. It is important that the doctors can tell people about the donor.* Bettina

In the early days of my involvement in the field of DI, 28 years ago, I was frequently asked to give talks to members of the public: service clubs, women's organisations, new parents' groups etc. The most frequently asked questions at all those meetings related to information about semen providers. Like many recipient couples, those who attended my talks seemed intrigued by what might motivate men to donate semen for infertile couples.

Traditionally, it has been very difficult for researchers to be able to talk with semen providers about their feelings towards their donation. Because of the closed model which has kept semen providers 'locked away in the closet', the people who have held the key have been reluctant to open the door and provide access for researchers. Fortunately this is changing and as a result, I have been able to carry out studies of semen providers in New Zealand, Australia, the United Kingdom and Sweden. My findings, along with those from studies carried out by other researchers, have now given us some information about men who provide the gift of a family and the gift of life.

The first and most significant feature to emerge from the studies is that there is not a typical type of man who provides sperm. It is impossible to say that all semen providers fit a certain profile, or that they provide semen for a certain reason, or have certain beliefs. In my attempts to understand why there is such a wide variety of differences among the views of semen providers (particularly regarding openness and sharing information), I have concluded that the major influences come from the attitudes, policies and practices of the staff members who recruit them. In other words, the views of semen providers are a reflection of the clinic's approach – whether they operate within an open or a closed model approach.

This is notable when comparing studies that have been carried out in different countries. In New Zealand, Australia and Sweden, there is a general culture amongst clinics that acknowledges and encourages openness, therefore, semen providers are recruited with the understanding that openness is a component of what they are doing. On the other hand, studies carried out in the United Kingdom, which has generally not had such an open approach, show that most semen providers are opposed to identity release and do not wish to provide information for offspring, or to have contact with them in the future.

Two other factors that play a part in the attitude of a semen provider are his age and his family status (i.e. whether he is single or married, and whether or not he has children). Generally, those who are reluctant to be open tend to be younger semen providers, who in a number of countries are often university students. These men seem to have more of a focus on the monetary returns, expecting to be paid for their contribution. They see it as a very simple process in which all they do is masturbate and as soon as they have been paid for their semen, that is the end of the transaction and the end of their involvement. They are also less likely to understand the rights and needs of potential offspring.

On the other hand, the semen providers who seem to be more committed to openness and have less interest in money are often more mature men, who are married or in partnerships, and have families of their own. It seems as if having their own children enables them to have more of an understanding of what their semen provision means from a child's perspective. They are more likely to have an insight into the long term issues than their younger counterparts, and also to recognise that conception is just the beginning of a lifelong process.

The combined importance of a donor's age and the clinic's approach was borne out significantly in a United Kingdom study that I undertook with others and which compared views of semen providers in two different clinics – one clinic encouraged secrecy and attracted younger men, while the other had a more liberal approach and attracted mainly older men. (Kings College Hospital in London is somewhat unique in the UK in this respect.)[4]

What is also interesting is that some men who provide semen when younger are likely to find in later years – either as a result of their own personal development or perhaps the birth and development of their own children – that their views change to fit the profile of an older donor.

Illustrating such a shift in perspective, two semen providers presented evidence in the recent High Court case in London, England, in which DI offspring Joanna Rose and a six year old person were seeking the right to have access to information about their semen providers. Both men said that since they had donated, their views had changed considerably. One in particular, said his views were very much influenced by the fact that he now had children of his own and as a result, he understood the issues that might arise for other children in terms of needing to have access to information.

Another example is Stephen Ferguson, a donor whose story appeared in the Scottish newspaper, *The Herald*.[5] He said that a few years earlier, when he was providing semen at the age of 25, anonymity was very important to him. However, on reflection, he is amazed that he hadn't seen the similarities between people who are adopted with people who are conceived through donor insemination, especially as he is an adopted person himself. Having since traced his birth mother, he says that 'being able to fill in the pieces of your genetic jigsaw is a wonderful feeling' and he now believes that adults conceived by DI should have full access to all information about their donors.

The changed views of these semen providers, and others like them, challenge the commonly held notion that men who have been guaranteed anonymity in the past must never be contacted in subsequent years about the possibility of supplying information or of having contact with their offspring.

As well as having different views on openness, men have different motivations for becoming a semen provider. Usually their reasons can be classified into three general areas:

1) an altruistic act to help others
2) a means of obtaining money
3) a combination of both of these

In most studies it is relatively rare to find men saying they provide semen only for the monetary reward - perhaps because there are more efficient ways of making money! However, it could also be argued that when asked, semen providers find it uncomfortable to acknowledge that they have provided semen only for financial reasons, and feel it is much more sociably acceptable to talk about helping people but also enjoying the monetary rewards at the same time.

The following quotes show just some of the many different reasons why men choose to become semen providers.

> *I have both relatives and personal friends who are unable to conceive because of one or the other partner. It saddens me when I see it affecting people who I know have so much to offer in the form of an excellent stable family life. I want to help such couples.* New Zealand policeman

> *I love children very much and it's not difficult to understand the situation for infertile couples who want children. It feels natural to help others – it is my desire. I am also a blood and organ donor.* Swedish lawyer

> *Money was the main reason for becoming a donor. I was totally penniless and needed a small regular income with which to continue my search for a job. I don't really mind contributing to conception (although perhaps I would prefer not to), especially if it is to help infertile fathers.* English economist

> *I was listening to a radio programme which was discussing donor*

> *insemination. A couple were interviewed, and for them, infertility was a personal tragedy. This was added to by the fact that there were not enough donors. Knowing that I already had healthy children, this seemed a way for me to help other people.* Australian mechanic

> *There were different reasons for becoming a donor – some of them, but not the most important, being financial. I decided to become a donor due to curiosity. It was something new to me.* Polish student

The mention of payment raises again the appropriateness of using certain terminology when discussing DI. I have frequently expressed concerns about referring to the semen provider as a 'donor' if he is in fact getting paid - a donor is usually somebody who makes a gift, without expecting anything in return.

The notion of being a donor, particularly of blood or organs, is valued in most societies, in that altruism and concern for others are desirable traits. However, while blood is seen as a donation in many countries, in others, such as the United States, payment is made for blood. Similarly, there is an expectation in the American culture for payment to be made for surrogacy, and semen or egg (oocyte) donation, although critics view these payments as commodifying gametes and potential children. What intrigues me is that there is not a similar system of payment operating in the growing field of embryo donation, or 'embryo adoption', as it is sometimes called. It is almost as if there is recognition that a certain boundary is crossed when moving from gametes to embryos, and that to pay for an embryo is much more akin to 'buying a baby'.

The Canadian government has recently decided that payments for gametes will not be made in the future, and this has led to claims by medical professionals that the supply of semen will 'dry up' as men only provide semen because they are paid. It is a similar argument to the one that has been made in relation to identity release – if anonymity is not guaranteed, then the supply will dry up – but this of course has not been the case in New Zealand, for example, where there is no anonymity, and payment is not made. The pragmatic focus of, 'If we don't pay, we don't get enough semen providers and therefore couples will miss out', assumes that the only way to recruit donors and the only way to value them is by paying them.

It is of course possible to value people without giving them money, which happens in the case of blood and organ donations in some countries. It has always seemed strange to me that this altruism isn't transferred more readily into gamete donation.

The issue of payment is separate from the reimbursement of costs sometimes paid to semen providers, such as petrol and parking charges relating to visits to the clinic. There are conflicting views, however, as to whether the cost of time lost from work is a reimbursement of expenses or whether it borders on payment.

Findings from some studies suggest that many medical professionals see donors only as a means to an end. With similar views to younger semen providers, they feel that once the semen is paid for, the transaction is finished, much like a business deal. The provision of semen is in many ways just the beginning of the arrangement, however, because the implications of that transaction continue well into the future, both for the provider and his family, as well as for the recipient family. As my New Zealand colleagues have said, a donor is only a donor for a short period of time. Thereafter he becomes a man with children in another family.[6]

Several studies have also shown that, contrary to claims by many doctors in the past, many semen providers do not provide their semen without an investment and interest in the outcomes. At some stage, the majority of semen providers do think about the children who may have been conceived – their traits, their family lives and their happiness.

A number of semen providers even talk about looking forward to the possibility of meeting offspring in the future, although in contrast, there are also those who have concerns about the consequences of their semen provision. In particular, they are anxious about what details of theirs, if any, might be made available to recipient families. There can also be concerns that offspring who want contact in the future may interfere in their family life, or perhaps expect something from the semen provider that he is not prepared to give. Although these are valid feelings, I believe that these types of issues should have already been addressed as part of the preparation semen providers undertake before deciding to provide semen. Donors need to have the opportunity to fully explore their uncertainties and anxieties, before being able to make a truly informed and responsible decision about becoming a giver of life.

To inform semen providers of the importance of their contribution, while also acknowledging the contribution they make to families, the Donor Conception Support Group in Australia, with several hundred members (parents, offspring and donors), has produced a leaflet *Not My Child – An Information Sheet for Potential Gamete Donors*. The following is an extract from that leaflet:

> You may have a very personal reason for wanting to help others in this way, and perhaps even know the people you want your donation to help... You may simply want to "help others", or share your good fortune as a parent, and not know or care who will benefit from your donation. The decision may seem a simple and uncomplicated one …
>
> You are to be congratulated for your desire to help others in this special way. However, if you do make a decision to donate, this will have an enormous impact on the couple who receive your donation, on the person who is born as a result of your donation, and even on you …
>
> As a first step, it is important that you leave information about yourself that both the parents and the child can have access to. Medical history is important, but so is information about your personal history, your personality and talents [and] how you feel about the donation … You can leave a letter, and even a photo, at the clinic at which you donate.
>
> It is also important that you are open to a possible request for information, and maybe even contact at some time in the future. To do this, it will probably be important for you to tell special people in your life about the donation, and the possibility that you have genetic offspring who may need some information and/or contact with you at some time.[7]

The importance of a semen provider telling special people in his life is due to the ongoing, long-term impact, namely the creation of another life. However, when questioning the extent to which his actions are shared with a partner or wife, it seems that some donors do not inform their partners that they are providing semen, while others, who have subsequently married, have not told their wife of previously being a donor. In many cases, even when he has informed his partner, he may not share this information with his children. One of the major themes throughout this book is how the culture of family building using DI is changing, and it is hoped that this will also include a move towards more openness on the semen provider's part.

Leonie and Warren had the opposite experience at a donor conception social, when they met a donor who they felt was too open.

> *We introduced ourselves and he announced that he had been a donor. His next words were, 'Oh, they could be my kids'. It just shocked me. I wasn't prepared for it. I remember being a little sharp with him. Here we were at a social, looking for support and ways to tell our child – remember our kids didn't know at that time – and I felt it was really inappropriate and insensitive of him to say that. Not just for himself but for everybody that was standing around me, most importantly, for us. He touched a raw nerve that I wasn't ready to have exposed.* Leonie

(Leonie felt relieved to discover he had provided semen at a different clinic from where she and Warren had undergone treatment, and there was no likelihood of this man being their donor.)

Related to the notion of semen providers being open – in an appropriate manner – is the way in which the need for their service is promoted. It is necessary to develop new strategies to recruit different kinds of people with different motives, particularly in countries where the traditional DI culture of anonymity and payment is in the process of change.

Certainly it is not easy to recruit semen providers, and more attention needs to be focused on the most effective means of reaching out to men – making them aware of the need for donors and then seeking their involvement in assisting people who otherwise would be unable to have children.

One of the most effective recruitment strategies seems to be for existing semen providers to talk to other men, including friends and relatives, about why they have done this and what it has meant for them. They are then in a good position to encourage these men to also become providers of semen.

Another strategy that I feel could be adopted is to present DI as an opportunity for couples to donate the gift of life to another couple, rather than it being solely the male partner's contribution. To present semen provision as a gift from one couple to another could be very helpful.

I am aware, too, of a growing number of couples who recruit their own donors, selecting and inviting a family member or friend who they see as being suitable. This method of recruitment clearly has a number of additional significant issues that need to be considered carefully, particularly the importance of defining the relationships between the parents, the donor, any children born as a result of his donation, and the donor's own family. One such story appeared in an Australian Donor Conception Support Group newsletter:

> … We believed it was imperative that any child we had was able to identify their parents, both parents, and so artificial insemination by unknown donor was not an alternative we wanted to consider.
>
> We considered our options – there was no near relative on my husband's side of the family whom we could approach. Fortunately though we have a wonderfully close friend who, coincidentally, looks very much like my husband … After some deliberation we decided that if we couldn't have a child that was biologically linked to my husband, then having one who was biologically linked to someone we both loved and respected would be our next preferred option.
>
> We explained to him our predicament and why we wanted his help; what it would mean to a child to have such a special person as his biological father; and what it might mean for him. We left him to think about it for a while and to talk it over with his girlfriend...
>
> We now have two healthy, well adjusted children. They have a wonderful relationship with their "special uncle", his wife and their son, and they know why he is special, and how they came into being...
>
> They have a positive relationship with the man who helped to make them. They can ask him at any time about his medical background. They'll grow up with a half brother who also knows why they're special.[8]

Using the semen from a known donor, with the intention of self-insemination, was one option Andrea and Bridget considered.

> *We were coming around to where we were eventually going to find the sperm because this is what it's all about. At the end of the day, 'How are we doing to do this?' Actually doing the mechanics of it aren't necessarily a big issue; it's just the raw products you need to get hold of to make it. Two guys at work approached me, privately, and both said, 'If you are looking for a donor, I would be willing to*

donate'. Then we read a few more books that said you need to protect yourself. Ask these potential donors, 'Are you willing to have HIV tests and any other tests that we may ask you to take, to establish Bridget's safety and the potential baby's safety, healthwise, along the way?' I think that's where this subconscious safety and legitimacy came in. We went around and around with this for a long time and because there didn't seem any other options, that's when we decided that we would use a clinic-user, anonymous donor. Andrea

When DI first started being written about many years ago, some people suggested that semen providers were of questionable psychological stability and that their morals were somewhat dubious (although it does seem that the moral concerns were more about the act of masturbation than the provision of semen). Some people still perceive these men to be in some way disturbed, strange or abnormal. After all, what could possibly lead a man to masturbate, collect the semen, and allow a clinic to use that semen so complete strangers could have a child or children? For most people, procreation occurs within a loving relationship, in which the partners know each other and share with each other at an intimate level. In the process of DI, however, there is of course no intimacy, no loving, and in most cases, the semen provider is not seen, let alone known.

As long as DI operates in a closed system, the positive attributes of semen providers very rarely see the light of day and donors are instead regarded by some with a degree of suspicion and perhaps fear. For some time I have wanted to write a paper (there are so many papers to be written!), tentatively entitled *In Praise of Donors*. The paper would focus on valuing donors for their gift, valuing them for their understanding and sensitivity, and valuing them for being prepared to reach out to help other couples. I see their gift of life as having a significant spiritual component when given out of concern and altruism.

While writing this chapter, I have coincidentally received two interesting and pertinent letters. One was from a fifteen-year-old schoolgirl, who asked if I could help her find out information about her donor. The other is from a couple who underwent DI treatment in two different New Zealand clinics and now have two sons, aged 20 and 15½. This couple and I had previously discussed their search for information concerning their donors and, in the case of their elder son, contact has already been made with the treating doctor, who has moved to another country. He informed me that all records had been destroyed and it was therefore impossible to obtain any additional information. However, there appear to be details available concerning the younger son's donor, as there is of the fifteen-year-old girl's donor. My task now is to make contact with the clinicians involved and to try to obtain that information, as well as raise the possibility of contact in the future. The fact that one brother can potentially access information, while the other can not, may have implications for the dynamics between the two brothers.

It is important to recognise that there is a distinction between the offspring seeking information and parents seeking information on behalf of their offspring – information concerning the semen provider is primarily for the offspring, although certainly parents will have an interest in this as well. There is also the possibility of the parents or offspring wanting to give information to the semen provider. The parents of the two brothers recognise this possibility, as they have written, 'It would be so nice for the donors to be able to meet [our sons] because they would be so proud of them. They are such fine young men.' Wanting to share their own pride of their two sons is another way of these parents expressing their gratitude – they want the donors to be able to see the good that has come from their donation, in a sense to reciprocate the initial gift.

The fifteen-year-old girl also shows how the request for information about her donor is part of a two-way process. In her letter she provided some information about herself, which she thinks might be important for the donor to know. As is often the case, she illustrates that, 'If I am interested in you, it is possible that you will have some interest in me as well'.

To give an example of the type of information offspring usually seek about their donor, I have reproduced the questions this young woman asked:

1. Where is the donor's family from? (England, Europe, etc.)
2. Where are they now?
3. What is the donor's name? (Would he be prepared to give his name?)
4. What does he look like? (Eyes, hair, skin colour)
5. Why did he choose to give a sperm donation in the first place?
6. Are there any other children born from his sperm donations?

7. What type of occupation does he have?
8. Would he be prepared to write to me? (Via you or directly)
9. Would he be prepared to meet me?

Parents play a significant part in their offspring's attempts to obtain information. Offspring will generally need their parents to be positive and emotionally supportive, as well as offering practical assistance. In the case of the fifteen-year-old girl, her mother had provided guidance and encouragement, but pointed out that her daughter had written the letter in her own capacity. She had not shown the letter to her mother, although they had discussed the content of it.

It is to be expected and only natural that many people who know about their DI conception will want information about their semen provider. The information sought, as this young woman has shown us and which has also been found in the field of adoption, is about physical characteristics, motivations and personality. Many also mention their desire to meet the man who has contributed to their genetic history, and question how he feels about this possibility.

As I have mentioned, as yet there is no formal system in New Zealand that enables offspring such as the three previously mentioned, to obtain information about their donors. However, because openness is very much the norm in New Zealand and profiles have been available for the past few years, it is highly likely that the doctors involved will be happy to try to locate donors who were recruited under the previous closed system and ask if they would provide the information that is being sought. If contact also becomes a possibility, a counsellor will no doubt help all parties prepare for this.

While offspring born in New Zealand are fortunate to have the support of doctors, the systems in place for offspring to access information vary a great deal around the world. In some countries, records with identifying information are required by legislation to be kept and to be made available to offspring when they reach a certain age, or earlier under certain circumstances, while other countries provide for access to non-identifying information at a certain age. The majority of countries, however, have systems that preclude access to any information, actively discouraging any interest in the semen provider.

My view is that doctors or other professionals who are asked for information, particularly non-identifying details, have a duty to make every effort to obtain the requested information and pass it on to the offspring. This does not breach the guarantee of anonymity that may have been given to the donor, as it is the doctor making contact with the semen provider again. It is then the semen provider's decision as to what, if any, information is supplied.

From an offspring's point of view, there have been disturbing stories of being told that records have been destroyed, only to find that when the issue is pursued, suddenly those records have been found. I have also heard stories of professionals who have threatened to destroy the records, should changes in the law require them to divulge the names of donors. It is, however, rare for policy makers to advocate that donors who were given a guarantee of anonymity should have this guarantee overridden by legislation. Where legislative changes have been made, instead of being retrospective, it has been on the basis that donors will be required to provide information from a certain date onwards.

For people interested in trying to make contact, the development of voluntary registers in some jurisdictions, such as the one in the State of Victoria in Australia, is an exciting move. Voluntary registers encourage donors and offspring to place their names on the register, and indicate their willingness/interest in contact or information, should a 'match' occur. Such a situation places the responsibility in the hands of the people who are mostly involved, namely the offspring and their semen providers, and removes the clinics from the controlling, key-holding role.

Contact between offspring and semen providers is still rare but instances are beginning to be reported. It is a new and evolving area, for which again, there are few scripts to follow. The contacts that have occurred have arisen from a variety of situations: the passing of new laws, the setting up of voluntary registers, or clinic staff making contact with semen providers on behalf of offspring. There have also been cases where offspring have appealed through the media for previous donors to come forward, with the hope that a match may be found. Although there are some instances where semen providers have initiated the possibility of contact, almost all attempts emanate from offspring, and have occurred with the full support and encouragement of their parents.

Most of the parents who have contributed to this book have not had the experience (or their offsprings' experience) of searching for their donor, but it is certainly an issue that they have considered.

> *I think you've got to give the child permission to ask to meet the donor.* Romana

> *I am looking forward one day to meeting the donor because I feel safe in my relationship with my child that he's my child and he's not going to want to go to this guy for a father because he's got a good relationship with his Dad.* Female, Melbourne Focus Group

> *I don't think we would ever trace the donor. I don't feel they are part of our lives but I can imagine a time when the children will want to know more and at the moment, all I can say is that I feel fine with that. What I don't know is how I would feel later on.* Female, London Focus Group

> *I have known adopted people and they know painfully that they cannot face that person because they feel it would desperately hurt the actual parents. It's only after their death they got in touch. I always felt that I couldn't shape my son as to how he would feel about this. If he could contact him in the future, that he may do.* Female, London Focus Group

> *David is eighteen and has shown no interest to find out who his donor is but maybe that is practicality talking because he can't find out.* Male, London Focus Group

> *I wouldn't like to downgrade the role of the person who has donated in case it goes down the track and the kids might get to meet the person. There may be some bonding that would come into it and I don't know how that bonding would affect the person that has actually brought him up.* Male, Sydney Focus Group

> *When they get to an age to do so, if they want to meet the donor, then I'm quite happy for them to do that and I'm not going to stop*

> *it. But for me, I don't want anything to do with him. He's given me something that I have and that's happy for me. But if my kids say they want to meet their donor, I will be quite happy to take them there but that's as far as it goes for me.* Male, Melbourne Focus Group

> *It's not a threat but I think I wouldn't particularly welcome the day when she found the donor. That would be the day when I think I'd feel it for her as much as anything, but I would feel it myself, what is this person going to be like?* Walter

Such curiosity is only natural, especially as the possibility of meeting the semen provider becomes more likely. Romana and Grant, together with their sons, decided to take a pro-active approach in attempting to locate their son's semen provider. Although in Australia at the time they had no legal access to information, Romana and Grant were fortunate that the clinic helped them exchange letters with the semen provider, which eventually led to their meeting with him. This is their story:

R: When Desmond was four, Grant was buttoning up his coat to get him outside and Des said, 'Who is the donor, Dada?' and Grant said, 'I don't know, mate'. We were in a rush so we left it at that. We revisited the situation later and Grant and I talked about what to do. At that point I started to want to meet the donor. I felt that it was important for us to do that with Desmond but I couldn't say anything to Grant. I didn't know how to phrase the words so that he could say, 'No' if he wanted to. It's easy for me to say, 'Let's meet the donor' because I'm biologically attached but I didn't know what he would feel. I should have known better because Grant one day just brought it up. 'I think we'd better make the search if we're going to do it.'

G: We'd become aware that if we let things slip too much longer, then we might not ever be able to contact him.

R: That was the original reason why we did it. We were afraid he might die or they would lose the information and Desmond would never be able to meet him.

G: We've changed the legislation here, granting offspring the right to some information but it's not retrospective. Desmond didn't have any legal entitlement, so we worried that if we didn't do anything, he might just lose that information. We weren't 100% sure about exactly what we were doing but we believed that in doing this, we were acting in his best interests.

G: We rang the social worker at the Royal Women's [Hospital]. We asked if we could meet the donor. That took a while; she facilitated an exchange of letters.

R: We wrote back and forth for two years. We just wanted to take our time; we wanted to work things out between letters.

G: Romana and I [first] met him with the social worker at Royal Women's. I wanted to check him out. I didn't want to introduce Desmond to someone who shouldn't have a place in his life. I don't know what I would have done if I'd taken a negative attitude to him.

R: We had talked about that. We were thinking worst possible scenarios and Grant said, 'It doesn't matter who he is because he is Desmond's biological father'.

G: We definitely were thinking about the way in which we would introduce him to Desmond and what sort of contact we would have – whether it would be having lunch together, whether we would occasionally get together once every six months for some minor social get-together or would it be once every two years in a more public situation. We went to check him out and to talk with him about what he wanted and what seemed to be a sensible way to proceed. He was very keen on having contact. He was willing to have whatever involvement was wanted.

R: I'm very happy about that. He is so accommodating and I hope that doesn't change.

G: We arranged for us, with Desmond and Maxwell, to meet him at the park one day. And then he came over here, and recently, we went over to his place for lunch.

R: When we went to the [first] meeting I was a bit nervous, but when he came into the room, he looked so much like Desmond that I felt instantly comfortable. He was familiar because he was so much like Desmond in mannerisms that it didn't feel a problem talking to him.

G: He's a very easy to get along with man. A very charming individual with a warm heart.

R: And he said really appropriate things. He said that he's afraid to have expectations, that if he becomes too emotional, just to let him know. And he was really appreciative of our contact with him.

G: I feel a sense of warmth and general friendship to him, partly because I feel like he's got a bit of Desmond in him, so I extend part of my friendship for Desmond to him.

R: He's got quite a philosophical bent, he says really good things. He was quite clear that he would do whatever we want, which is really nice. He's very generous and not intrusive in any respect. Even his comments about his parents when he told them about Desmond, they wanted to know what contribution they could make to the family. It was just a really nice way of wording things. We're really lucky.

G: When we went to meet him, to my mind, it was just something you need to do, like going to the dentist or the doctor. It's like security for the future, it might make things easier for Desmond, but there is no immediate impact.

R: It was totally different for me. I think it's tied up with family. I was worried; I didn't know where he would fit. I was worried about Desmond's reaction and I can tell by the way I answer Desmond's questions that I'm still a bit worried. When Desmond asked me recently, 'So is [the donor] extended family?' I said, 'Well what would you like him to be?'

G: I told everybody he was family but it wasn't like immediate family.

R: And then Desmond said, 'If he came to live with us, would he be my Dad?'

G: He obviously had a number of questions about it.

R: Millions of them!

G: When we went and visited [the donor] in his house, I was more anxious about seeing what Desmond's reaction was going to be and I must confess, I was a little bit relieved that evening, when I asked him where he preferred best, that he said he would be much happier staying here. I was happier that he wasn't asking me if he could go and live with [the donor]. It's not a major worry but I guess the donor parent is a threat to the stability of the family and I was relieved that Desmond expressed clearly that he likes it here.

It's really good for Desmond. It's interesting for him, just seeing his biological father; he does have a lot of physical similarities. He and his brother talk about what they're going to be like when they're older. Maxwell talks about whether or not he'll be like me and Desmond has now got some sort of little chart in the Universe, some idea of what he's going to be like when he grows up.

* * * * *

In addition to Romana and Grant, one of the couples at the Sydney Focus Group briefly mentioned the contact they had experienced with their semen provider.

> *We have contacted our donor and we have a letter and photos from him. It takes the mystery away. He hasn't offered to meet us yet but that's okay. It's just wonderful to see photos of the donor and I remember there was a photo of him when he was ten and when*

> *I first saw it – when I was reading the letter – I thought it was a photo of Pam's family. It was like her father when he was younger.*
> Female and Male, Sydney Focus Group

The many issues surrounding contact between offspring and donors were highlighted at two workshops, *Towards Contact,* which were held in Perth, Western Australia.[9] Counsellors, fertility clinic staff members, two members of the Donor Conception Support Group, and a legal officer participated.

The following summary of the discussions at the workshops is very comprehensive and very helpful, although I have to say I find it interesting that the order of consideration was donors, recipients and then offspring. This perhaps reflects some of the thinking of the time, namely that the most vulnerable party in any possible contact was the donor, whereas I feel that the main focus should be concern for the offspring and their need for information.

1) Issues facing donors:

a) If donor initiating contact

- may want to know if they are fertile or not; may be alarmed if they have no donor offspring
- may want to know how many families/offspring they have contributed to and the sex of offspring
- may have curiosity about the offspring's well being
- may have a growing awareness of the needs and responsibilities of children
- need to consider the potential impact on their own family e.g. a fear about accidental incest for their own children, may want to replace their own children if they die or become separated
- if have no children of their own, they may have an emotional need for a child or have other identity issues
- may risk rejection from offspring

b) If offspring or recipient initiates contact

- may have possible concern over motives e.g. a son of a single woman may

be annoyed at having no 'father', recipients may desire financial support
- donors may not be well prepared for dealing with the reality of offspring

2) Issues facing recipients

- parents need to agree on level of contact
- depending on quality of relationship between parents and children, some parents may welcome the contact
- others may fear intrusion into family and the impact on family relationships e.g. parents may feel threatened that their children will reject them and turn to donor
- in particular, may be difficult for the male partner to meet the donor who 'inseminated' his wife
- mother may want to protect the male partner
- parents may feel a need to prepare and safeguard children from rejection/ hurt by the donor
- may have to deal with an extended time frame e.g. if the child's curiosity is immediate and intense but process to make contact is slow and may not eventuate
- if parents have not told the children, this will cause layers of difficult issues

3) Issues facing offspring

- some offspring may not want any more information at all and others will not rest until they have contact
- contact dependent on age of offspring - if under 18, parents have responsibility; if over 18, they can decide for themselves
- may have curiosity over why he donated - may be devastating to find out he donated just for money
- may have curiosity about his physical and personality traits, and whether he has any children
- offspring's fantasy about the donor may not match reality
- concerned about parents' feeling over offspring's desire for more information or contact with donor
- could be additional problems for child if parents not fully comfortable about contact

- concern over donor's motives if he initiates contact e.g. parents of donor who was killed may want to give their inheritance to donor children, may be seeking to become 'father figure'
- if offspring is not aware of DI conception and receives a letter regarding donor's desire for contact, huge implications to deal with

4) Issues facing staff at clinics

- should consider compulsory counselling for recipients prior to use of donor, regarding possible future contact
- may be divided loyalties – may seek to protect donors who donated in a different spirit
- need very clear information about what information is available so those seeking information that is not available do not feel rejected or singled out
- frustration at the limited information that is actually held
- concerned by differences in available information for offspring, especially where this affects offspring from one family
- frustration at being unable to locate past donors

Because of the number of significant issues for all relevant parties – offspring, donors and parents – it always seems wise to have the assistance of a counsellor when considering the process of making contact. Counsellors are able to help the individual parties clarify the implications, work through any issues they may have, and act as facilitator during initial meeting/s and any discussions that result from this contact. They can also organise the exchange of letters, as with Romana and Grant.

It is not only the question of potential contact with the donor that arises, but as with the fifteen-year-old who wrote to me, there is often the desire to know if there are other children conceived from the sperm of the same donor. Not all offspring, of course, will be interested in finding out this information or in making contact with any half-siblings, but some may want to fully explore all genetic relationships.

I'm waiting for the day when it hits them that they might have some half-siblings out there. I reckon that will be a big shock. Male, Melbourne Focus Group

The potential of having half-siblings, perhaps in the same community, is an area of growing interest, and one that will undoubtedly become significant as more people join donor conception organisations. It is a possibility that parents who meet up through these organisations could find they have received treatment at the same clinic at approximately the same time as another couple. This may well lead to thoughts regarding the possibility of genetic linkages via the donor, particularly if their offspring have physical similarities.

As a result of a pilot voluntary register being set up in New Zealand, a meeting took place between two families, whose children were conceived by the sperm of the same donor. They shared their experience in a story that appeared in the *New Zealand Infertility Society Newsletter*, entitled 'Sisters – A Donor Sibling story':

Making the Connection

Right from before our first daughter was born, we'd planned to be very open with her about her donor insemination conception... Both [our] girls shared the same donor, a man that we'd never met, but had once exchanged letters with via the clinic after the first treasured arrival. But after our house move, and the loss of this precious letter, along with a house move on the donor's part, now out of contact with the clinic, we were more than ready to enlist in the pilot of the Donor Family Register established by Sylvia Nixon from Fertility Associates.

We anxiously awaited the return of information with details of other families who had shared the same donor. When the information did arrive in the post, although we were disappointed that more families had not wanted to make a connection, it was gratifying that there was one other family who had identified themselves, along with their only daughter, close in age to our eldest.

We called Sylvia, thanking her for the details, and advised her that we intended to go ahead and make contact with the other family. 'Did we want to make that contact via an intermediary?' enquired Sylvia. It didn't seem at all necessary to us; both families had registered their contact details for the sole purpose of making contact. And as I'd previously been through the experience of contacting and meeting my birth mother without any third party intervention, it didn't seem like a major challenge.

That's not to say that there wasn't a degree of nervousness when we made the initial phone call. However, right from that first conversation, we got on exceedingly well with [the other parents], related to us in the sense of sharing the same sperm donor. It wasn't too long before we arranged our first trip to visit them. Our toddler was blissfully unaware of the implications of the trip but our five year old was well informed, and became very anxious before we left on the last leg of our journey.

Upon arrival however, the anxiety completely disappeared; lots of outdoor space, pet lambs, and the trampoline at the school over the road, along with a warming relationship between the two five year olds soon calmed any fears there had been. We were overwhelmed with our hosts' hospitality, and our afternoon visit too soon came to an end, although we were fortunate to take away with us a video of the girls playing.

Email is a wonderful invention, and since that first visit we have remained in close contact, with the girls exchanging their own messages complete with updates on rabbits, guinea pigs, and other important happenings in their lives. This last summer, we paid another visit, but this time extending over a couple of days, and the half-sisters cemented their relationship whilst digging for fossils on a nearby farmland hill, gambolling in the picturesque river, and blobbing out in front of a video in a darkened bedroom.

Where this relationship will go, what paths it will take the girls down, will now be largely driven by the girls themselves. But we feel sure that the experience will add to their perception of who they are, and of how they came to be conceived.

Sisters get it together

Whilst we felt that our honesty and open attitude would be conducive towards an easy and positive acceptance for our child, there were still two areas which could possibly be areas of concern. The first was that the donor should be available, should the child wish for some reason to contact him at a later stage of life. Our donor had indicated on his profile that this was acceptable to him. Until last year this was no longer considered an issue, then when last year it was brought up again, it was found he was at this present time untraceable. We are hoping this is a temporary situation, however it accentuated the importance of the

> second issue – the possibility of co-incidental meetings with half siblings.
>
> Whilst we appreciate that each donor recipient family is a separate entity, there is still undeniably the factor that these children are blood related, by a common donor.
>
> When we first heard of the possibility of a Donor register, we greeted it with excitement and enthusiasm, keen to surrender our identifying information for the sake of our daughter's 'identity' and the other children involved.
>
> The night we received the long awaited call from [the other parents] was extremely exciting for us all. The call was great, mainly consisting of little tidbits about the girls and arranging to get the children together to get to know each other.
>
> My husband was very accepting of the meeting, taking it in his stride as he usually does and same as me, he was excited for our daughter. I was feeling excited, but also a little scared that the children would not enjoy the meeting. Our daughter was excited when told and expressed curiosity as to whether they would look alike. She did tell the kids at school 'her two sisters were coming to play with her'.
>
> The visit went extremely well from our point of view and it seemed to flow very easily because we had so many things in common. We had a fun time exchanging photos for the children to keep and they left with promises from both sides to meet again.
>
> We consider the get-togethers to be successful because our original reason for both families was for the sake of the children. The fact that we have so much in common and have become friends is a bonus.[10]

Voluntary registers to facilitate contact are beginning to be established in various countries around the world, including the United Kingdom (www.ukdonorlink.org.uk). Funded by the government's Department of Health, the register helps people over the age of 18, who were conceived through donor sperm and/or eggs, to exchange information and make contact, if desired, with their donors and their half-siblings.

In the United States, 'Single Mothers by Choice' established a database (www.singlemothersbychoice.com) after several mothers of the group coincidentally learned that they had used the same donor and that their children were half siblings. This confidential registry is open to any parents, whether single or married, of children conceived through donor sperm, egg or embryo and it enables them to locate other children conceived from the same donor. The registry operates on a similar basis to adoption registries that help children/offspring find their genetic parents. Parents are encouraged to provide their child's name, sex and date of birth (or offspring can register their own details), along with the donor information, and the name and address of the clinic used.

Another donor sibling registry (www.donorsiblingregistry.com) was set up in the United States by a mother and her son, who was conceived through DI. As at February 2004, 2336 families had registered with their website and 500 offspring (that they knew of) had already found half siblings through the site. As I write this book, an American television programme is soon to share the story of how two families met through this registry. One family has a set of eight-year-old fraternal twins and the other has a nine-year-old girl, all conceived from the same donor.

Clearly, while some people may have fears and anxieties about what such openness could mean to them, many others are becoming more accepting of information sharing, and more understanding of the desire by some offspring to have the opportunity for contact with their donors and siblings. Such openness is potentially of huge benefit for the emotional development and well-being of offspring – and also perhaps for their parents and their donors.

Exploring the issues associated with the semen provider's contribution to your family and especially if there is going to be information shared and possible contact, are consequences of making the decision to be open with your children/offspring about the way in which your family was built.

This chapter has covered a stage of family building with the assistance of DI that is less well charted than the others stages covered. This is primarily because of the relatively recent move to information sharing and the 'opening up' of DI. There is simply not a lot of experience to draw on but what has been attempted is an overview of the issues that need to be considered. Some may seem more relevant than others. Some may be appropriate at certain ages of offspring. Some may also raise anxieties and tensions but these should not necessarily be seen as negatives, but rather as opportunities for enhancing the health and well-being of the family.

10 Confident and healthy families – some concluding thoughts

I expect that, having reached the final chapter in this book, you will have experienced a variety of emotions as you have journeyed through the previous chapters. If you are anything like me, some of the comments of parents and other people who have featured in this book will have moved you to tears. Some of their experiences have been very powerful and I again want to thank them for being prepared to share many personal and intimate experiences with us.

The book has no doubt engendered a variety of responses for different people. The predominant reaction for some readers may be, 'Wow, that is just how I feel' or 'I am not the only one who feels this way after all'. If this is how you feel, I hope that by identifying with someone else's feelings, some of the isolation you have experienced may have disappeared.

Some readers may feel deeply appreciative of what they have learnt. Gaining some insights into how other parents have dealt with certain issues may have assisted you in your own journey and in the construction of your own scripts of sharing.

For others, reading this book may have raised anxieties and uncertainties. You may say, 'I recognise the importance of having an open and honest relationship with my offspring, but...' And it is the 'but' that challenges readers to contemplate the possibility of acting in the way that the parents featured in this book have.

Yet for others, the book may have provoked outright fear. If you are living with a decision that you would not share information with your children/offspring and are now faced with the belief that you should be open, there is possibly the fear of what the changing of that decision might mean, especially for your family relationships.

Without doubt, this is a challenging book. It challenges parents or would-be parents to think and explore in depth the issues that are associated with building a family with the assistance of DI. It asks you to acknowledge the past, live in the present, and anticipate the future.

For those of you who are offspring, the fact that you are reading the book probably indicates that you know your family beginnings. It is my hope that you learned this information as a result of your parents having had sufficient confidence in themselves and your family as a whole to know that love is the cement that builds and binds you together. There will be books written by, for and with you in the future and this will be great. In the meantime, my hope is that what is contained within these covers will enable you to understand and appreciate even more the journey undertaken by parents using DI.

For readers who have contributed semen to enable family building to occur, you will have been made aware of the deep appreciation there has been for your 'gift': the gift of life, the gift of a child, the gift of a family. Without your contribution the lives of many people would not have been so full and rich. Your contribution did not end when you provided your semen, however, and this book presents a challenge to you to think about how you might meet the needs of offspring who may want information and/or contact.

This book may be no less challenging to many professionals, than it is to parents and would-be parents. Parents place a great deal of trust in professionals but sometimes find their DI experience to be disempowering. A growing number of parents at DI consumer group meetings are calling for professionals to listen to them and their experiences, and to reflect on how they can best meet the needs of would-be parents and their future families. Managing the relationship between patients and professionals in a way that is both respectful and empowering is therefore an ideal to be constantly strived for.

It has been encouraging to see policy makers in a growing number of countries beginning to 'rethink' the culture of secrecy that has dominated

DI for so long. It is never easy to change a strongly-held ideology, but the recognition that some parties in DI family building are rendered vulnerable and powerless by the actions of others demands attention. How to manage policy change however, is a matter of conflict and debate and the various countries cited in this book give a small insight into this.

Having made the above comments regarding the various parties involved in DI family building and the possible impact this book may have on them, let me conclude by focusing on seven central themes that, in my view, parents and would-be parents will find helpful to consider.

1. Of critical importance is being able to acknowledge and learn to manage the range of feelings, thoughts and behaviours that emerge when you are unable to build your family without assistance from others. Whatever the reason for needing assistance, it represents the loss of something that is highly valued in all societies – the ability to become a family in the way that most families are formed. Losses are invariably accompanied by sadness and grief and in the case of infertility, lead to a reassessment of self-identity. It is only natural to question "Who am I, and what is the basis of the relationship with my partner?" Acknowledging the loss and all that accompanies it will be painful and often disturbing, but it is only with this acknowledgement that a start can be made (often after some time) on deciding how to manage this new-found and unwanted 'state'.

   This book does not presume to tell you how to do this. What it does do is provide you with insights into other people's experiences, which are shared on the basis that they may offer support and act as a possible guide. For each individual and couple, however, the journey will be unique. Some will move slowly, while others move more quickly; some will want regular signposts, while others will be guided more by intuition; and some will be pre-occupied with looking over their shoulders, while others will be future-focused. These differences are also likely to occur within a partnership.

   Family building using DI is challenging enough (and the same could be said for family building in general), without being constantly pulled back and having to use a lot of energy on past phases of our lives.

2. DI is not appropriate for everyone who needs assistance but having the knowledge that DI is the right way for *you* to build your own family lays a sound foundation. To reach this point of knowing it is the right decision for you will, as the parents in this book indicate, occur in different ways and at different times. The issues and implications will ideally have been fully explored and considered, which is why Petra Thorn (Germany) and I place such a heavy emphasis on the value of what we call 'preparation for DI family building'. Yes, we are counsellors and yes, at our preparation seminars we do use our counselling skills, but more importantly, we provide an educational experience, in which information is put in front of participants so they can make their own informed decisions. The information is extensive and comes from a variety of sources, including professionals, parents and of course from group members as they share with each other. Some participants leave these weekend seminars deciding that DI is not for them, which is great, as they have acknowledged, considered and then decided.

   The goal for couples or individuals beginning DI treatment is to feel confident about their decision making and confident that they are fully informed not only about the treatment, but also the family building that occurs post treatment. DI is different from other kinds of family building and the differences will not suddenly disappear when pregnancy occurs, or a child is born.

3. Following the decision to use DI, the next biggest decision facing couples or individuals will be whether they share the origins of their family with their children. This author and all the parents who have contributed to this book are clear that if you want a healthy and well-functioning family then sharing this information is vital.

   The decision to share information is of course closely related to the preceding discussion concerning confidence. Insecure parents who are not confident in the decision to use DI may feel some shame about using this treatment and therefore want to hide the information. They may feel that it is taking a risk to share information with a child.

Confident parents on the other hand will feel pride in the children they have and the family they have created. They will be thankful for the assistance of others – especially the donor – and see no need to hide this fact. Confident parents will be those who know that love is always stronger than fear, and that a loving parent is an honest and open parent. They will know that communication between parents and children needs to be free of defensiveness and avoidance. They will also know the children are very resilient and manage truth and honesty much better than they do secrets and deceit.

4. It may seem superfluous to say, but family building is a continuous journey. The family never reaches the stage of being built as there are always new developments to be incorporated into the family thinking and culture. In their stories of sharing, parents have talked of how they shared information at different stages of their children's lives and how the information sharing developed over time.

   The children/offspring interviewed in the excellent video *A Different Story*, produced by the Donor Conception Network in the UK, provides outstanding examples of the value of growing up with the knowledge of their family origins. The language that they use at different ages gives a fascinating insight into their journeys of understanding. The video also illustrates their journey of maturation and how it is necessary when considering DI to look beyond the focus on a baby, to also include the needs of the teenager and adult that baby will become.

   It is also helpful to remember that there are likely to be certain times and events that add richness and developments to the journey. The desire to discover information concerning the man who provided his semen and perhaps the possibility of a meeting are events that will be full of importance and significance for all involved. The decision for offspring to marry and have children of their own may also raise new issues for themselves and their parents.

   The central focus of this book is the family, rather than just the parents, or the child or the donor. All of course are individuals and need to be seen as such. However, they come together in a web of relationships and it is these relationships that play a significant part in the building of the family. Considering the needs of all those parties involved with DI means that a holistic approach is followed.

5. Because DI is still relatively unknown, there is not a lot of information available to parents and would-be parents as they start and then pursue their journey. The growing number of sources of information is to be welcomed, but unless it is known where to find these, there can be a feeling of isolation and loneliness.

There are three major sources of support and information available and they have all been found to be helpful by parents in this book: other parents, family and friends, and professionals.

The most valuable of these sources of support seems to be the experiences of those parents who have already commenced and are part-way through their DI journey. The evolution of support groups and consumer organisations has been of tremendous benefit to would-be travellers, giving them the ability to develop confidence in their own journey. Increasingly, consumer groups are producing written material that, like this book, seeks to inform and work towards reducing the marginalisation of those who use DI. The Internet is also playing an increasingly important role in this connection.

Providing the second source of support are those people who form your network of family and friends. They may not have experienced infertility personally; they may know little about DI; but their love for you should enable them to seek to be understanding and supportive. Sometimes there is a fear that some relatives or friends may not understand, but when sharing of information does occur, it is usually discovered that the fear is unfounded. This is not to say that there will be some people who won't know what to say and how to react, but then your self-confidence will hopefully enable you to educate them as to how to be supportive to you! This however, is a challenging task.

The other potential source of support is professionals who work with you. They can be extremely significant in the way they respond to you, the information they share, and the confidence that they instil concerning family building with the assistance of DI. This leads to the next point to be considered.

6. Learning to manage the professionals. When a person is in any situation where they need something from someone else, there is the risk of vulnerability. The vulnerability may be due to being dependent on the other person, it may be due to the pain and distress that has led to the need for help, or it may be due to the response of the person who can meet those needs. (It may be of course that all three factors are operating at the same time.) The need for assistance with family building is a prime example of how professionals have the potential to create vulnerability and there are many examples of this throughout the book.

   We have already discussed the importance of developing confidence and how professionals can play a part in strengthening that confidence. This does not mean, however, that professionals will not still ask you to reflect on the way you have made your decisions and on your understanding of the implications of those decisions. The task however should be to assist you reflect. It should not be too prescriptive, telling you what you are to think and how you are to behave. I have also sought not to make this book prescriptive but it does, however, strongly argue that if you are committed to the health and well-being of your family, then the issues raised need to be reflected on before you will be able to make the decisions that are appropriate for you.

   In the past, many professionals advised patients to adopt certain positions and behave in certain ways, but times are changing, albeit faster in some countries than others. These changes suggest that the role of the professional is now more to facilitate rather than control; to share information to enable patients to make informed decisions rather than to advise them what to do; and to develop, rather than undermine, patient confidence. Many consumer organisations are working hard to have all professionals function in these ways and it seems appropriate that if difficulties are encountered with a professional, then support and assistance should be sought from a consumer organisation.

7. The final theme relates to terminology. Treatment was originally known as 'artificial insemination by donor' (AID) before the word 'artificial' was recognised to be inappropriate. By that time, the letters AID were being of course also being used to describe another condition. There are many other words that continue to be used in DI that need to change but the difficulty in moving to new words and terminology, is that it is much easier to fall back on words we have used over many years and are comfortable with. A central issue in this connection is that we face the challenge of redefining or broadening definitions of words like 'parent, mother, father, and family'. Because it has been traditional to associate these terms with genetic connectedness – for instance, a father is someone who has contributed semen – we struggle to shift our thinking to accommodate those fathers who have made no genetic contribution yet are loving and nurturing fathers to their children. As Rona Achilles from Canada has said:

> The solution is logically simple but socially complex. We need to redefine parental roles; we need to be able to hold two different images of fatherhood in our mind's eye at the same time. One, the social father – the man who will nurture, guide and take legal responsibility for the child – is clearly the most significant role. The other – the genetic father – cannot, however, be dismissed or denied. Although his contribution seems only genetic, his role must also be understood in social terms since knowledge of his identity may be essential to the child's mental health. These two roles should not necessarily be a threat to each other if clarity is achieved about their respective features, rights, and responsibilities. This is exactly the process that has taken place in the case of adoption. Open adoption, in which all participants actually know each other, is now frequently practised. [1]

Clearly the issue of terminology is one that is challenging – to all parties involved – and it may well be that it is the parents and offspring who move us forward in our thinking.

Building a confident and healthy family is an ongoing process and one that is very much shaped by the attitude, nurturing and commitment of the parents. As Irene Ryll has said, 'A family is what you grow once you have it, not about who planted the seed.'[2]

Using DI to start the growth of your family may emerge out of different circumstances and may differ from the way most families are built, but the use of this method is not better or worse; it is merely different. A male member of the Melbourne focus group succinctly summarises the overall experience of using DI:

> *It wasn't our ideal way of having a family but it was our ideal family. They are here and we are proud of them.*

Chapter Notes

Chapter One Notes

[1] Emma Lycett, Ken Daniels, Susan Golombok, Ruth Curson (2004) (Non) Disclosure in Donor Insemination Families. *Fertility and Sterility* vol. 82, no.2:172–179.

[2] Ken Daniels (1999) Donor Insemination New Zealand: from Early Beginnings to the Millenium [sic]. *Pathways* (the Magazine of the New Zealand Infertility Society)

[3] Gottlieb C, Lalos O, Lindblad F. (2000) Disclosure of donor insemination to the child: the impact of Swedish legislation on couples' attitudes. *Human Reproduction* 15:2052–56

[4] Ken Daniels and Othon Lalos (1995) The Swedish Insemination Act and the availability of donors. *Human Reproduction* 10:1871–74

Chapter Two Notes

[1] Elisabeth Kübler-Ross (1970) *On death and dying*. Macmillan: New York

[2] Uli and Valeria Stockey, quoted in 'The Unknown Fourth' by Christiane Grefe (2000) *Die Zeit* Nr.29 13 July

[3] Tony Ferns (1998) Untitled. *DI Network Newsletter* No. 11, May

[4] Anonymous (1990) Bombarded by Blunders! *Christchurch Infertility Society Inc newsletter*

Chapter Three Notes

[1] Anonymous (2002) Personal Story: Our Decision to Tell. *Australian Donor Conception Support Group Newsletter*, November

[2] Shirley Brailey, quoted in 'The mother and father of all dilemmas' by Margaret

Mallon (2002). *The Scotsman*. Retrieved 26 September 2002 from http://lifestyle.scotsman.com/home/headlines specific.cfm?articleid=6557

3 Anonymous (1995) 'Infertility: a Personal Perspective' in *Donor Families: Raising the issues*. Forum presented by the Victorian Standing Committee on Adoption and Alternative Families, and the Victorian Infertility Counsellors Group pp.22-24

4 New Zealand Infertility Society Inc (1991) 'Why Me'?

Chapter Four Notes

1 Lynne Spencer (1996) Personal correspondence, 27 January

2 Margaret R. Brown (1994) Whose Eyes are These, Whose Nose? *Newsweek* March 7

3 A. William Cordray, personal correspondence, undated

4 Anonymous. (1997) *Let the Offspring Speak: Discussions on Donor Conception*. The Donor Insemination Support Group of Australia. p.19

5 Ken Daniels and Karyn Taylor (1993) Secrecy and Openness in Donor Insemination *Politics and the Life Sciences*, 12(2):155–170

6 Shirley Pratten (2000) Letter to *The Ottawa Citizen*, 17 October

7 Mary Braid (2002) Your Daddy was a sperm donor. *The Observer*, 20 January. Retrieved 20 January 2002 from www.observer.co.uk/review/story/0,6903,636020,00.html

8 A. William Cordray (2000) Speaking for Ourselves in Report to Health Canada on The Offspring Speak – An International Conference of Donor Offspring. Prepared by Sherry Franz and Diane Allen. p.91

9 A.T. Gregoire and Robert C. Mayer (1965) The impregnators. *Fertility and Sterility* 16(1):130–4.

10 Commission Appointed by His Grace the Archbishop of Canterbury (1948) Artificial Human Insemination, London: *Society for the Propagation of Christian Knowledge*

11 Simone Bateman Novaes (1998) Chapter 6 'The medical management of donor insemination' in *Donor Insemination: International Social Science Perspectives* edited by Ken Daniels and Erica Haimes. Cambridge University Press: United Kingdom p.110

12 Feversham Committee (1960) Human Artificial Insemination: Feversham Committee's Report. *British Medical Journal* July 1960. pp.379–80.

13 Dr Arthur Leader (1999) Quoted in Dynamics of Secrecy by Paul McKeague, *Southam Newspapers*, 2 October.

14 Ken Daniels (1998) Chapter 5 'The semen providers' in *Donor Insemination: International Social Science Perspectives* edited by Ken Daniels and Erica Haimes. Cambridge University Press: United Kingdom

15 Louise Priday (2000) Open letter to the Minister for Public Health. *Journal of Fertility Counselling* No. 7, pp.25–26

16 Anonymous. (2002) How it feels to be a child of donor insemination. *British Medical Journal* 324:797

17 A. William Cordray, personal correspondence

18 Susannah Merricks, personal communication

19 Louise Priday (2000) Open letter to the Minister for Public Health. *Journal of Fertility Counselling* No. 7, pp.25–26

20 Susannah Merricks, personal communication

21 Julia Feast, quoted in The Mother and Father of all Dilemmas by Margaret Mallon (2002). *The Scotsman*. Retrieved 26 September 2002 from http://lifestyle.scotsman.com/home/headlines specific.cfm?articleid=6557

22 Lynne Spencer, personal communication

23 Louise Priday (2000) Open letter to the Minister for Public Health. *Journal of Fertility Counselling* No. 7, pp.25–26

24 Amanda Turner (1999) My Story, *DI Network News*, Spring

25 A. William Cordray (1998) Personal correspondence, 2 July

26 Barry Steven (2000) Letter to *The Ottawa Citizen*, 17 October

27 United Nations (1989). *Convention on the Rights of the Child*. New York: United Nations

Chapter Five Notes

1 Suzanne Midford (1988) How to tell your child that he or she is not your biological child: A guide for adoptive parents, step parents, parents of children born via the new birth technologies and other guardians. Presented at Adoption and Permanent Care International Conference, the University of Melbourne, Australia

2 Nicole Williams (1996) Family Secrets. *PB* pp8–9

3 Harriet Lerner (1998) *The Mother Dance: How Children Change Your Life*. New York: HarperCollins Publishers

4 Claire Wells (1998) Untitled. *DI Network Newsletter* No. 11, May

5 Golombok S, Cook R, Bish A, Murray C: Families Created by the New Reproductive Technologies: Quality of Parenting and Social and Emotional Development of the Children. *Child Development* 64:285–98, 1995

6 Gottlieb C, Lalos O, Lindblad F. (2000) Disclosure of donor insemination to the child: the impact of Swedish legislation on couples' attitudes. *Human Reproduction*;15:2052–6
7 Leiblum SR, Aviv AL: Disclosure issues and decisions of couples who conceived via donor insemination. *Journal of Psychosomatic Obstetrics and Gynaecology* 18:292-300, 1997

Chapter Six Notes

1 Uli and Valeria Stockey, quoted in 'The Unknown Fourth' by Christiane Grefe (2000) *Die Zeit* Nr.29 13 July

Chapter Seven Notes

1 Clare Murray (2000) What do we know about the children? Presented at a conference on Gamete privacy: should egg and sperm donors be anonymous? Organised by Progress Educational Trust and Dr Françoise Shenfield
2 Anna Rumball and Vivienne Adair (1999) Telling the story: parents' scripts for donor offspring. *Human Reproduction* vol14 no. 5 pp 1392–99
3 Aline Zoldbrod and Sharon Covington (1999) 'Recipient Counseling for Donor Insemination' in *Infertility Counseling: A Comprehensive Handbook for Clinicians*. The Parthenon Publishing Group: New York. pp.325–344
4 Leonie and Warren Hewitt (1998) Telling our children about their donor conception. Unpublished paper presented at the Donor Issues Forum, Adelaide, South Australia
5 Clare Murray (2000) What do we know about the children? Presented at a conference on Gamete privacy: should egg and sperm donors be anonymous? Organised by Progress Educational Trust and Dr Françoise Shenfield
6 The Victorian Standing Committee on Adoption and Alternative Families, and the Victorian Infertility Counsellors Group. (1995) *Donor Families: Raising the issues*
7 Suzanne Midford (1988) How to tell your child that he or she is not your biological child: A guide for adoptive parents, step parents, parents of children born via the new birth technologies and other guardians. Presented at Adoption and Permanent Care International Conference, the University of Melbourne, Australia

Chapter Nine Notes

1 Leonie Hewitt and Caroline Lorbach (1997) Donors: Dispelling the Myths. The Donor Conception Support Group of Australia Inc.

2 Anonymous. (2002) How it feels to be a child of donor insemination. *British Medical Journal* 324:797

3 Forum presented by the Victorian Standing Committee on Adoption and Alternative Families, and the Victorian Infertility Counsellors Group. (1995) 'Infertility: a Personal Perspective' in *Donor Families: Raising the issues.* pp.22–24

4 Ken Daniels, Ruth Curson and Gillian Lewis (1996) Semen donor recruitment: a study of donors in two clinics. *Human Reproduction* vol.11 no.4 pp.746–751

5 Jennifer Cunningham (2002) I didn't consider the implications of donor anonymity. *The Herald*, Glasgow, p14. Retrieved 27 May 2002 from www.theherald.co.uk/living/archive/22-5-19102-21-47-22.html

6 Purdie A, Peek J C, Adair V, *et al.* (1994) Attitudes of parents of young children to sperm donation – implications for donor recruitment. *Human Reproduction* 9(7)1355–1358.

7 Donor Conception Support Group of Australia Inc. Not my child – an information sheet for potential gamete donors

8 Anonymous (2000) Personal Story. *Donor Conception Support Group Newsletter* July

9 Reproductive Technology Council of Western Australia (1997 and 1998) Summaries of *Towards Contact* Workshops

10 Anonymous. (circa 2000) 'Sisters – A Donor Sibling story'. *Pathways* (newsletter of FertilityNZ)

Chapter Ten Notes

1 Rona Achilles (1993) Protection from What? The Secret Life of Donor Insemination. *Politics and the Life Sciences* 12(2) p.171

2 Irene Ryll (1996) Our Nest is Now Complete. *Journal of Infertility Awareness Association of Canada Inc./L'association canadienne de sensibilisation à l'infertilité inc.* Vol.3 October.

Pen Pictures

Bridget Moss and Andrea Prout – United Kingdom

Our eldest child is six years old now and we also have a little boy, aged two. It is interesting to think back over the years and acknowledge the experience we have gained, as when we first began discussing having a family by DI, it was impossible to imagine being where we are now.

Being parents as Lesbians brings us the same challenges and joys as any family. This is particularly evident now our daughter is at school. Her desire to be 'just like all the other kids' is very strong, and we feel that's how it should be.

Our family is different because the two adults are both women, but although our relationship varies from the majority of people in our local community, it isn't seen as an issue by any one around us. At times we can find ourselves in the position of educator and information-giver if people want to understand more about how we built our family, but this happens very rarely now. It was more frequent during the pregnancies and when the children were newborn.

Sometimes we find it necessary to assert that we are both the parents to the children because people such as doctors and school staff sometimes address Bridget as the mother, rather than us both. Once these professionals are informed then they treat us as unit, but it can be an occasional stumbling block.

Above all it is deeply satisfying and rewarding to be parents and we are proud of how we built our family. We are open with all our relatives and friends and of course with the children. The children, especially our daughter, understand their origins and we discuss their questions as they arise, but these discussions always occur within the general chaos of everyday family life.

Bettina and Sven Williamson – Germany

Bettina is now 41, Sven is 46, our son is 9 and our daughter is 6. We are a very normal family, with all the same small and medium-sized worries and problems, but also with the same happy moments and events. Our family was built differently from others but that does not mean that it is better or worse.

At the moment, it is not at all important to our children that they are not genetically related to Sven. He is their daddy whom they look forward to seeing in the evening and for whose attention there is typical sibling rivalry. We are still glad that we have informed them about their conception and that we do not have to have any anxiety that they may learn via a third party or by accident.

We do not know how they will manage the fact that they do not know their genitor when they reach puberty but we will help them, should it really become important for them to find the donor and to meet him.

We hope that more and more people will talk openly about assisted human reproduction and especially about donor insemination and the children resulting from it. Only like this can the public be informed in a factual way, so that DI would no longer be taboo and DI families would not need to make it a family secret.

Adoption indicates that a change in the public attitude is possible. The confident way in which adoptive families manage their special situation gives us hope that such a development is possible in the area of DI as well. The examples of other countries also raise hopes that in a few years, in Germany, every DI-family can live without a family secret as well.

Laurie and Evelyn Taylor – Australia

We are the parents of two adult donor offspring. We had been married for eight years when we discovered Laurie was infertile. At the time, we lived in a small country town, where people were not open-minded and they had very set views on what a family consists of. A doctor suggested that we look at donor insemination as a way of starting a family, so for several months we travelled down to the city for treatment. During this time we received little or no counselling and when we successfully conceived after nine months, we were advised not to tell our child of his birth origins.

In 1974, our first child, a son, was born. Laurie was confused and opted out of the relationship for a brief period to consider his place in the family. On his return, he accepted our son with much love. In April 1977, our second child, a daughter, was born.

As time went by, we realised that we must tell our children of their conception, however, we did not have a clue how to go about this. We returned to the clinic and were told they couldn't help us and that we were the first couple who had approached them with the intention of telling our children.

When our children were 12 and 9 and were old enough to understand, we sat them down and told them together. They have since grown into well-adjusted adults.

Leonie & Warren Hewitt – Australia

Warren and I have been married for 30 years and are the parents of three children conceived using three different donors: Geraldine 20, Kieron 16, and Genevieve 13.

When we were thinking about having our children by DI, Warren was ready long before me. However, he gave me the space to make my own decision and it took me another 13 months before I was ready to make the commitment to have a family by donor. I really questioned my ability to love and mother a child, as I was raised in a children's Home and had no experience of family life.

Warren is a most remarkable man; he is the success story in our family. He took on a 'Home' girl with all her issues, has given her love, security, the chance to be herself, and that is what he has given to our children as well. We have both worked to ensure that our children feel loved by both of us, and that they know they were wanted and are valued in their own way.

We both wanted to raise our children in an open and honest relationship. From my own experience, people had lied to me and kept information from me about my family, and I was determined that we would not repeat the mistakes of the past.

DI is a great way to have a family; however, there are many issues for parents, and the children/adults who are created this way. We, as the parents, have the responsibility to help our children deal with these issues. My advice to parents is to be honest with yourselves, with your family and friends, and most importantly, with your children.

Please don't wait for your children to actually ask for information about their donors; make sure you have the information and tell them you have it. Children may not ask questions, as they may be afraid of hurting your feelings.

Some people may not agree with your choice to have a family this way, but we have told our children that we live in a democracy and people are allowed to disagree with our choices and hopefully this will assist a little when they come up against people who are against the way we created our families.

Marie Kikoyne – United Kingdom

My DI son, Lee, was 14 at the time of the interview and my older son was 18.

Looking back on my experience of DI, I am so glad for the help of DI and of course, the donor. Without him, I would not have my lovely son, Lee. His social father left 10 years ago with little contact since, and I have worried a lot over the years about the effect it would have on my son, not knowing who his biological father is. As he is now approaching 18, I am really worried about it.

There are three points I would like to make:

1. I would like to see counselling readily available for the parents and children of DI.
2. I would advise parents to tell their children very early in life, at age two or three.
3. If possible, I would choose a known donor so as not to have to face

that brick wall.

The clinic in London where my son was conceived has closed down. All records are lost; I have no information at all to give him about his donor. I find this very sad and I do feel very guilty sometimes. If I had one wish, it would be that he could get some information about his donor and that he could have the choice to meet him if he so wished. It should be his basic right as a human being to be able to have this information.

Olivia Montouschi and Walter Merricks – United Kingdom

Over twenty years ago we discovered that we would not be able to parent children together unless we adopted or used donor assisted conception. After nine months of grieving for the child that could never be, we decided that DI was the way forward for us. We wanted to be able to go through pregnancy and birth together and welcome a child who had been wanted and nurtured from conception. Our first child William, now age 19, was conceived at the first insemination. It took five attempts two years later to conceive his sister Susannah, 16. Because we planned only one child at a time and in 1982 sperm was not being frozen on a regular basis in the UK, they are from different donors.

It never occurred to us not to tell the children about their origins. We were surprised when our clinic clearly thought we were slightly mad to be planning to tell. But why would we keep something as important as this a secret? We did not consider infertility to be shameful in any way so why would we want to deceive our children?

Now that Will and 'Zannah are old enough to let us know how they feel, they have confirmed that we made the right decision. Will does not have any interest in having information about his donor at the moment, but is very clear that he feels respected as an individual to have known from an early age that he was conceived with the aid of DI. Susannah, whilst acknowledging that it is very unlikely she will ever have any information about her donor, is very curious about who this man might be and about any possible half-siblings. She is also adamant that it is her right to know about her conception and to not be misled into assuming genetic connections that are not there.

We are lucky to enjoy really good relationships with both kids and our sense of fulfilment and completeness could really not be greater if they were fully genetically connected to us both.

Romana Rossi and Grant Cairns – Australia

We live in Melbourne, Australia, with our children Desmond and Maxwell, but our extended family is scattered over the world. Romana was born in Italy in a family that immigrated to Canada, so she has immediate family in Canada and cousins, aunts and uncles in Italy. Grant grew up in Queensland, where his parents still live, but he spent nine years in Europe and Canada and his closest friends live overseas. So Desmond and Maxwell have a network of relatives and family friends across the globe.

Our family is now further enriched by meeting Desmond's biological father Kevin, and through him, his mother Irene and father John, and Kevin's brother Eddie, his wife Kerri and their family. Like Kevin, they all live in Victoria. Through their generosity, we are now all part of an extended family and we meet regularly so that Desmond and Maxwell can build these family ties. This winter Kevin has been coming down to Melbourne every Sunday to watch Desmond and Maxwell play football.

This family building was driven by the idea of "doing the right thing" for Desmond. At first it proceeded cautiously, but now it has a relaxed, natural feel and no doubt, it will develop further in the future.

Susan and Greg Byers – United States of America

As the years go by, we are more and more convinced that being honest and open about DI is one of the single most important decisions we have ever made. There is no doubt in our minds that life would be much more complex, stressful, and lonely if we had to worry about maintaining secrecy, or orchestrating some sort of dreaded truth-telling event.

As the boys have grown up, they seem to see their mysterious origins as a way that they are unique. Rowan, now 14, doesn't seem to be conflicted or particularly concerned about it. I think the fact that we are forthright has given him reason to trust that he can expect us to be straightforward in other ways as well; that's a good card to hold with teenagers!

Eli, our 11 year old, has always been more interested in relationships and social connections. He occasionally says that he wishes he knew what his donor looks like, or something about him. When he speaks about this, he doesn't seem sad, angry, or upset in any way; he is just sharing his feelings. He knows it isn't really possible to find out and it seems just a momentary disappointment, not a major problem. We told him the donor probably looks a little bit like him, and that thought seemed to resonate with him in a peaceful way.

Neither of the boys seem at all tormented by the awareness that they were conceived through DI. If anything, it gives them more fuel for the typical children's battle cry "I didn't ask to be born!" No, we counter, you didn't, but we wanted you enough to move mountains for you. We think they really do understand that, and the gratitude that we have for the donors. I can't imagine that they would love Greg more if he were their biological father, or he them. I see no difference in our relationships in that way, even though I am the one with a biological connection.

In looking back, we realized that what we did together was actually courageous and remarkable in a way, although it didn't seem so at the time. That gives us a feeling of personal gratification. We wish that all couples who choose DI could feel the same sense of grace and comfort about it that we do now, simply because we chose to tell our children the truth.

Tom and Ali Reid – Canada

When we discovered in 1983 that Tom was, for all intents and purposes, sterile, the news was devastating. The decision to use DI brought tremendous hope to our lives; however, we often say that we worked hard to achieve our dream.

So began two and a half years of driving 200 kilometres each way to the University Hospital. At that time inseminations were done twice during the week of ovulation and the hospital required me to be there early in the morning.

The day we found out that I was finally pregnant with our first son was unforgettable. Our prayers had been answered and we were blessed with a beautiful baby boy. When he was six months old we decided to try for baby number two. Fortunately I was pregnant three months later and in 1987 we had another gorgeous son.

Two years later it was time to try again for our third baby and, after only two attempts, we were successful. Our dream of our country home filled with kids was shattered when I miscarried. The thought of going through the whole process and starting over again was devastating.

Nine months later we decided that our family didn't feel complete and again I became pregnant quickly and our precious daughter was born. As soon as I saw her, I felt a sense of peace and understanding about my miscarriage. If I had had that baby I would not have had this very special baby girl who completed the circle that is our family.

We have always been open and honest with our children about their conception. The subject comes up occasionally, and we are always careful to give them the information they are looking for without making it complicated for them.

Our children are each other's best friends and they love each other dearly. While they may not yet realise the full impact of being three siblings conceived through three different donors, we feel that they have the confidence of our love and the love of each other, so they may take this in their stride. If, at some point, any of them feels they need to pursue background information on their donor we would support them and do what we could to fulfil this need.

Our family has been through many transitions, some heartbreaking, some challenging, but Tom and I believe that no matter what challenges life throws at us, we have faced them, remembering our dream. Our children are the focus of our lives and, as they move quickly toward young adulthood, we say again and again that without them, our lives would be empty.

(At the time of the interview Eric was 14, Adam was 13 and Carly had just turned 9.)

Resources

First books for children:

Our Story: How We Became a Family

Perfect for building confidence in sharing this information with your child.

Our Story is a unique range of colourful, illustrated books designed to be read to and with babies and young children up to 7 yrs. They explain in a simple, positive and age-appropriate way how the child was conceived and became part of their family.

Telling and Talking

A series of booklets for parents based on children's developmental stages: 0-7 yrs, 8-11yrs, 12-16yrs, 17+ and 'Continuing the Conversation'. These books provide parents with a source of practical guidance and emotional support in finding the right time and the right language to 'tell' and continue conversations with their children over the years.

Telling and Talking with Family & Friends

This booklet explores how to explain to relatives and friends why you might be considering or have used donor conception. It helps parents and prospective parents think about how to share information with their wider community and what sort of reactions they might get.

Our Family

Our Family is a companion guide, designed to give to family and friends to help them understand your situation better.

Mixed Blessings

A booklet for those who have non-donor conceived children and also have (or are planning to have) children conceived with the help of a donor.

Emily Engel

Going It Alone : A Guide for Solo Mums in the UK

Lightning source UK 2019

Available to buy from DC Network

A comprehensive resource for anyone considering solo motherhood as well as solo mums with children

Jana Rupnow

Three Makes Baby: How to parent your donor conceived child

Rupnow Associates Publishing, Texas, 2018

Available to buy from DC Network

Excellent and supportive advice from an experienced American psychotherapist. Mostly for potential parents and those parenting young children but with a short section on teenagers.

Diane Ehrensaft

Mommies, daddies, donors, surrogates: answering tough questions and building strong families

Guildford Press New York, London 2005

Diane brings the insight of a developmental and clinical psychologist to all the painful grey areas of donor conception, shining a light that is supportive of parents but puts the needs of the children first.

Wendy Kramer and Naomi Cahn, J.D.

Finding Our Families: A first-of-it's-kind book for donor conceived people and their families

Penguin Group, New York, 2013

First 'how to tell' and then questions and strategies for donor conceived adults and their parents around searching for and connecting with genetic relatives. The first author is the founder of the Donor Sibling Registry based in the US.

Wendy Kramer

Donor Family Matters: My story of raising a profoundly gifted donor conceived child, Redefining Family, and Building the Donor Sibling Registry

Wendy Kramer and Donor Sibling Registry, Colorado, 2020

An honest and heartwarming account of Wendy's path to parenthood by sperm donation, the challenges of raising a gifted child and how the Donor Sibling Registry came to be started and developed into a national and international resource for DC families.

Petra Nordqvist and Carol Smart

Relative Strangers: Family Life, genes and donor conception

Palgrave MacMillan Hampshire, 2014

Beautifully written and very accessible account of research study looking at the family life of both heterosexual and lesbian couples, including interviews with grandparents.

Katherine Fine (editor)

Donor Conception for Life: Psychoanalyitic Reflections on New Ways of Conceiving the Family

Routledge London, 2015

Available to buy from DC Network

Much more accessible than the title would suggest, the chapters in this book reflect by way of research and personal experiences on the many ways in which becoming a parent by donor conception has changed over the years, what has stayed the same and what is different and also what the future may look like.

Susan Golombok

Modern Families: Parents and Children in New Family Forms

Cambridge University Press, Cambridge 2015.

Professor Golombok's teams, first at City University and then at the Centre for Family Research at the University of Cambridge, have led the way in researching DC children in different family types and are conducting the first longitudinal study of donor conceived children's wellbeing.

Rosanna Hertz and Margaret K. Nelson

Random Families: Genetic Strangers, Sperm Donor Siblings and the Creation of New Kin

Oxford University Press 2019

This fascinating American research looks at how families with young donor conceived children are connecting with each other in a variety of ways. At its heart is the question Do shared genes make you a family?

Dani Shapiro

Inheritance: A memoir of Genealogy, Paternity and Love

Daunt Books 2019

This wonderful and beautifully written book contains the story of how Dani Shapiro discovered after taking a DNA test in her fifties, that she was donor conceived, found the donor and eventually made peace with her heritage from both genetic and non-genetic sources.

Further research into the experiences of donor conceived adults and DC families can be found via the following links:

https://www.donorsiblingregistry.com/sites/default/files/2019OffspringResearchpdf.pdf

https://www.researchgate.net/publication/280122837_Sperm_donors_describe_the_experience_of_contact_with_their_donor-conceived_offspring

Also see the website of the Victorian Assisted Reproduction Treatment Authority (VARTA) for excellent video films of donor conceived adults, parents by DC and donors all speaking about their lives and experiences. https://www.varta.org.au/information-and-support/donor-conception

Daniels, K.R. The perspective of adult donor conceived persons. In Assistierte Reproduktion mit Hilfe Dritter. (eds) Beier, Brugge Thorn and Wiesemann. Springer .1/1/2020

Daniels,Ken. Understanding and managing relationships in donor assisted families. In Donor conception for life. Kate Fine.(ed) London. Karnac. 2015. 181-208

Contacts in the UK

Human Fertilisation and Embryology Authority

For enquiries from parents of under 16s and donor conceived people from age 16:

https://www.hfea.gov.uk/contact-us

Surrogacy UK have created a Parents Through Surrogacy group for members, which provides social events and workshops (including partnering with DCN) so that children born through surrogacy can meet with others and parent can share experiences. https://surrogacyuk.org/aboutus/membership-benefits/

The Donor Sibling Registry based in the United States has a website https://donorsiblingregistry.com but also a secret Facebook page that you can access via Wendy Kramer: wendy@donorsiblingregistry.org

This register, although largely US focussed, has entries from people hoping to find genetic relatives from all over the world, including the UK.

About the Author

Dr.Ken Daniels has been working in the field of donor insemination (DI) and assisted human reproduction for 44 years. He has provided counselling for parents, families and donors, co-conducted preparation seminars for those considering DI, spoken to numerous consumer groups and organisations, conducted research in seven countries, written extensively and acted as a consultant on policy development in several countries. He has published over 150 papers in academic and professional journals. He was Deputy Chair of the National Ethics Committee on Assisted Human Reproduction and the New Zealand Government Advisory Committee on Assisted Human Reproduction for 14 years. Ken is Adjunct Professor of Social Work at the University of Canterbury in Christchurch, New Zealand. In 2014 he was appointed as an Officer of the New Zealand Order of Merit (ONZM) in recognition of his work in assisted human reproduction and mental health.

"Ken Daniels has been an inspiration to DC Network almost since the beginning of our organisation. He helped us understand that donor conception was as much the story of the family as it was of the child and we changed the name of our children's story books to Our Story in response to this. We are very proud to be taking over the publishing of Ken's important book which remains as relevant today for all families using sperm donation, as it was when first published in 2004."
Donor Conception Network

About The Donor Conception Network

The Donor Conception Network provides support and resources to anyone who is thinking about using or who has used egg, sperm or embryo donation to have children. We work directly with families and donor conceived people but also advocate on their behalf, advising clinics, policy makers and other professional bodies.

We are primarily a membership organisation offering contact, community, support and information to donor conception families around the world. Our members range from people at the very early stages of thinking about donor conception to those with adult children now having families of their own.

Our website also provides a wealth of information and guidance. We have an online shop selling books and films for donor conception families including books for young children – the Our Story range – and our book for 8–12yr olds "Archie Nolan: Family Detective".

We publish our Journal twice a year, have a monthly newsletter, run two family conferences in the UK for members each year as well as organising a range of local groups all around the UK. We also offer online contact to members who don't live in the UK or near a local group. We run workshops for those considering donor conception as well as Telling and Talking Workshops for those who have children. Our range of books will continue to expand as our resources allow.

Most importantly we work hard to ensure that donor conception families are represented, their voices are heard, and that donor conception is openly understood by the wider community as one of many ways a family can be created or expanded.

DONOR CONCEPTION NETWORK

Join us to be part of an organisation proudly supporting and championing you and families like yours.

For information about membership or to make a donation towards our work please visit our website.

Lightning Source UK Ltd.
Milton Keynes UK
UKHW022020151120
373432UK00005B/153

9 781912 886074